SWORDS AND REMAINS

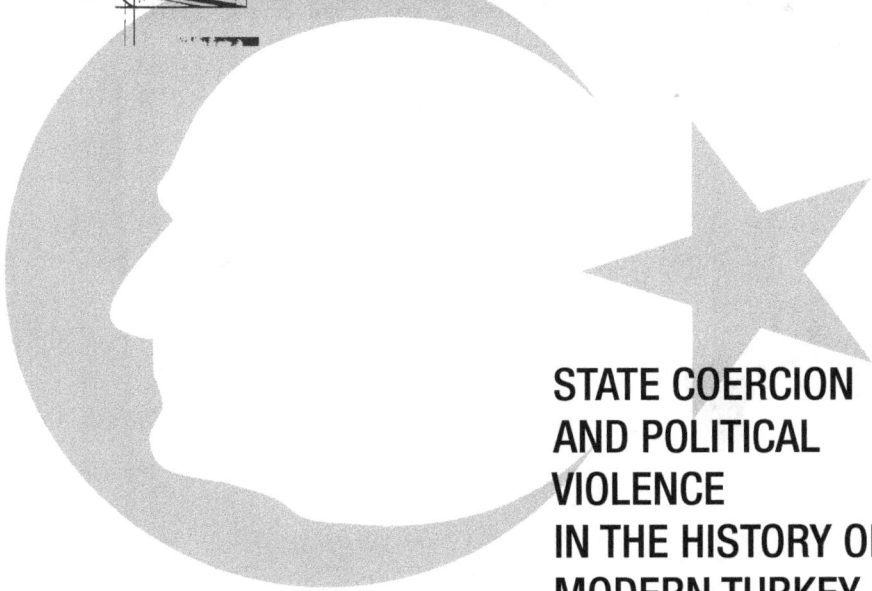

STATE COERCION
AND POLITICAL
VIOLENCE
IN THE HISTORY OF
MODERN TURKEY

VEFA SAYGIN ÖĞÜTLE & GÜNEY ÇEĞİN

RED QUILL BOOKS

© Red Quill Books Ltd. 2017
Ottawa

www.redquillbooks.com
ISBN 978-1-926958-35-4

Library and Archives Canada Cataloguing in Publication

Öğütle, Vefa Saygın, author Swords and remains : state coercion and political violence in the history of modern Turkey / Vefa Saygın Öğütle & Güney Çeğin.

Includes bibliographical references. ISBN 978-1-926958-35-4 (softcover)

1. Political violence—Turkey—History. 2. Protest movements—Turkey—History. 3. Turkey—Politics and government. I. Çeğin, Güney, author II. Title.

DR576.O38 2017 956.1'02 C2017-905537-2

TABLE OF CONTENTS

INTRODUCTION

Van was a strategic city in eastern Anatolia near the Russian and Persian borders, the biggest city with a substantial Armenian population. A moderate governor, Tahsin Pasha, was replaced at the end of 1914 by a radical Ittihadist, Djevdet Bey, the brother-in-law of Enver. Returning defeated and angry from the front, he blamed the Armenians for the defeat. On April 16, he tricked five local Armenian leaders into meeting him and had them killed. The alarmed Armenian community erected barricades. Both sides dug in. Sporadic killings began of isolated Armenians in villages around the lake. On the 20th, an attempted rape of an Armenian woman flared up into mass shooting, and a bloody siege of the Armenian quarter began. This gradually merged into the war as the Russian advance neared the city, headed by Armenian volunteer detachments. They took the city on June 19, but it was retaken by the Turkish Army and Kurdish irregulars in August. Van was the site of a full-scale ethnic civil war in which the front and rear dissolved into one (Mann, 2005: 147).

The Sheikh Said rebellion was suppressed with too much blood. Hundreds of villages were ravaged, and thousands of innocent men, women, children were murdered. Special courts were held according to the law on the maintenance of order. Many people were condemned to death, including some men of weight who had no dealings with the rebellion. Sheikh Said and 47 Kurdish leaders were executed by hanging in Diyarbakır on 4 September 1925. Many less influential people were murdered without any hearing. All the people who lived in the rebellion region were exiled to the west. All lodges, shrines, and places of pilgrimage were shut down on 25 December 1925 due to the role of sheikhs in the rebellion (van Bruinessen, 2013: 429).

720 Commandos Are Going to Hunt Bandits in the East (Milliyet, Daily Newspaper, April 3, 1967).

The law limiting union rights has ensanguined Istanbul. 3 workers and 1 riot police died in fight (Günaydın, Daily Newspaper, June 17, 1970).

On 22 December 1978, in Kahramanmaraş, men holding weapons, sticks, axes, hatchets and gas cans went to neighbourhoods where Alevi communities lived. To kill everyone coming their way... they took people out of their homes and stuck bullets in their heads. They beat them to death, poured gasoline and burned them [...] the result was unbelievable on 25 December: 111 people were dead, over 1000 people were injured. 552 houses, 289 shops and 8 vehicles were burned (Akçura, 2006: 209).

1 February 1979. Editor in Chief and Editorial Writer of Milliyet, Abdi İpekçi was shot 300 meters away from his home (...) Uğur Mumcu, a writer and researcher who was working in the Cumhuriyet Newspaper, was murdered at 24 January 1993 by the bomb planted in his car (Akçura, 2006: 212, 238).

15 August 1984: The PKK's guerilla force, the HRK (Kurdistan Liberation Force) launched the movement's first military attacks (White, 2000: 222).

Terrifying losses! 12 March Gaziosmanpaşa: 2 people are dead, 60 people are injured. 13 March Gaziosmanpaşa: 14 people are dead, 350 people are injured. 15 March Ümraniye: 4 people are dead, 30 people are injured (Milliyet, Daily Newspaper, March 16, 1995).

Sabancı Holding Board Member and The President of Automotive Group Özdemir Sabancı, General Manager of ToyotaSA Haluk Görgün and secretary Nilgün Hasefe were murdered by the assassination in Sabancı Centre (Zaman, Daily Newspaper, January 10, 1996).

On the 19th of December 2000, 28 prisoners and convicts died in the operation called "Return to Life," which was carried out simultaneously against 20 prisons. A total number of 122 people died and over 600 people became permanently disabled in the ongoing process and during the death fasts (The Report entitled "December 19, 2000 Massacre in the Prisons of Turkey").

F-16s which took off upon the images taken by Unmanned Air Vehicles shot smugglers who were thought as PKK members. 35 people are dead, 17 people are missing (Radikal, Daily Newspaper, December 30, 2011).[1]

Is it possible to form a conceptual and illustrative *sociological* framework that covers this chain of acts of violence narrated with a journalistic tone? An analysis that can cover this chain of acts of violence has to be based on an historical-sociological approach, which is the basic characteristic of this study. This means that the construction process of violence monopoly and consequently political violence movements conducted by the state should be dealt with a relational and contextual manner. Human communities resort to violence not because of their ideas, motives, or a contextless discontent, but because of the certain dynamics of political field that are detectable and of the struggles that have a centrifugal effect in the field.

According to Tilly, the only violence confirmed in history is the one connected with incidents leading a government to reconstruct. If so, it is possible that there is a direct connection between social violence types and the state field. He claims that, "inequality based on control of goverments figures significantly in collective violence – both because it makes control of goverments worth fighting for or defending and because it almost always includes differences in access to violent means" (Tilly, 2003: 10).

The state field always has a capacity capable of transforming social actors into the target of state coercion. Therefore, individuals or groups can easily participate in different types of social violence when they want to express their political demands or feel that they will become an object of the state coercion. In the words of Goodwin: people, like an electrical current, are

---

1   All quotations from Turkish sources are translated to English by us.

always able to choose the less resistive path (2005: 404-422). On this point, forms of political violence can become a mechanism mostly encouraged by exclusivist state authorities. As Tilly (2003) has demonstrated very clearly, the collective, civil violence occurs within societies managed by oppressive and lawless states (authoritarian regimes with low capacity) that seem to have unlimited power.

In this study, focusing on the relation between state coercion and political violence specific to Turkey, it is necessary to clarify what is meant by "the state." As we demonstrate in this book, the power system and institutional architecture of the state, the way that the dominant class and elites define their own interests, the conflicts between different powers and variables within the state field, and the geopolitical position of the state are *mostly* decisive for the formation of violence practices. Therefore, focusing on domination mechanisms and furthermore using historical-sociological literature related to the state's morphology are required to comprehend the political violence issue. In particular, implications of that renowned operation in the '80s ("Bringing the State Back In"), which brought state phenomenon to the agenda of social studies again, serves as a milestone for many researchers even today. The reason is surely that the state is always located on one end of a political violence and/or terrorism issue. Proof of this phenomenon were discussions that started with a sophisticated analyses of a state-making moment and then of processes in which states' own legitimate violence monopolies were enforced by establishing governmental, financial, legal, and military tools on a certain territory and making social scientists from all around the world direct their own state-making processes.

A large literature that started with scholars such as Marx, Weber, and Hintze and continued at the second half of the last century with Bendix, Tilly, Rokkan, Anderson, Mann, and others has focused on the historical anatomy of the *weird body* named the state, revealing that the modern state differs in many aspects from prioritizing structurings: (a) being a body of institutions dissociated from other social areas, (b) having an administrative personnel who manage these institutions, (c) being organized as a central power within a bordered field, and (d) its capacity to make binding decisions supported by a some kind of organized physical power on which it asserts itself (Weber, 2004; Mann, 1993; Tilly, 1990; Giddens, 1985; Jessop, 2008).

When those features are considered, the modern state, as Mann suggests, is a state that has developed its "infrastructural government quite powerfully in terms of its ability to literally penetrate into civil society and to logistically implement political decisions within its jurisdiction" (1992: 9). This advanced literature in which a rehabilitated Weberianism and a rehabilitated Marxism become partners has also reinforced the idea of the state being *a field of hostile powers*, not an organization or a system as functionalists satirized, by emphasizing the conflicting dynamic of politics. This operation, which helped to immobilize analysis tools that have made the idea of the "state" free of history or transformed the state into an absolute *Geist* by absolutising the state, as is usually seen in the Turkish social science field, provides important opportunities for our study. Hence, our main goal here is to provide a brief argument about how to make the state phenomenon functional in the course of analysis on political violence practices, regardless of having an absolute theoretical position on the importance of the state's relationship with social classes. Meta-theoretical principles established below will be utilized in analyzing the socio-historical background of the political violence in Turkey:

(i) First the state should be conceived as a *field*, not as a monolithic organ. In other words, "field" is very close to Norbert Elias' (1978) "tension field" concept because there are numerous benefits to envisioning the state as a place where many actors interact with each other. The state as a field could draw the analyzer from essentialist thinking, by laying emphasis on the plurality of power relations. Therefore, the social scientist who works to reveal *generative structures* that have a special effect on tendencies and morphologies of particular events within the field may know that he/she should always start with these relations and pass over to the one related (Elias, 1978: 127).

(ii) Second, the analyzer can make the state phenomenon more readable by focusing on the interlocked, unsystematic development of capitalist, symbolic, national, and militarist state crystallizations recommended by Michael Mann for researchers who study Western countries (Mann, 1993: 88),[2] since it is not possible to talk about *a single* hierarchical principle that can determine the holistic character of the state. However, this type of a methodological measure against the state's spatialisation should not destroy the analysis object in a conceptual chaos (Bozarslan, 2012: 85). Therefore, the first definition is: the state is a dynamics that differentiates itself from all other power types, has a relavite autonomy, and can constantly reproduce its ability to mobilise both its coercive capacity and executors.

(iii) However, it would be wrong to envision the state as a mere field, since the state is also an *actor*. As a whole of administrative, military organizations, and law enforcers coordinated to a certain extent, it is an autonomous structure managed by an executive authority and has its own logic and interests (Skocpol, 1979: 29-30). This autonomy, which is vital for the existence of the state, operates with its ability to determine when and where it will get involved, not through mere physical monopolization of the violence (Bozarslan, 2012: 87).

(iv) However, the "capacity to get involved" is not enough to maintain the state single-handedly; the state offers a structure that activates *coercive practices,* particulary in crisis stages. Use of coercion is dealt within the scope of its *legal form* in the shape of a constitution, public law, and civil law. It therefore makes an alliance with limitations to guarantee private property. Hence, the legal form has an evident contradiction: it both restricts the access area of state coercion and is based on violence. Therefore, the legality of state practices always carries its opposite, the illegal violence practice with itself. In this sense, we believe that the thesis on the "state's violence monopoly" should be studied as a special historical form of social exploitation and oppression conditions (Hirsch, 2005).

---

2   Mann's argument can be confirmed by the example of Turkey elaborated below: The founder cadre of the modern state established through the discharge of emperorship has designed the dynamics of the field according to capitalist development, has established a parliamentary system within the scope of social classes being caged by the course of the nation state, and has equipped its governmental apparatus with a militarist autonomy in its formation stage.

(v) What mobilizes violence practices used against citizens is the state *personnel.* The violence used by state personnel is more extensive, effective, and active than the violence used by other organizations, and the state also has more approval from its people (Tilly, 1985: 173). However, we must note that the approval is always a blind spot in the socio-scientific sense. We claim that legitimacy is a misrecognition of arbitrariness in the sense of Bourdieu's *méconnaissance* concept: faith in the existence of legitimate state violence with no strings attached, reproduction of that faith within society by imposing it upon citizens through members of the state, and a misrecognition from not being able to come up against institutions and processes that establish the benefit at a macro level.

(vi) The essential product of uniformity and exclusion strategies developed by centralized state coercion is the notion of *nationality.* A cultural-biological imaginary union of origin would be imposed through an ethnicization strategy. As we will discuss later, the Kemalist project, on the one hand, has based national existence upon both Turkishness and an Islamic, or rather a Sunni, identity that has been intertwined with Turkishness, giving it a status and raison d'être compared to other factors; on the other hand, it has also activated the economy of violence within the scope of Turkey.

(vii) Each state with its historicity should also be analyzed within a system of states, i.e. its geopolitical position, because constitutive development of capitalism across the world has been determined by various nation states all along. Inter-state conflict or conflict between alignments of the state is, despite its tendencies to become internationalized, the characteristic of international politics. In other words, endless competition within the system of states has shaken the worldwide development of capitalism to its foundations. Therefore, since the system of states is a structural manifestation of the capitalist class and competition equilibria, i.e., since the pressure of competition within the world's markets will reflect upon domestic policy processes, the social scientist who studies the political violence issue has to consider interactions of any regime with other countries, facts of imitation, and the cyclical importance of physical conditions of each country.[3]

By being simultaneously an arena and an actor and a totality of institutions, the state executes its physical formation through a *constitutive violence*. This indicates the law-making process and, as with the inconsistent character of legal form, it is vitally important to consider "law" itself as the essential form of violence. Enacting a law is to use violence itself.

Ground swells created by constitutive violence expand into social domains circinately. Within inner circles, there are conflicts between groups, in Gramsci's words, between historical complexes, that somehow got involved in law-making processes. Depending on the strength of participation, there is a repertory here ranging from governmental exclusion to ideological isolation and gradually to physical destruction. The more intense the participation is, the more intense the violence will be. These types of "cleansings" have happened quite often during the foundational processes of both Soviet Russia and the Turkish state in the 20th century. However, Tilly (1985) reminds us that this is not limited to the 20th century only; there is also a strong connection between the establishment process of violence monopoly, which is managed by the founders of the modern state and these types of cleansings. the monopolization process of the violence managed by state makers is basically the process to distinguish "legitimate" and "illegitimate" executors of the violence. It is surely possible that this distinction has become clear to a certain extent regarding a state completely built, but this distinction is extremely ambiguous and elastic during foundational phases. In the early stages of the state-making process, many different parties have had the right to use violence and put this right into practice to reach their own goals: "The distinctions between 'legitimate' and 'illegitimate' users of violence came clear only very slowly, in the process during which the states' armed forces became relatively unified and permanent" (Tilly, 1985: 173). In that case, one of the most important and first steps of state-making is the demilitarization of various local power groups, i.e. the elimination of potential state makers. This is exactly what happened to certain Unionist groups and also to several resistance movements and gangs during

---

3   Colin Barker suggests that the state should be considered as an institutional embodiment of an international network composed of class relations and balances of power. See Barker, 1991.

the process of making the Turkish state. On the other hand, we will see what kinds of tranformations the hereditary partisan tradition withstood during the practical execution of state coercion.

While this is the case for inner circles, moving towards outer circles are groups, classes, or identities systematically excluded from the law-making process. Those are objects of *the nation as a project* and also potential social focal points on which the violence monopoly, i.e. state coercion, will be executed. A suppression-absorbing pendulum becomes apparent from the state's aspect. We will reveal coercive practices in detail generated within this pendulum.

It is important to place emphasis on the distinction between state coercion-political violence that we borrowed from Tilly. This distinction allows us at first to distinguish executors and subjects of the suppression-absorbing pendulum because Turkish political history is full of political acts of violence developed by ethnic, religious, and class groups that have been systematically excluded from the state-making process and have become objects of coercive practices. There is a relational causality here that cannot be resolved with the distinction of legitimate-illegitimate violence.

We will try to solve this relation here through historical-sociological content and mechanisms, accordingly. That is, our analysis will take its shape not over *essences* such as "Turkish state," "Turks," "Kurds," "proletariat," "the congregation" etc., but over *collective political actors* and/or *rival variants* who appear in several representations as a result of actual execution and socialization of the violence performed by the state coercion. In that case, political violence is in a direct causal relationship with the state field and is literally both social and political.

Political violence directions in Turkey present a clear continuity in certain aspects. Narratives of political violence actors in Turkey persistently underline this continuity. This continuity, on the one hand, reveals a basic symptom that has motivated this study: Narratives about the beginning of a "struggle," whether told by the modern Kurdish national movement or radical left traditions or Islamic movements, are always dated from the last years of the Ottoman Empire, which correspond to the early stages of the state-making process. The political project, embodied within the Committee of Union and Progress, as a *classless and united modern Turkish nation* has explicit implications about the question of who the state coercion, which will grow into its most consolidated form through the Republic, will gravitate to.

On the other hand, if every political movement has to consolidate its members to build a consistent history, standing only on this level of continuities will pose a risk for us to transform the history at hand into a theater stage for certain friends and foes. If it is possible to make a socio-historical analysis of Turkey's last 150 years, then we must decide not to fictionalize that history as a theater stage of good and evil, friends and foes, acted on by imperialism and the Turkish nation, international bourgeoisie and Turkish proletariat, Turkist elites and Kurdish people or secularistic elites and Muslim people. Although relevant political actors have acted and still act at the heart of those distinctions, we hope that we can show in this study that the state field is not only made up of a static complex, but also that state coercion (along with its basic components) has had a hand in both Kurds and leftists and also Islamists. State coercion is not made up of a simple mechanical procedure.

The formation and completion processes of the state's violence monopoly differentiate two most general momentums of political violence in Turkey. We name those political violence momentums, which are based on analytical dating pre- and post-1960 as *civil-reactional violence* and *radical-constitutive violence,* respectively. Civil-reactional violence includes rebellions with Islamic motives that occurred in the first years of the Republic as well as Kurdish riots such as the Sheikh Said rebellion. The distinguishing feature here is that state coercion has been put into action, but the state-making process is *still* ongoing. Therefore, the effort of social identites, which were excluded from the state-making process, to participate in this process is in question here. Regarding Kurdish rebellions, this effort started with the law on the maintenance of order in 1924 and finished with the Dersim rebellions in 1937-38 (Dersim is also vitally important for the construction of modern Alevi identity). Rebellions with Islamic motives finished with the proclamation of the Republic (1923), and then sects and congregations, and bearers of the Islamic opposition movement went underground. Movements based on class (e.g., strikes) were weak and suppressed in a short span of time.

The fact that the period between 1940 and 1960 was an off-peak period in terms of political violence movements is generally acknowledged, and it is true in general. However, we believe that certain dynamics should not be overlooked to present continuity because in this period some movements were either political and do not show a tendency to violence or have a violent content but do not have a clear political character, without which it would not be possible to fully comprehend the violence spiral that ascended after the 1960s. Therefore, in parts of the study relevant to this period, we will assess movements such as the anti-Democrat Party student youth movements and the Kurdish banditry, the participants of whom could be called "social rebels" (Hobsbawm, 2000), within this context.

It seems that political violence entered into a new moment, which we call radical-constitutive violence, starting from the 1960s. The distinguishing feature here is that the foundation of state-making was laid completely and political violence actors appeared in stages of history through their construction projects for a radical society or an independent state. Many social and political factors have directly or indirectly affected the formation and embodiment processes of those projects that have been sine qua non for the formation of the political memory of today's Turkey. Two of the most effective sociological reasons are blooming urbanization and the gradual increase in numbers of college students. The primary political factors are surely the 1960 Constitution and that many political actors organized and became visible through some partial rights given by this constitution.[4] However, the international context is an elemental determinative factor here. Guerilla movements in the Third World and their global effects resulted in two essential facts regarding our subject. The first is that the sequence of military coups, which occurred as a political phenomenon and involved many countries between 1960 and 1980, indicates a concept of international civil war. Secondly and correspondingly, it is the existence of both an international and domestic climate in which political violence was considered notably legitimate. These two factors provided the formation of a politicization that put Third World adaptations of Leninism into practice (through experiences gained from China and Latin America cases). Although these types of political violence organizations existed in countries in Europe such as Germany and Italy, the fact that they have become part of the main streams within the Turkish socialist movement

---

4   In our opinion, the fact that political debates about whether the 1960 Constitution is a "progressive" constitution are still running even today is a symptomatic indicator of its historical significance. Answers to this question will play a paradigmatic role in the sense of political positions that will take shape and become clearer in the next periods of time. This, with regard to our subject, will bring the significance of the Turkish left's relationship with Kemalism to the fore, as we will discuss in detail later.

shows us the most important difference between '68 in Turkey and '68 in Europe. Revolutionary political actors of Turkey positioned Turkey as a colonized country, and this has returned as a notion of counter-authority in political rhetoric, not as the anti-authority notion that left its mark on '68 in Europe. There is a project here designed to construct a radical society that perceives political violence instruments as the essential political tool, and this type of policy making would mostly leave its mark on the period between 1975 and 1980 in Turkey.

On the other hand, the Kurdish national movement has canalized this notion of counter-authority obtained from radical left understanding into a project to make an independent Kurdish state by combining it with a Fanonist national/individual existence notion, and it is perhaps the most genuine synthesis of Turkish political violence history. Kurdish socialists found their own independent organizations and parties by gradually becoming distant from revolutionary organizations in Turkey during the 1970s. The fermentation period of the PKK (Kurdistan Workers' Party), which has become the leading actor of Kurdish politics today, falls on these years. Therefore, analysing the process in which the PKK has gradually monopolized the violence in Kurdish regions during the 1980s and '90s will also enlighten the original content of this synthesis.

The post-1960 period clarifies that the political violence repertory in Turkey fundamentally changed in accordance with the goals of radical-constitutive violence because, in this period of time, we see a repertory ranging from mass movements with a varying violence content to guerila war and terrorism, rather than the repertory[5] based on mass rebellion in the 1920s and '30s. This also means *continuation* of the political violence via central and stable political organizations.

The 12 September 1980 Military Coup was the most radical and extensive military coup in Turkish political history. This military coup caused a sudden reduction and transformation in political violence organizations, as distinct from 12 March. This military coup process in which most of the pre-1980 political violence actors were discharged is also a resource for "new" political violence organizations. The 1990s would witness the second biggest political violence campaign in Turkish political history after the 1975-80 momentum.

---

5   As we will explain, we apply the term of "terrorism" in its original meaning developed in historical sociology literature, not in its common sense meaning.

This radical-constitutive violence momentum, which included the most organized, most comprehensive, and most dirty counter-guerilla tactics of Turkish political history, finished late in the 1990s. Our main question about the 2000s is: Is Turkey in a post-political violence period now?

It should be obvious that this story, with such a deep historical context, does not include a detailed analysis of every event and organization that occurred within the same history. The only purpose of this study is to present the main lines of making and remaking processes conducted by state coercion in their formation and development periods and of political violence movements in return, and to identify essential actors. Political violence practices occurred within the Turkish left at first, and then actors within the Kurdish movement and the Islamic movement followed in its footsteps respectively. Therefore, when analyzing political violence movements and organizational actors who have actualized political violence, we will base our work on the periods in which they show up and their levels of activity/continuity.

On the other hand, this study should be read as the product of an attitude that is against *dominant doxic rhetoric* that becomes prominent for comprehending the history of Turkey by being a symptom of current nationalist historiography in Turkey. After all, we believe that the scientific activity has an ethico-political aspect, and this seems the most important movitation that drives us to write this study. To build any incident on a historical-sociological ground, an absolute condition of this aspect is to place that incident into the context in which it happened, and then to understand its structural transformations while isolating it within its singularity. However, official Turkish historiography blatantly falsifies many historical incidents through a trap-paradigm that we call the *dehumanization process*. This alteration creates a high-level reductionism sometimes: For instance, a revolutionary activity engaged in by a group of militants with an ethnic (Armenian or Kurdish) identity, would be reduced to their identities. In this way, that group would be converted to an essential threat for the nation, and following this acceptance everything performed by the state would have become legalized easily.

Another appearance of the dehumanization process is the analogy of "mass crimes" through numbers. As we have witnessed in many cases that have a civil war characteristic, dead people have been endlessly transformed into an object on which political dispute/discussion has been made. The dynamic that feeds this social-Darwinist pattern is the constant activation of "betrayal," the most striking term of political syntax. In this regard, *production and reproduction of the betrayer* are litmus papers of Turkish historiography, so to speak. Person (Çerkes Ethem) or people (Armenian, Kurdish, and Rum) would never be emancipated from this labelling by any means.

This doxic and criminalising rhetoric operates like a legal proceeding, not like a socio-scientific investigation. What we mean here by legal proceeding is the search of executor by starting from the results. Instead of investigating the target and the objective of the executors' actions, an executor is searched for the intention derived from the result. First dehumanized then criminalized persons, groups and people have become legitimate addressees of state coercion that way. This study is an attempt to systematically break away from this trap-paradigm: Its central focus is on *actors*, not on criminals or victims.

CHAPTER ONE

The Incubation Period of Political Violence Repertories: Abandoning the Emperorship

We have already emphasized in the introduction that narratives about political violence in modern Turkey can always be explained by reaching out to the Ottoman's last period and this should be directly associated with early periods of state-making. Our claim is based on the fact that the founders of the new state have been described by conventional Turkish historiography for a long time as deus ex machina that creates Turkey out of nothing (Zürcher, 1984). This approach, although it has become weaker today, has taken place in and out of the academic field as one of the most insistent fixed ideas (*doxa*) of political disputes for years. This approach, which is basically derived from an historical document called *Nutuk* that serves as the Kemalist establishment's credo, relied on a historiography that was confined to a disengagement/ continuity pseudo-opposition by dealing with the foundation processes of the Republic from a *modernization paradigm* perspective and through a linear conception of history. Therefore, they have ignored the *relational ontology* of an historical process that is multilayered, complex and that hosts disengagement and continuity simultaneously within.[6] In terms of the purpose of our study, the critical problem that constitutes the deactivation of this relationality is: To miss the resemblance of practices that Unionism after 1913 and Kemalism in the founding period are applied when putting "state coercion" on, which

---

6   These types of studies, due to their ideological reserves, ignore the determinant dynamics of role and cultural practices that Islam takes over in social courses and they also disregard penetrating into the multilayered historical-social texture of this geography. On the other hand, they get stuck in an Orientalist perspective that deactivates the dynamics of social upheaval by taking West Europe's secularization process as an essential taking-off point, by assuming that Anatolian geography must have similar changes, by being confined to a Euro-centralist approach and by considering Ottoman and Republic periods as detached, immobile and homogeneous "entireties." Another common ground for those who approach the subject from modernization theory's influence and defend the disengagement argument is that a state structure that goes on for ages collapsed entirely in 1923, and lost its independence, and the "ill fate of nation" has been inverted only by the leadership of a genius. Herein, a whole historical course is being designed around a highly idealistic myth and the fact that multilayered social and historical events have changed the historical course is being denied.

shows a clear continuity in terms of coercive practices of Ottoman and the Republic of Turkey. For instance, both governmentalities – as we will expand on later – consolidated a significant force to their coercive capacities through mobilizing paramilitary groups as they tried to monopolize the coercion they legitimated.

But continuist history reading that was averse before and is hegemonical now in the field of Turkish social studies after 1980, and which claims this type of eccentricity characterization as an ahistorical argument imputed to a new nation state, also has similar problems. This approach, which speaks with a *state-centric* paradigm as much as the Kemalist-nationalist historiography of which it attempts to rarefy from the field, still attempts to make some sense out of the modernization/westernization duo, and to our knowledge, has failed to build a new historical ontology. Even worse, it has activated the implicit *ideological function* into historiography by shifting the pioneer of modernization course from the state bureaucracy that Kemalism has created to the Ottoman bureaucracy and elites.

At this point, we accept the fact that both historiographies have made significant contributions to Turkish political history and should be understood with the intent of revealing explicative structural dynamics of political violence that are interactive and show continuity in due course. As a result, we suggest analyzing *founder moments* and *breaking points* in the historical course of Turkish modernization apprehension and its historical-social practices together. To understand political violence repertories in the socio-political history of Turkey, we should go back to an historical course from emperorship to the Republic and especially should go back to centralization and modernization movements starting with the Reorganization reforms.

I. FROM REFORM TO DISSOLUTION: DISRUPTIONS IN RULERSHIP CONFIGURATION

On the subject of how a modern centric state managed to be built and to what extent, Reorganization reforms executed by the late period Ottoman Empire at the start of the 19th century have a critical role. However, the essence of Reorganization (declared in 1839) is not its being a starting point for a large reforms programme that turned the institutional, economic, and social appearance of the whole country upside-down within only a few decades. This new organization of the empire that reached the top with the first Ottoman constitution in 1876, through a number of projected principles (centralization of ruling, westernization of society, modernization of state affairs, fields of education and law partially gaining authority from religion), caused the *dissolution* of the empire rather than putting it in *order*. In this regard, according to the primary objectives of this study, we will focus on the parameters of the dissolution discussed in this chapter and how this long-range period helped political violence repertories incubate.

Before the Tanzimat reforms, the rulership configuration of the Ottoman Empire had been built on a basic mechanism providing that conquered lands were assimilated and articulated to the ruling domain. This mechanism provided a flexible political framework that included numerous power groups unlike each other in terms of quality in the influence domain of the state on the one hand. On the other hand, this mechanism enabled these power groups as *potential violence producers* to have contact with the state. Powers and variables that might decentralise the rulership could be passivized within a certain control and balance mechanism. In this regard, the most centric motive of the configuration was political-ideological monism:

> The original transcendentalism of Islam's message was transformed by the military success and political symbolism of the Ottoman caliph into an immanent ideological infrastructure flexible enough to absorb, or at least administer, the socially heterogeneous periphery. Structured by the omnipresent *askeri*[7] hierarchy, the Ottomans' political–ideological monism thus gave the imperial state a level of territoriality hitherto unattained (Jacoby, 2005a: 47).

Therefore, in this large territoriality, the Ottoman political culture conducted itself through a mechanism that had two notions performed in synch: *justice* and *coercion*. The first notion was crystallized around the *al asabiyya* notion of Abdul Rahman Ibn Khaldoun who was widely read especially by the Ottoman Elite. *Asabiyya* formed a basis for the primary objective of the

---

7   "This ruling group, headed by the sultan, was the *askeri* which, in addition to the office of the monarch and the grand vizier, consisted of three branches. The first two, the *kalemiyye*, or scribal service, and the *seyfiyye*, or military, were staffed by prisoners of war and 'slaves' augmented by the *devsirme* system in which predominantly non-Muslim children were recruited from the periphery" (Jacoby, 2005a: 31).

state to maintain the social order. The balance between the ruled and the ruler could only occur through the "circle of justice" on which this balance depended (Berkes, 1974: 295): state without wealth, wealth without prosperity of people, prosperity without justice, and once again state without wealth were not possible. Thus justice was provided by the state for the sake of *order*. This was providing that the Ottoman *nation*, a notion used to imply a non-Muslim community in particular, remained as a relatively atomized factor and it also emancipated the state from the obligation of imposing a national ideology (Jacoby, 2005a: 32–33).

Another important factor in the mechanics of the Ottoman political and ideological organization was state violence as coercion. The state, through the "classical rulership engineering" that Şerif Mardin named the Ottoman implied agreement, allowed the representation right of different ethnic, religious, and vocational categories by appealing an indirect ruling. Also by this established obedience mechanism, it pledged to use minimum violence in its relations with "peripherical" regions and herewith acted as an arbitration body for potential disputes in the periphery. The center's power before Tanzimat was based on its disconnection with the periphery, which it agreed to give autonomy (Bozarslan, 1999). But when it came to the 19th century, the capacity of the Ottoman Emperorship to fortify this ancient structure for factors under its sovereignty was thoroughly reduced. Since the imperial edict brought a "self-limitation" to the rulership of the Ottoman sultan, a radical change was foreseen too (Tunçay, 1989: 10-11). Decentralized socio-economic groups, which were created for a long time by the separation between the ruler and the ruled, were politicized under the influence of new movements of thought. On the ruler layer, a particularist patrimonialism came into existence. In addition to these two processes,

> Utilising the official channel of the state bureaucracy and the nascent literacy networks existent within sections of civil society, the Young Ottomans and then the Young Turks institutionalised, first, an elite and, second, a provincial challenge to further central-isation. This diminished the religious proto-nationalist efficacy of the ulema without institutionalising a viable alternative. As a result and in contrast to Western patterns of social change, the state's infrastructural reach diminished. Concurrently, the *ayan*

were able to increase their influence over mercantile channels of ideological communication within the periphery eventually decentralising a limited amount of political power and thus, by the early nineteenth century, taking on many of the characteristics of a semi-extensive intermediary 'class'. As a result of the expansion of the state's bureaucracy, they were able to build on these provincial networks to gain a foothold in the educational establishments of the core. (Jacoby, 2005a: 50)

The period of centralization, modernization, and becoming a bureaucratic state, which came from the sense of rulership that was running within the frame of the Ottoman's "emperorship" power, was deeply involved in those upheavals fundamentally. Therefore, this quickly accelerated a reformist wave in the Ottoman Empire after 1839, which, to our knowledge, should be interpreted as *a strategy intended to increase the capacity of state*. The most essential output of this strategy that will reveal important historical sequences in the development of gradual political violence repertoires is that: The state interacted more with informal colonialism that performed with free trade agreements and legal privileges. In this context, the state took steps to save itself from the imperialist coercion, but at the same time by imitating methods of colonial powers it attempted once again conquerings in its own sovereignty through "a borrowed colonialism" (Deringil, 1998).[8]

II. THE CONSTRUCTION OF COLONIAL OTTOMANISM AS A FORM OF STRUCTURAL VIOLENCE

The efforts to reverse the process that navigated from reform to dissolution started with the ascent of Abdul Hamid II to the throne. In an attempt to provide a new basis for the legitimacy of the state, the first move of the sultan was to protect the empire against internal and external threats with the help of a centralizing, authoritarian, and Pan-Islamic policy. Having increased loyalty to his own personality, he started a cultural battle (*Kulturkampf*) intended to develop an Ottoman culture in Islamic geography. This religious-political

---

8   For a very important study that narrates this colonization process by comparing the practices of France in Algerian colonies, see Ünlü, 2014.

battle also harbored an intention to barricade the growing foreign influence for a while (Yasamee, 1993: 20–36).[9]

However, we essentially see that the state that went into the orbit of a paternalistic and patriotic political discourse at this stage put into action a new strategy composed of imperial and new colonial techniques: *Colonial Ottomanism*, through the caliphate ideology that was brought forward with the argument that it protected the Islamic World from Christian imperialist forces (Kühn, 2007: 331). According to Edhem Eldem, this strategy virtually denoted a struggle for survival from the viewpoint of state elites:

> Within its remaining territories, the Ottoman state began imitating western colonial empires. The state consolidated the homogeneity of the core region - i.e. the Anatolian peninsula and the eastern regions of Thrace - along a proto-nationalist line even as it gradually pushed the periphery - principally the Arab provinces - into a colonial status (1999: 200).

This "borrowed colonialism" was composed on the one hand of caliphate, sharia, Hanaffiyah fiqh, Turkish-Islamic laws, and the Ottoman's ancient empire practices such as guilds, and on the other hand, of centralizing reforms representing the enlightening and positivist side of the 19th century. According to Selim Deringil's argument, this colonial technique was a "civilizing mission" comprised of the synthesis of the Ibn Khaldounist view and Troisieme Republique (Third Republic). This mission hosted "a spiritual estrangement" in which being a Muslim was no longer the preferred currency among the community as it had been. On one hand, an attempt to create Islamic solidarity was being made by stimulating religious sentiments of the community with the concern of averting the threat of Christian occupation, and, on the other hand, on a positivist plane, the peripheral population was being regarded as a tangible resource. With this in mind, Ottomans refused the "subordinate" role that was deemed suitable for them by the West, however, only by inviting "their

---

9   David Kushner argues that "the concept of being Turkish" that would occupy the center of Ottoman/ Turkish political life in subsequent years started its spread during the term of Abdul Hamid in relation with the strategy of barricading foreign influence. This period in which Pan-Islamism became prominent also coincided with the time when Ottoman media agencies put the idea of a cultural Turkish union forward. For a detailed discussion, see Kushner, 1977.

own" subordinates to the stage of history (for detailed analysis, see Deringil, 2003: 311–343). In line with this technique, two subordinates were turned into the actual victims of structural violence: first the sultan, who sought the continuity and strengthening of the emperorship by assimilating the Muslim lands, put the strategy of assimilating and colonizing Kurdistan into action. The second strategy that was followed later by the Unionists in a more determined way was the dissolution of non-Muslims. The relatedness of the Armenian and Kurdish issues emerged essentially in this period. Actually, heading towards this colonial technique (and hence towards a new kind of structural violence) was directly related to the fact that the sultan realized that the empire was forced to retract to Anatolia. He sought to homogenize the *core* in Anatolia and to protect this core via peripheral regions inhabited by populations that were Muslim but not Turkish, such as the Kurds and Arabs. We should read the Armenian massacres between 1894 and 1896 as a concrete step towards the reestablishment of Anatolia as a Turkish and Muslim community (Kushner, 1977).

In this context, *Hamidiye Regiments* were established as a symptomatic manifestation of these two strategies. Kurdish tribes that debilitated the rulership were made to massacre Armenians, the main component of Ottoman periphery, since they were regarded as "allies that do not inspire any confidence" (we will approach this subject in detail in the following pages). This state strategy, one of the multifaceted manifestations of the "last castle Anatolia idea," ran the project for the dissolution of non-Muslims by resulting in organized massacres between the years of 1895 and 1896 and consolidated the assimilation and colonization strategy by integrating the Kurdish tribes in the state. Therefore, this organized violence spiral that became concrete at the periphery had turned into one of the most important triggers of the process of Islamization and Turkification of Anatolia (Klein, 2011).

Shutting down the parliament by creating a psychology of a continuous state of crisis and martial law followed by abandoning the Reform Ottomanism via the techniques of Abdul Hamid II who provided the emperorship with a short term of political stability could not overcome the disengagement between the palace and the new military and civilian elites brought on by the reforms despite all these attempts. A new class of intellectuals very different from Ottoman Ulama emerged. This class that was always on bad terms with the Palace, finding the revolutionary action attractive, adhered to the idea of "progress" rather than the idea of "order" (Bozarslan, 2004: 21). This way, the center of the military-ideological complex state quickly started to depend on decentralized elements with regards to its control. The west-centered organization of bureucracy and consecutive defeats exerted a prohibitive effect on the center in carrying its ideological structure to the surrounding areas. Due to these advantages, state-like elements got the chance to form an organizational alternative against the imperial superstructure, and this situation especially enabled the foundations for the disassembly of segmental cosmopolitanism in favour of a national-state Gesellschaft (Jacoby, 2005a: 51).

The principal actors that would to provide the historical route to the Republic, "Young Turks," emerged from this disassembly in Europe after 1895 (Hanioğlu, 1986). Pursuant to a "reform theory" with a systematic and an internal consistency even unimaginable to the administrators of the Reform (Mardin, 1991: 59), this group remained as a movement divided into several fragments until the Second Constitutional Era. However, Young Turks, whose ethnic composition was mainly comprised of Muslim Ottomans, gave birth to two different movements that would affect the Ottoman and Turkish political life substantially. The first of these movements was the Committee of Ottoman Union that would later be named the CUP (Committee of Union and Progress – İttihat ve Terakki Cemiyeti) founded by Ahmet Rıza. This group, that initially possessed a positivism-oriented mentality in terms of reform suggestions and was devoid of an integral political project, gradually grew stronger with the participation of soldiers and the inclusion of successfully organizing individuals into its structure after 1906. The second movement was the Private Enterprise and Decentralization Association that was established by Prince Sabahaddin and advocated for the ruling of the empire entirely through decentralization. Being swept to a marginal level against the hegemonic political strategies of the CUP that aimed to unite nations of Turkish origin, this movement was not going to have much effect on the formation of Turkish political life during the subsequent periods.

The incident that changed the political destiny of the Young Turks took place in 1908. Young Turks exercised power over the Palace with the escape of a small group of young soldiers led by senior captain Niyazi Bey from Resne into the surrounding mountains, enabling the restoration of the constitution that was in suspension for thirty years. The 24th of July was reclaimed as the "Declaration of Freedom" and combined corteges comprised of Muslims, Christians, and Jews festively celebrated the political ideals of the autocratic regime. However, this event that was evaluated in Paris as the "French Revolution of the East" would further accelerate the disintegration of the Empire (Bozarslan, 2004: 23-25). In no time, in order to overthrow the constitution, Abdul Hamid II started to secretly provide financial assistance to pan-Islamist groups that were the dissenters of the western modernism of Young Turks. The reserved attitude of the Young Turk leaders in direct takeover of the control and the elections that carried over 137 non-Turkish representatives (the total number of representatives was 288) to the Assembly further ignited the fears of being prone to European influence. Following the tremendous impact of the success of the CUP, an antagonist alliance organized within religious students, low-middle ranking ulama, and traditionalists made a move from the Taksim Military Barracks in the capital, seizing control for a little while; however, the rebellion was suppressed by a military unit that was connected to the Third Army and also contained an officer named Mustafa Kemal from Salonica. As a result, deposing Abdul Hamid II and replacing him with Mehmed V both weakened the conservatives and hence provided a means for a radical reform period (Jacoby, 2005a: 72). The annexing of Bosnia and Herzegovina by Austria with an opportunistic move, and the invasion of Libya by Italians in 1911, and a major part of Rumelia by Balkan countries in 1913 consolidated the already strong position of the military-ideological wing and allowed for the government to prepare a widely centralist reform program (Landau, 1981: 46-47). These regulations had the objective to limit the efforts of public debate, press freedom following the revolution, and the autonomy of the *millet.*[10] The support provided to the Ottomanism of Ahmet Rıza and bureaucratic modernists thereby lost its influence gradually, in a way to empower the centralism of Gökalp and Akçura. This also enabled federalism that was advocated by the group of Prince Sabahaddin to be regarded as "a dangerous formula, if not suicidal" (Lewis, 1993: 277).

---

10   The millet system in the Ottoman Empire points to an authentic social structure arising from the interpretation of Islamic Dhimmi law by the Turk/Islam administrative traditions in accordance with the requirements of an empire that presents variations regarding ethnicity and religion. For detailed analysis, refer to Findley, 1980.

III. FROM VIOLENCE AGAINST THE STATE TO COERCION IN THE NAME OF THE STATE: "UNIONIST DICTATORSHIP"

"Unionist mentality is to risk everything, head in the lion's mouth, with respect to the formation of national identity." [Zafer Toprak][11]

During this period, the CUP initiated an attempt to establish an even more powerful authoritarian structure with a reform program that almost completely destroyed the gradually weakening Ottoman pluralism and put the Turkish ethnocentrism to its focal point. Structural changes such as the acceptance of Turkish language lessons as a part of the compulsory curriculum with the 17th article of the 1909 Constitution, the binding of the language of classical judicial opinion as Turkish instead of Arabic in the legal system, and thereby the relating of linguistic segregation with ethnicity by the state instruments clearly showed the intentions of the major actor of the newly emerging political field (Karpat, 1985: 164–168). These and similar changes signified a progressive shift from reform movements intended at Ottoman unity (it could also be read as an effort to strengthen the ties required for a multinational country, as attempted by Abdul Hamid II) to Turkification policies (Eriksen, 1991: 392–395).

The leader profile of the Committee that started to regard itself as the *soul of the state* changed substantially following Constitutionalism. People with high intellectual capacities under the standards of that period such as Ahmet Rıza, İshak Sükuti, Prince Sabahaddin, Abdullah Cevdet, and Yusuf Akçura gave way to second generation Unionists who could be regarded as activists such as Talat Pasha, Enver Pasha, Cemal Pasha, Bahaeddin Şakir, Dr. Nazım, and Yakup Cemil. This alteration presented a property that could radically change the political perspective of the Committee as well as its political practices. Within the context of an understanding that considered all kinds of violence legitimate for the survival of the state, Unionism was "described as an eternal meta-category that materializes in itself, legitimizing coup d'etat, coercion, and when necessary internal war with the concerns for the 'survival of the nation'" (Bozarslan, 2009d: 372). Rooted as a secret organization all across the country after 1906 and specializing in guerilla activities thanks to

---

11   See Düzel, 2008.

the struggle they had with the Balkan resistance movements, the Committee did not abandon the utilization of political violence even after becoming a political party after 1908. Therefore, as an essential argument, partisan and revolutionary qualities comprised a structural character of Unionists.

With the Balkan wars, the government that reformulated Abdul Hamid's strategy of assimilation and colonization of Kurdistan and his project of dissolution of non-Muslims in line with an exclusivist Turkism[12] rapidly put into effect a project directed at Turkification of the remnants of the Empire and clearance of non-Turkish and non-Muslim elements. Providing State-Party coalescence in a short period of time, the Unionist troika initially resorted to compulsory settlement since the destruction of masses that were spread throughout a large territory was not easy. The law that enabled compulsory settlement and provided the cabinet with the authorization of decision making without counseling the Parliament was adopted at the 1913 CUP general assembly. The law would only be imposed "in case of need" and the target would be the Armenian community as discussed in the next section.

On the other hand, the open pro-British politics of Unionists in the initial periods had to change its direction due to the conjuncture working continuously against them on the axis of inter-imperialist competition. This pro-British political strategy was only able to continue until World War I in 1914 because the leaders of Union and Progress were continuously being let down by Britain's adverse politics. The thoughts of Unionists had already started to change with the 31st March Incident that was suspected of being supported by the British Embassy. In the words of Çağlar Keyder, "When Bulgaria and Greece invaded the European soil of the Empire, the British government adopted a strict policy of impartiality and the attempts made by the Istanbul Government in joining the Triple Entete were turned down by England and France with the justification that this alliance would have constituted a reason for war in the eyes of Germany. In a world where impartiality became almost impossible, the government of Union and Progress had no other chance but to ally with Central Powers" (Keyder, 2004: 83-84).

Due to German foreign politics in favor of the Ottoman Empire (the politics intended to prevent the strategies of the British and French regarding the Arab provinces and the intention of Russia to establish an Armenian state),

---

12   According to Fuat Dündar, contrary to the establishment of other nation-states, Turkish nationalism evolved as a form of ideology stimulated by incidences uniting the people with the same ethnic properties, rather than the ideology of the burgeoisie during the process of independence (2011: 245).

the strengthening military and economic influence of Germany within the Ottoman territory, and an increase of separatist movements, the Committee of Union and Progress decided to build an alliance with Germany. Following the settlement law and the alliance with Germany, the Parliament was dissolved indefinitely. Accordingly, the decision mechanism fell entirely into the hands of the cabinet, and especially to some of the ministers. According to Hamit Bozarslan, there were of course other factors influencing the participation of Unionists in the war: (1) The war would have strengthened the single-party regime and provided a means for the prohibition of all political formations that were not allowed by the nationalistic ideologists; (2) the Troika had complete confidence in a German victory, a victory that could have abolished the Ottoman Public Debt Administration, enabled retaliation from Russia, and provided an opportunity to conquer Middle Asia, the legendary cradle of Turkish nationalism (2004: 34). To efficaciously realize this utopia that was designed along the axis of a Social-Darwinist idea, it was necessary to achieve clarification of non-Muslim elements towards Turkification of Anatolia (and Islamification in parallel). The Armenian community was codified as the ideal scapegoat that was featured in this issue.

IV. ARMENIAN CRISIS, "SPECIAL ORGANIZATION", AND THE LIQUIDATION OF CHRISTIAN ELEMENTS

"Do not defame our nation. There is no Armenian massacre in Turkey. There is a combat between the Turks and Armenian. They stabbed us in the back, so we did the same." [Ziya Gökalp][13]

In this section, we will argue that the mass massacre directed at the Armenian people can be analyzed through two different stages. Massacres that correspond to the first stage present a *local* character within the scope of a suppression policy directed at different religious and ethnic groups that live under the auspices of the Ottoman state (Akçam, 2003: 61). We see four prominent actors in this first stage directly related to state politics carried out in East Anatolia and spanning the years especially between 1894 and 1896: Ottoman government staff, Turkish notables in cities, nomadic Kurdish tribe leaders, and Armenians. Tension that existed among these actors grew stronger with

---

13   See Sapolya, 1974: 184.

three issues: (a) The conflict of interest between Armenian farmers and Kurdish nomads, (b) The efforts of the state in subduing Kurdish tribes as a part of the state politics regarding centralization, and (c) the 61st clause of the Berlin Agreement that would transform the relationship between the Ottoman state and Armenians tremendously.[14]

Although Armenian communities living in the Eastern provinces were secured to some extent through international watch, this position that was acquired via the Berlin Agreement was not sufficient in preventing the organization of radical Armenian groups in political space. Land issues, confiscations, double taxation, and armed tribal oppression throughout the term of Abdul Hamid II also helped create Armenian revolutionary organizations. With the influence of populist movements in Russia, the socialist Hunchakian Party and the nationalist Dashnaktsutyun Party were founded in 1887 and 1890 respectively (Suny, 1993: 77–78). A strong violent wave (1894–1896) that was going to destroy Ottoman-Armenian solidarity had begun as a result of activities of the militants of these two formations in East Anatolia. The first incident took place in Sason when Armenians responded to the exaction request of Kurdish nomads with weapons. As a result of collaboration between Hamidiye Regiments and the Ottoman army, Hunchakian militants were defeated. The second stage of the local crisis took place when the Hunchakian Party organized a protest in Istanbul in September of 1895, requesting the promised reforms to be put into practice. Since Hunchakian militants had come to the protest armed and the government had responded to that with military force, the event transformed into a total act of violence. Especially when madrasa students [blind followers] stepped in, Armenians were terrorized for days all over the city. The third crisis began once again in Istanbul when Dashnaktsutyun militants threatened to blow up the Ottoman Bank. The objective was to occupy this building that was the stronghold of European finance centers to convince both Abdul Hamid II and major powers to a reform in the East. Simultaneously, another group attacked the Sublime Port and attempted to kill Halil Rıfat Pasha, carrying the Dashnaktsutyun organization to success. However, the tragic role of this event was going to be the triggering of pogrom against Istanbul Armenians (Eldem, 2007: 113–146). After these events that were apparently influenced by several resentments such as religious, local, and economic, the

---

14   The Berlin Agreement (Clause 61), concerning the protection of Armenians was regarded as 'a step towards the establishment of an independent Armenian state' not only by the government but also by several neighboring social groups. See McDowall, 1992: 56.

Dashnaktsutyun Party decided to make an alliance with the CUP especially to retrieve the goods confiscated by the Kurds. Therefore, this series of events rendered Abdul Hamid II strong, albeit for a certain period of time, while weakening Armenian nationalists. The Armenian population in East Anatolia was significantly reduced due to massacres and immigrations. The second stage of mass massacres of Armenian people started with the *1909 Adana Incidents* that triggered the process going from the local plane towards the "final resolution." There was more than one reason behind these events that also proved the confusion the state regarding decision mechanisms after 1908. One of the most important reasons was that Cilicia Armenians were getting richer in commercial life as well as with agricultural investments. After the 31st March incident, the vulnerability of the central government, the incompetence of local authorities, and the participation of soldiers coming from Rumelia following the dethroning of Abdul Hamid II as well as the responsibility of the CUP are among factors accelerating this disaster (Toksöz, 2007: 148). However, despite this event during which approximately 20,000 Armenians (plus around 1000 Muslims) died, many laws and drafts were approved by the assembly during the April and August months of 1909 with the collaboration of the CUP and Dashnaktsutyun, indicating that the Armenian side was still faithful to the strategy of uniting with the Ottoman state. However, among these laws, the one that concerned military recruitment divided Armenians in half (Minassian & Avagyan, 2013).

In 1911, the relationship between the state and the Armenian community adopted a new course with the *de facto* acknowledgement of Turkism at the 4th Congress of the CUP in Salonica. In addition, the battling of Hunchakian and Dashnaktsutyun militants in Serbian and Bulgarian armies against the Ottoman army during the Balkan wars quickly radicalized the nationalistic perspective of Unionist leaders. Although a product of central politics, Armenian massacres that were characterized as *local* until approximately 1915 started to adopt a new character from that date forward. When the Unionist Troika started to dominate the field of power completely, the decision was made regarding the settlement of Armenian issue conclusively and the Special Organization that they established with this respect became the gunman of this unfortunate project.

Before attempting to analyze the Armenian massacre, we will open a short parenthesis regarding the Special Organization. This parenthesis is not only being opened because the paramilitary organization is located at the core of, in Erik J. Zürcher's words, "a centrally controlled policy of eradicating Armenians" (1998: 121). Above all, the Special Organization, principally named the "Eastern Affairs Office," is important in understanding the specificity of the Turkish paramilitary. According to Stoddard's argument, the organization that approached thirty thousand members during the process of *murderous ethnic cleansing*[15] towards Armenians was a paramilitary political formation equipped with special objectives.

> The cadre of these new guerrilla bands (*çetes*) was to be made up of convicts, Kurdish tribesmen and Muslim immigrants, and were to be led by the same gangsters the CUP had used in the Balkan wars and in prior political competition. The convicts, named "savages and criminals" even by CUP officials, were very often Kurdish tribesmen, or local outlaws and bandits who had committed crimes of theft or manslaughter. (Üngör, 2005: 36)

In a short time, the organization that became the striking power of the Emperorship's official politics moving from Pan-Islamism towards Pan-Turkism conducted activities in a field ranging from the Balkans to the Middle East and Caucasus. These units, equipped with all kinds of special funds, ammunition, logistics, and administrative advantages of the state, organized especially in places where Christian elements were to be liquidated. This formation, of which the principal cadre was made up of a Muslim faction that had to flee to Anatolia due to the Balkan defeat shouldering the severity of mass massacres they experienced, was designed as a somewhat more advanced version of the Hamidiye Regiment. According to Ahmet Refik, the historian referred to by Mete Tunçay, the main goal of the organization was to bring forced displacement into life (Tunçay, 2007).

Then how did this murderous ethnic cleansing take place through this goal that had become the national ideal of CUP leaders? The security organization of the Troika decided on organized massacres under the guise

---

15   For differences between ethnic cleansing and genocide, one can refer to Michael Mann's terminological collection. For Mann, in determination of the difference between these two offences that he recognizes as mass massacre and crime against humanity, the principal criterion is geography/location. According to Mann, ethnic cleansing is an attempt to exterminate an opposing ethnical element by an ethnical element that regards itself as an absolute ruler and worth and is self-righteous in a certain geography, region, on a piece of land, or location. See Mann, 2002: 3.

of forced displacement towards Armenian communities on March 1915, and mass massacres gradually intensified. Fuat Dündar's argument is important regarding the stages of this process. Forced displacement was framed through four important breaking points: the decision of exiling Armenians to deserts on April; partial evacuation of Van, Bitlis, and Erzurum on May; evacuation of six provinces on the coast and the regions on the Russian border at the end of May; and the decision of exiling "all Armenians without any exceptions" (2008: 275). During this gradual process, Armenian populations were annihilated via the continuous operation of the state's compulsory practices as well as the participation of Muslim immigrants due to their hatred and ressentiment towards Christians. *Ressentiments* that evolved with the Balkan wars facilitated the work of Unionist political elites and in this sense they did not have any trouble finding perpetrators for the spreading of massacres as continuous waves. The following words of Hamit Bozarslan who suggested reading this process as a natural continuation of the conflicts experienced between the nations in the Balkans regarding the "rationality of massacres" are substantially meaningful:

> Following the Russian-Ottoman and Balkan wars that resulted in Muslim community to be subjected to pogroms and their mass immigration, Ottoman politics were based on a generation of an Anatolia where no non-Muslim communities could pose any threat and the fixation of the attempts to uniform this newly established unit. This standardization was a certainly a source of obsession and paranoia. It consisted of a symbolic universe covered by a nationalistic mysticism that was embellished with elements such as Ergenekon, Bozkurt, or Turan Empire. The project of the Turan Empire was mentioned openly back in 1906 by Dr. Nazım and Bahaeddin Shakir, two influential men of the organization. But basically, it obeyed a perfect rationalism at the service of the establishment of a nation-state. (2005a: 70)

As a result of ethnic cleansing, the state somewhat achieved the goal of Turkification and Islamization of the region by also providing numerical superiority; also the assets of the liquidated community were transferred to the national economy and bureaucracy. All Armenian assets were confiscated via well-thought-out legal legislations such as Derelict Laws.[16] Michael Mann argued that a slaughter operation towards Armenians resulted in a successful outcome for the Turks in the long-term, an argument we agree with:

> [T]he disappearance of Armenians made it easier after the war to unite and centralize Turkey. Yet the country remains bedeviled by two Young Turk legacies: military authoritarianism and an organic nationalism that now repress Kurds rather than Armenians. (Mann, 2005: 179)

Eradication of Armenians resulted in the substantial loss of fighting power of the Ottoman Empire that participated in World War I along with Germany, a substantial factor in their defeat. The dream of Enver, Talat, and Cemal Pashas turned into a total collapse for the Ottoman state. Just as the desire to conquer Middle Asia that was designed in the scope of Turanism by Ziya Gökalp went up in smoke, the symbolic empery over the Muslim population came to the brink of bankruptcy with the loss of all Arab provinces in 1916. When the Armistice of Mudros was being signed, the three pashas abandoned the country after destroying CUP archives. Talat and Cemal Pashas were killed by Armenian militants, while Enver Pasha died at the hands of Bolsheviks. The parameters of the route towards the Republic would be fed directly via these dynamics between the years 1908 and 1918. Decision making processes and operating mechanisms throughout these ten long years would provide the backbone of state making.

Finally, we think that the socio-historical structure of the new nation state should be read according to the arguments listed below.

(1)   The Republic regime rose above a legal system that consisted of the Derelict Law that aimed to exterminate a community (Armenian) and internalized this law. The policy of forced displacement, economic dispossession, and eradication applied to Armenians was also applied to other Christian elements especially Rum and Assyrian. In this context, the Kemalist paradigm carries traces of an organic continuity with Unionism, so modern Turkey identified itself as opposed to non-Muslims on the basis of being Turkish.

---

16   For a detailed study regarding this subject, see Akçam and Kurt, 2012.

(2) Besides the Turks and Turkist staff, Kurdish people also participated in the dissolution of non-Muslims as well as the extortion of Armenian goods. This complicity strengthened their ties with Unionism, and as appointed by Taner Akçam (1992), this alliance formed the social basis of the Independence War after 1919.

(3) We stated in the beginning that during times of crisis, the state survives only by providing actors other than itself with the authority of using force, abandoning its monopoly on violence tools, and expanding the syntax of its hegemony in a way to legitimize these actors. In this regard, the Special Organization that was a prototype of Turkish paramilitarism had become another central motif of the continuity between Unionism and Kemalism with its special kind of organization and comprised a model for paramilitary formations in Turkey in subsequent periods, even though these were of different tones.

CHAPTER TWO

Formation of the Turkish State: Construction of Violence Monopoly, Manufacturing Consent, and the Political Composition of Breach of Legitimacy

In line with our major objectives, this chapter will not only focus on the Turkish State formation, but also build the investigation of the "omnipotent" state attributed to Kemalism as a problem crosscutting our analyses. Established as a remnant of the Ottoman state, the State of the Republic of Turkey, in our opinion, can be neither analyzed as an entirely specific project inspired by the standard interpretations of Kemalism nor reduced to a shadow phenomenon of Ottoman reform activities as presented by some critical history readings.

Instead, we think that a reading manner composed of *a disengagement and continuity dialectic* and essentially centered on the following argument is more efficient with respect to the social-scientific perspective: The founding cadre of the Turkish state, while constructing a kind of mutual transcendent historicity immanent to all its nationals with the help of Kemalism (the principal source of performative discourse that generates the state) that is established as the successor of Unionism and as a religious govern-mentality, designed its material reality/state area by means of concentration within secular practices that exclude physical power capital. This government configuration was structured against existing or potential other states on the outside and counter-attacks of the counter-government variants (Kurdish rebellions, uprisings based on religion, and secret activities of dissenter Unionist cadres) on the inside. Two main levers of the configuration work in sync: the first one concerns the gradual installation of force instruments as emphasized by Charles Tilly as a part of nation-state formation. In other words, the process of conversion from "private monopoly" embodied in the personality of the caliph-sultan to the public monopoly of the modern state. During this process, the state designed its force practices towards Kurdish areas that were subjected to a different regime after 1924, "reaction" in 1925,

Unionists other than Kemalists and dissenters in 1926, religious cults after the "Menemen" incident in 1930, and Thracian Jews in 1934 (Bozarslan, 2009d: 373). The second base of our narrative will be focused on the projection of the following identification voiced by Pierre Bourdieu during the lectures he gave in *College de France* on the generation of the Turkish state:

> Depicting the birth of the state is to depict the birth of a relatively autonomous social microcosm inside a wider social world, a social sphere in which a private game, the legitimate political game, is played [...] Resorting to the theater metaphor, to the consensus to become theatrical, conceals the fact that there are people holding the strings of the puppets and the work is performed elsewhere, the real power is some place else. Studying the birth of the state is to work on the birth of an area where politics will be duly played, symbolized, become theatrical, and hence the people who have the privilege of entering this game will have the privilege of appropriating a private kind of resource that we could call a "universal" resource to themselves. (Bourdieu, 2012: 161-162)

The implication of this paragraph in the context of the narrative that we will build is as follows: Any study focused on the socio-genetics of the Turkish state should conceive Kemalism as the name of a *practical logic* that changes its form continuously until today, rather than an *essence* floating freely. More precisely, Kemalist governmentality, the name of the performative that built the modern Turkish nation-state, is essentially the producing matrix of the "classification principles" of the state ("universal" in Bourdieu's language). When and where a violence monopoly generated by banning violence to its citizens was insufficient, this producing matrix (Kemalism) maintained its presence by both determining the rules of the game and producing/reproducing the cognitive world of the societal accompanied by the mental categories it approved. Therefore, in our opinion, it is impossible to read Turkish history critically without analyzing this symbolic dimension (together with constitutive physical violence) that influenced the determinative semantic categories of the political field in Turkey. For this reason, we will include the state violence that was systematized during the formation of the state and the activities of the opponent variants of the state below. Additionally, based on the postulate that *obedience acts are informational acts*, we will present arguments regarding the characteristics of Kemalism.

I. TWO PILLARS OF MONOPOLIZATION: ESTABLISHMENT OF POLITICAL AUTHORITARIANISM AND THE KEMALIST MODERNIZATION VIEW

With the Armistice of Mudros signed at the end of 1918, the imperialist forces provided a means for the Western powers (English, Italian, French, and Greek) to maintain control over the emperorship resources by destroying the Ottoman military structure. On the other hand, the Chartage-esque treaty (Jacoby, 2005a: 77) signed in Sèvres on the 10th of August 1920 was the declaration of an even bigger destruction from the viewpoint of the Ottoman state/empire. Ottoman land was to be shared by the victors also on a legitimate plane from then on. This destructive nature of the treaty triggered the local resistance in no time. The Independence battle led by the army that was going to rise – in G. Harris's words – to the rank of "*de jure* source of progressive practices" (1965: 55) in a few years and unite the Turkish-Muslim mercantile class, provincial notables, and bureaucratic elites started in this context. Following the dissolution of Armenians and Greeks, local rulership networks comprised of Turkish merchants and provincial notables that intended to seize their property supported the movement gathered around Mustafa Kemal. The Independence War that was mobilized quickly with the help of the newly fledgling Turkish bourgeoisie started in Kurdistan with the action of Kurdish corps commanded by Turkish officers under the banner of Islam (Jacoby, 2005a: 77).

The first stage of the war took place between the Armenian forces that had established a republic in Caucasia and Turkish nationalists. With the Sovietization of Armenia and as a result of the peace treaty signed with the Soviets on April 1921, the forces were shifted to the west. This war, in which an estimated 400 thousand people from the Armenian community in Southwest Caucasia had died, also went down in history as the last stage of the annihilation process of the Armenians. When Italy and France decided to withdraw from the country as a result of the resistance of the local notables in Anatolia, the Turkish army found the opportunity to use all its force against the Greek army. Greek armies deprived of the protective shield of the imperial powers with the Conference of London on April 1921 were defeated by consecutive attacks (Bozarslan, 2008: 40-41). With the ending of the war, after the renegotiation of Turkey's geopolitical position in Lausanne, the resistance movement started to dissolve and "A tension started to surface between the rural supporters of Ankara and the ultimate masters of the structural interpretation" (Jacoby, 2005a: 79).

At the backdrop of the resistance, there was also an internal struggle for power that was not resolved completely even after the restoration of peace with the imperial powers. Success on the battlefield provided Mustafa Kemal and his proponents with the opportunity to overcome their opponents. First,

> To reduce traditionalist influence still further, the officer corps was purged and loyalists were appointed to the leadership of a nationwide 'Peoples Party' (*Halk Firkası*) which, with the extension of the Treason Laws to include pro-sultanate agitation, gave ex-members of the military an institutionalised political role. So much so that in the elections of June 1923 only three members of the 'second group' were returned to the assembly. Indeed, it is indicative of the enduring importance of the military to Kemal's vision of social reform that he only felt secure enough to announce the abolition of the caliphate in March 1924 after insisting upon a pay raise for the entire armed forces against the wishes of the civilian members of his cabinet. (Jacoby, 2005a: 79)

Soon after, Mustafa Kemal took a series of precautions to prevent any kind of actions of potential confrontations. With an appearance that complies with the modernism of the CUP based on representation, he strengthened a nationalistic organization that was embryonic in Ankara. The revolutionary action that started with the abolition of the sultanate on the 1st of October 1922 gradually became radicalized with the passivization of Islamist and liberal focuses of opposition that lacked a partisan structure and the killing of Mustafa Suphi that was going to drive the Communist opposition underground for a prolonged period. All these moves were clear proof that the institutional and ideological structure of the newly established nation-state would be shaped within *an essential continuum* with the ten-year ruling of the CUP. The most apparent parameter of this continuity motif was that "The First Group" identified themselves as being Turkish and being the state, despite

Mustafa Kemal's introduction of the multi-party system at the first stage as in the case of the Committee of Union and Progress. The Kemalist government had been utilizing the legal and the illegal, the established parliament and "special organizations" together. At the same time, continuing the tradition of the Special Organization, the government initially used famous gangs. In fact, human resources of the Kemalist Republic were comprised of teams that played the leading role in the "Armenian Slaughter." However, in 1921, at least a part of these units whose members mostly originated from the Organization was replaced by the army (Bozarslan, 2004: 42-43).

Another one of the most determinative indicators regarding the continuity theme was that the Unionist Turkish nationalism had permeated the core of the nationalism description of Kemalists (Koçak, 2009: 43). Additionally, the maintenance of centralist tendencies with regards to the political practices by governmentality, the design of the Westernization objective from top to bottom, and legal regulations to obviate all kinds of centrifugal tendencies would determine the contents of an authoritarian political structure. On the other hand, the Republican government that did not get its legitimacy from an ultra-society place, as in the case of the Ottoman state/empire, could have only stayed alive on a "wertrational" (value-rational) legitimacy ground, a Weberian notion, namely, a new nation that would be established as the modern carrier of a value-rationalist motive (Aktar, 2009: 77).[17]

This situation left the Republican elites confronted with the task of building the grounds for pulling something out of thin air. In line with this objective, Kemalist cadres initiated a series of reform movements. The inner structure of the single-party regime was shaped through several improvements such as the abolition of the sultanate, acceptance of the Latin alphabet, adoption of the style of "civil attire," inclusion of women in the public space via professionalization, featuring of polyphony in music, establishment of a secular education system, abrogating Islam from being the official religion of the state, shutting down of Islamic lodges and monasteries. In this regard, Republican elites that enabled *instructive-normative strategies* in reaching the goals of nationalization and civilization through the structuring role of

---

17   Mustafa Kemal believed, just like Durkheim, that the modern state could be supported by "the religion of citizenship." To ensure commitment of the citizens in Turkey, it was necessary to establish institutions that would encourage the development of the religion of citizenship and improve the personal responsibility that this religion is based on. This is the reason for his secularism politics to appear as if a series of new institutions were imported from the West as a bulk, something that was done neither by the Reformists nor the Young Turks (Mardin, 1991: 119-120).

the instrument of bureaucracy centralized nationalist cultural reproduction and made the symbolic area open to the determinations of the nation-state (Açıkel, 2009: 119).[18]

CONSTRUCTION OF POLITICAL MONISM

After the foundation of the People's Party that would be named the Republican People's Party (CHP) later, the Progressive Republican Party *(Terakkiperver Cumhuriyet Fırkası* -TCF)[19] was established as an antagonist organization with the leadership of Kazım Karabekir. The disintegration process that started with the parliamentary question directed at Refet Bey, the Representative of Exchange, Reconstruction, and Housing, on the 20th of October 1924 accelerated with the resignations of Kazım Karabekir and Ali Fuat Pasha from the military in the same month. The reaction of Mustafa Kemal to this process that he called the "Pashas Conspiracy" was to assign officers about whom he did not have any doubts to the highest ranks of the military and to delay the attendance of two dissenter pashas to the assembly (Zürcher, 2007: 73-75). Subsequent to the motion of no confidence on the 8th of November, Rauf Pasha and ten of his colleagues resigned from HF and officially founded TCF on the 17th of November 1924.

The establishment of a new party by the opposing group made Mustafa Kemal quite angry and he voiced his ideas clearly during the interview he gave to the *The Times* Istanbul correspondent Maxwell Macartney on the 24th of November 1924: A character analysis of the people who established the party reveals that there are people among them who could never be "real republicans." For him, TCF was the work of treacherous minds who wished to render the Republic premature (Zürcher, 2007: 197-198).

---

18 According to Kadir Cangızbay, with these attempts, the Republic reproduced its continuity with the Ottoman Empire in the most indissoluble way in the name of detaching from it and putting a distance in between. "After all it is a government that established a Fez Supervision to subdue counter-revolutionaries and regulate fez wearing. The fact that transitioning to a phonetic alphabet like the one we use today was also a reform considered by Abdul Hamid II and that the views in accordance with the Turkish History Thesis and Sun Language Theory were made the subject of humor in Ömer Seyfettin's stories before the 1910s displays the links of intermittency and continuity dialect in flesh" (Cangızbay, 2000: 18-19).

19 The thesis that it is not possible to establish national unity without mentioning the past of the Ottoman Empire is at the forefront of the program of Progressive Republican Party. The representatives of this movement that are not directly religious advocate that religion should be regarded as a social tool that consolidates the society and provides it with a moral foundation. In this respect, according to Şerif Mardin, we call them "Durkheimists" (Mardin, 1991: 29).

Of these two parties that diverged from each other in terms of their principles and programs, the Progressive Republican Party was closed down a while later for inducing the Sheik Said rebellion that started in line with Kurdish national objectives. The Single Party System was established definitively by completely silencing the opposition (2001/2002: 282), especially through the law of *Takrir-i Sükûn*[20] (Restoration of Peace) that was described by Mete Tunçay as the end of the period of "politics" and the beginning of the period of "administration." Erik J. Zürcher's comment is very explanatory on this point:

> Exertion of the decision for two years resulted in the silencing of whole political opposition and the press, oppression of Kurdish ethnic and religious identities, and the elimination of all potential power rivals apart from the Kemalist circle via the trials that were conducted in Ankara and İzmir in 1926. When this two-year period ended, Kemalists were feeling secure enough to let this law remain in force. However, the political system, climate, and culture brought on by this law were going to stay the same for the next twenty years. (2007: 123-124)

INNER AREA CLEANING: CLEARING OFF THE OLD UNIONIST CADRES

A topic emphasized in the Zürcher citation is also a candidate for being a subheading. In terms of the power configurations after 1923, one of the most important dangers was probably the presence of old Unionist cadres. The CUP had not been a single-structured organization since its establishment and presented a structure that consisted of groups and fractions with separate leaders who were sufficient enough to keep the Unionist threat alive even after the establishment of the Republic. The assassination attempt (15 Haziran 1926) towards Mustafa Kemal that took place after the closing down of the TCF played into the hands of the rulers for an inner area cleaning within the domination syntax of the state. The trial process that aimed to dispose of all dissenters that would confront Mustafa Kemal, including the members of the

---

20 The declaration of the Takrir-i Sükûn law should be considered as an event as important as the announcement of the Republic regarding the foundation moments of the political area. This process that could be regarded as the reproduction of the Unionist "governmentality" in Kemalism would be determinative in the organization of the Turkish political area in three respects: (1) Attempts were made to provide social legitimacy to the order brought on by the repression of the Sheik Said rebellion; (2) Transition from the multi-party regime to a monolithic regime was made by the elimination of the opposition, and (3) revolutions were started in connection with the construction of the regime (Öngider, 2009: 316).

TCF, manifested in the form of a "payback for the past periods" instead of punishing the perpetrators of the assassination attempt (Tunçay, 2005: 170). More than fifty Unionists were arrested and tried during the second hearing of the trial without considering their involvement with the assassination. Both a group of parliamentary members that remained from the TCF and old Unionist political cadres that were trying to gather strength outside the parliament were discharged (Koçak, 1997: 104). According to Keyder, this process in which the obvious opponents within the bureaucrats were disabled also designed the possible conditions of the Single Party regime (Keyder, 2004: 110). This clearance operation built a barricade, though for a little while, to the discontent brought on by the defeat in Musul Issue and reforms made after 1926. On the other hand, with this process, not only were the opponents isolated, but also the press was barricaded. According to Hakan Özoğul:

> All kinds of opposing lines of thought including the Leftist and Islamist press were targeted. Due to the Islamist character of the Sheik Said rebellion, Islamist press became an easy target since they were publishing articles criticizing the Ankara government. Several potential Islamist leaders were arrested and tried in the Independence Tribunals that reinforced the undertaking of the government towards the disciplining of antagonist ulama that is regarded as a big obstacle on the way to progress and modernization. On the other hand, with the same allegation, the government also targeted the leftists that endangered the safety of the new regime with their new intellectual tendencies and political commitments. (2011: 217-218)

Following all these cleansing operations, the construction of the legal area of the state was initiated. In 1926, the Code of Civil Law and the Code of Obligations, the Criminal Code, and the Commercial Code that were obtained from Switzerland, Italy, and Germany, respectively were accepted almost exactly with slight revisions. A year later, a transition was made to a period of "compulsory consent" by relieving the public of their election right. With a new amendment within CHF, the task of appointing the parliamentary member candidates was left to the sole selection of Mustafa Kemal (Demirel, 2007: 728).

On the other hand, the *instructive-normative strategies* were quickly implemented in such an atmosphere. As a result of the social reforms as well as the struggles in the state apparatus, in 1925 Mustafa Kemal settled a cyclical and pragmatic understanding of the Republic in accordance with the military—party—state composition. With this process that was defined as the "Kemalist Single-Party state" by Erik Jan Zürcher and summarized as "There are no other -isms other than Kemalism and all other -isms are foreign and harmful" by Taha Parla (2004: 313), the "political field" transformed into a field where an authoritarian style of ruling became permanent. [21] In other words, the practical logic of *nationalistic doxa* started to function much faster with the transition from the pluralist political discourse of the Independence Struggle period to the homogenizing-unitary discourse of the Kemalist Republic (Özbudun, 1997: 66).[22]

According to Şerif Mardin (1983: 24), all attempts towards the construction of a political authoritarian structure were based on these social phenomena that fundamentally contained disengagement elements as well: (1) Transition from a regime based on personal authority to a new understanding of national honor based on laws and norms; (2) Transition from Islamic transcendence to the materialism of positive sciences; (3) Transition from a communitarian social structure to a homogenous society, or in other words solidarism; (4) Transition from a religious community to a national society and state. On the other hand, according to Şerif Mardin, during this period, the position of religion in the field had a 'double function': The function of contact of administrators with the low classes and in terms of the governed, the function of being an alternative to the political structure and a buffer against state officials (Mardin, 1971: 197-221). This double function continued its

---

21   One dimension of the conflict axis in the political field revealed itself on the subject of participation of women in the field. In the leadership of Nezihe Muhittin who led the women's movements during the Ottoman Constitutionalism period, women asked to participate in the construction of the new Turkey and took actions to establish the first political party of the regime (Women's Public Party) a few days before the establishment of the HF. However, this was not found appropriate by M. Kemal and his colleagues, and women had to establish an association named the Turkish Women Association instead of a party in Ankara. During the 1927 elections, the attempts to nominate women candidates from the party were also not found appropriate by the elites (Tekeli, 2009: 253-254).

22   What Norbert Elias stated about the history of the formation of the German national identity could sound striking for us regarding the shaping of the Ottoman-Turkish identity: "The weakness of a country relative to the other countries could create special and extraordinary conditions for people who are affected from this weakness. These people are psychologically overwhelmed by the feeling of uncertainty, they become doubtful about their own value, they feel humiliated and feel like their dignity was bruised and they look forward to getting their revenge from the creators of this situation (Elias, 1996: 15).

influence during the early periods of the construction of the nation-state in terms of the co-establishment of intellectual and social structures. Contrary to Gökalp's prediction, the state did not break its pragmatic connection with religion in any way. Rather, the Republic gained an infinite control power over religious issues in the country, as also identified by Dumont (Dumont, 1987: 2). This way, bureaucratic-statist-nationalist doxa "secularized the 'past' in the name of forming a secular now" in the words of Ahmet Yıldız (2004: 119). All political practices were framed within the paradigm of the Republic through an understanding that was isolated from Islamic motifs. [23]

In this context, in the political and cultural life of the 1930s, a *Gleichschaltung*[24] occurred in which the CHP took over all forms of socio-cultural practices and one that spread through the educational system of official *doxa*. Therefore, we summarize the story of the Single-Party regime that was designed in accordance with the Six Arrows of the CHP that was shaped by Mustafa Kemal and later by İsmet İnönü until 1950 and the revised (in 1937) provisions of the 1924 Constitution as the story of a regime in which the *political capital* spent its resources.

II. 30S: THE SYMPTOMS OF EXTREMISM

When it came to the 1930s, state actors resorted to a method of making Fethi Okyar establish a new party to appease the discontent brought on by the economic collapse resulting from the Great Depression in 1929. The Liberal Republican Party (Serbest Cumhuriyet Fırkası – SCF), which could be considered as the first popular party in terms of the political field of Modern Turkey, announced its liberal and anti-authoritarian tendencies in the fields of economics and politics, respectively. In this context, the Liberal Republican Party that was founded in 1930 appeared as the voice of social groups that fell outside the coalition formed by the CHP and experienced the authoritarian sides of the reforms the most. However, although formed as an "integrated opposition," the Liberal Republican Party was closed down after

---

23 Halil Berktay has important claims regarding the persistence of history writing during the Single-Party period towards severing all its ties with Islam and the Ottoman regime/empire/state: In his work named *Republican Ideology and Fuat Köprülü*, he claims that the history thesis commissioned to Köprülü was not approved since it consisted of groundings based on the Seljuks and Islam. Köprülü was not credited during that period since he believed in a mild Ottomanism that seeks continuity in the cultural field (Berktay, 1983: 43).

24 In the terminology of the Nazi Germany, this is the name given to the silencing of all opponent groups and ensuring the whole society to think identically and prevent them from questioning some events.

a short lifetime spanning three months and members of the CHP were left free to formulate the new role of the state and the governmentality that lay behind the social and economic implementations (Keyder, 2003: 49). Through the achieved continuity of the Single-Party regime in the political field and the statist understanding in the field of economics, the *bureaucratic power* exacted its own perception of national will to society, and hence established a social-political structure that is defined as "class-free, concession-free, and united" without the need for institutionalizing the mechanisms of social representation (Jacoby, 2005a: 100).

According to Faruk Birtek, social mobility within the urban- and semi-urban-based professional middle class and the possibility to become affiliated with this class were dependent on serving the spread of the Kemalist state. This way, acquired high social status was dependent on the compulsory rejection of local hierarchies, organizations, and traditional bonds. The government that based its power on limited social participation as well as the incorporation of a major part of local elites controlled the state by keeping the cultural surrounding rural areas away from the center (Birtek, 1994: 225). This success that was accomplished by the bureaucracy during the struggle in the field of economics revealed "an uninterrupted coalition" shaped by the leaders in the field of industry. Developments such as the enactment of a labor act patterning the fascist Italian legislation in 1936, oppression of union activities, encouragement of cartelization in industry, worked towards the strengthening of the present corporatism. Capital owners lacking international contact areas became full supporters of the state's centralizing politics as the capitalist class became an exceptional example that did not challenge the normative concerns of the bureaucracy (Keyder, 2003: 49–52). The statist method, at the same time, meant to follow a strategy towards decreasing the dominance of comprador actors in the surrounding areas. This situation meant to take the economic development project in the tow of a political integration strategy. As Şerif Mardin also stated, although this strategy prevented the autonomy of comprador commercial groups, it still could not provide "an influential power" towards the implementation of a Western-style capitalist development model in the state (1980: 43).

Although the Kemalist governmentality differs from German Nazism and Italian Fascism in many ways, it also undertook other activities that carried profound traces of these two political regimes *de facto* and were not limited to practices in the economic-political area. Governors that followed the archeology-anthropology methodology institutionalized in Germany attempted to build a perspective that created a synthesis of the understanding of a nation of German historicism and organic society understanding of French positivism (Aydın, 2006: 344–369). The scientific field (especially the field of historiography), was seen as ideally suited for the fortification of the new style of the regime with the direct influences of the fascist discourses ravaging the West. Thinking that the past is a "burden" for a nation that would like to join the Western world, Kemalist historiography preferred to put Ottoman history into parenthesis. And when it rejected the Ottoman, it had to take shelter in a *mythic past*. Scientists set out for the invention of local ancestors to circumvent the claims that Turks extorted by force Little Asia that belonged to the ancient Greeks and Byzantium. Hittites, an ancient civilization in Anatolia, was the first choice for this fiction; however, when it was understood that they were of Indo-European origin, Kemalist historiography clung to the idea of a pre-civilization that was the cradle of all civilizations in Central Asia (Yerasimos, 2009: 53-54). The rise of this racist paradigm emerged from Republican ideals that were not fully internalized by the society and led to the structural appreciation of a mythic and so-called scientific national continuity thesis based on race-lineage that found a common ground in the feeling of a common ancestry within the Turkish national identity (Yıldız, 2006: 225).

The last connecting ring of the dissolution of non-Muslims would be written in history as a tragic output of this period. In 1934, provocation attempts towards Jews began in Thrace. As a result of the anti-Semitic campaign started by Cevat Rifat Atılhan who received his political education from Julius Streicher, the famous anti-Semitic ideologist and demagogue in Nazi Germany, approximately 15,000 Jews were forced to leave their homes. During the event in which paramilitary practices were put in place, many Jews were killed. The law of Wealth Tax that was accepted unanimously by TBMM on the 11th of October 1942 was also designed as an extension of this period and non-Muslims were also eliminated on an economic plane for the Turkification of the market. In the subsequent years, events of September 6-7 that are pointed out as "the end of imperial culture in Istanbul and the beginning of provincialization" by Mete Tunçay were to be experienced as the last stage of this process. Even though the Kemalist experience did not present a *sui generis* feature on these subjects, when compared to the experiences in

Europe, Turkey displayed a *post facto* character that was going to aggravate the outcome of these social-Darwinist projects. According to Bozarslan,

> Mustafa Kemal acquired a divine character post-mortem, his Anıtkabir (memorial tomb) became the sanctuary of a new sense of past; the role of sanctuary guards was entrusted to the soldiers and "the fresh forces of the country" (Kemalist intellectuals, youth). Political pluralism was accepted to an extent at which it did not overshadow Kemalism, the syntax of the state. (2009b: 228)

III. OPPONENT VARIANTS: THE KURDISH POLITICAL MOVEMENT AND RELIGIOUS ATTEMPTS

OLD ALLY, NEW ENEMY: THE KURDS

After the foundation of the Republic, without a doubt the most important threat with respect to the Turkish state was the Kurdish rebellions. The events of 1924-25 were recorded as a serious uprising that targeted the central government and its ally, the tribal oligarchy, and carried both religious and ethnic motifs. Within this context, although it still remains unclear whether the rebels acted on demands for land or not, one thing was clear: that the rebellion reminded the elites that the state had not yet achieved national homogeneity (Keyder, 2004: 118). In fact, at the beginning of the struggle for independence, Ottoman land was envisioned as a "Kurdish and Turkish national border" in the words of Mustafa Kemal, and Kurds accepted to be a part of the Ottoman community within the scope of the principles announced as the National Pact (Misak-ı Milli) (Hakan, 2013: 359). However, in reality, what lay beneath this alliance was the concern that Armenians who survived the massacres might come back and get the land and goods seized by Kurds after 1915.

After 1923, Kurds (together with several other groups) were exposed to the disciplining and education of the regime. The alliance between the two sides shattered when the founding elites of the Turkish Republic decided to keep all non-Turkish elements outside the syntax of sovereignty by defining Turkey on the basis of being Turkish and continuing the Turkification policy initiated by the Unionists; in parallel, the state strengthened a perspective comprised of the social-Darwinist views of Unionism. Henceforth the Kurds were encoded as – in Mesut Yeğen's words – "prospective Turks" by the state elites. According to Yeğen, this codification would transform into one of the main parameters of Turkish nationalism:

> A compulsory or 'normal' assimilation practice would be quickly put into practice, but a while later, there would not be any need to 'invite' the Kurds to be Turkish; the resistance shown by the Kurds to the fortification of the nation-state and the 'lineage Turkism' that had to be dealt with during the authoritarian climate of the thirties led the Turkish nationalism to the denial of Kurdish tribal existence. According to this famous dictum that it still owned by some varieties of the "lineage Turkism" and carefully protected by the main stream Turkish nationalism until the nineties, Kurds do not exist. (2003: 884)

This ignoring strategy met an absolute refusal on two routes. The first route was opened when some of the Kurdish intellectuals such as Celadet Ali Bedirxan and Doktor Şükrü Mehmet Sekban emphasized that Kurds could definitely not be Turkified, assimilation politics would not yield any results, and the Kurds should become acquainted with their Kurdishness both ethnically and linguistically. Already presenting an Ottomanist character during the years of the Second Constitutional Period, Kurdish Nationalism entered a course of radicalism in intellectual terms as a result of the activities of some organizations such as *Society for the Rise of Kurdistan* (1918), *Azadi* (1923), and *Xoybun* (1927).

The second route was related to the course of political processes: while the abolition of the Caliphate and some reforms made in the field of religion assured Islamist Kurds that it was not possible to be brothers with the Turks anymore (van Bruinessen, 1992), Kemalist elites who regarded this radicalization process as a threat of the first order in terms of the establishment of the state were engaged in relentless activities for the state to attain a militarist authority. According to Hamit Bozarslan, this break that turned the state violence towards the Kurds progressed based on three factors: (1) Kemalists regarded the new state as the result of a Turkish victory over other nations of the Ottoman Empire, (2) the abolition of the Caliphate that was the principal pillar of the Kemalist-Kurdish alliance, and (3) the anger felt by the Kurdish leaders due to the premature ending of the Struggle for Independence before the retrieval of South Kurdistan that was left to the English, as promised by Mustafa Kemal (Bozarslan, 2012: 358).

The first serious indication of the disengagement was the rebellion of Sheik Said, a recognized Nakshbandi sheik in the Bingöl area. The secret organization named Azadi that gathered its first congress in 1924 decided to initiate a general rebellion on the scale of Turkish Kurdistan; however, the abolition of the Caliphate in March of the same year resulted in an increased utilization of religious motifs in Azadi's propaganda. The rebellion that was partially comprised of nationalistic tones was mobilized by putting Islamic symbols forward. As understood from Mesut Yeğen's claim that "The Caliphate was an institution that ensured the weak-bonding between the political center of Ottoman and the Muslim elements of the 'surrounding areas'" (1996: 221), the abolition of this institution was perceived as a serious move that would cast a shadow on both the ideological legitimacy and the relative autonomy of the Kurdish traditionalists and notables (Jacoby, 2005a: 79).

In addition to the discrediting of this present representation on the countryside, banning the Kurdish language in both the legal and education systems gave rise to a serious discomfort on the perimeter. The revolt was suppressed by the Kemalist forces in a short period of time. The leaders and their followers were arrested and many rebels were put to death, starting with Sheik Said. However, the circumvention of the rebellion by the state force would yield two birds with one stone for Kemalist elites: both the demands of the establishment of a separate Kurdish identity were suppressed and the organized resistance and opposition was broken completely in favor of Mustafa Kemal through the shutting down of the *Progressive Republican Party* by the Independence Tribunals – by showing this revolt as an excuse – and the dissolution of the leader cadres (McDowall, 1993: 37).

This rebellion also gave the state the legitimacy to categorize people as 'the ones that are close to the Kurds', 'the ones that sympathized with the Kurdish nationalism', or 'the ones that embrace the ideology that would fortify the Kurdish ethnic power' (see Olson, 1992: 237). Turkish state elites that defined the Sheik Said rebellion as the first battle undertook by the Turkish as an "ideology" (Bozarslan, 2003: 848) must have considered that the nationalism they imposed (if we say in reference to another important Tillian notion) would have resulted in a "state-seeking nationalism" in Kurds,[25]

---

25   For detailed conceptualization see Tilly, 1998.

so they tried to provide the militarist autonomy of the regime in the region after 1925. Violence that was put in place towards the Kurds was now being converted into the official ideology of the state because:

> The events that initiated with the Sheik Said rebellion and continued with Mutki Rebellion, the Second Ağrı Operation, Bicar Tenkil Operation, Zeylan Rebellion, Oramar Rebellion, the Third Ağrı Operation, Pülümür Operation, and Dersim Rebellion proved that the settings were not ready yet for the *project of establishment of a nation homologous to the state*. The reaction of the state executives to the rebellions could not have obviously been limited to force; alongside, "population engineering" practices were also quickly put into practice. Although using a nationalistic rhetoric, the government chose the path to exercise compulsory immigration and resettlement towards factions they thought posed an internal and external security threat and saw the need to keep under control in a despotic and selective way to an extent allowed by the infrastructural government. This engineering project that was virtually a *symbol of punishment* from the viewpoint of the Kurds became an area where the central, national, and militarist crystallizations of the modern state were articulated. (Çeğin, 2014: 49)

The year 1927 caused the initiation of a new period in the form of struggle with respect to both the new state and the Kurdish rebellions. A "General Inspectorship" was established in a way to cover most of the areas where the Kurds live, and İbrahim Tali (Öngören), one of the important figures of the Special Organization for a period of time, was appointed to this job. On the other hand, a year later, the *Xoybun* Association that united opponent tribal leaders living in Turkey, Iraq, and Syria started a serious war of propaganda against the General Inspectorship in an alliance with the Tashnak organization that was forced to leave Armenia upon adoption by the Soviet government. When İhsan Nuri Bey who fled to Iraq during the Nasturi uprising contacted *Xoybun* in Ağrı, he quickly transformed this chaotic situation into an armed public uprising. When no results were obtained from the diplomatic meetings that continued until 1930, the İsmet Pasha Government decided to take military action. When no significant success was achieved against the forces of İhsan Nuri, the government changed its tactic and besieged Ağrı via the Iraqi border. With the diplomatic pressure of the Soviets, Iran agreed to stop the aid to Kurds and to get a portion of land in Van from Turkey in return for the region of Little Ağrı (Olson, 2000: 67-94). This way, the second important Kurdish rebellion spanning the years from 1927 to 1930 was suppressed with a large military operation in close collaboration with Iran, the Soviet Union, and partially Iraq. The rebellion that carried the model defined by the Sheik Said rebellion to a more advanced level provided a means for the heavy destruction of Kurdish countryside (Bozarslan, 2000: 359-360).

Subsequently, the state apparatus began resorting to more nuanced methods, especially around the East Anatolia region, against Kurdish attempts that endangered its sovereignty. The first of these methods was "cartographic violence and accompanying official reports that were prepared by the authorized units of the state," the primary strategy of the state towards rendering the public readable (Çeğin, 2013: 232). These reports as a whole were prepared to restore state authority in the geography, so the first target was Dersim that had been regarded as a "nuisance" for the state since the Ottoman era. Within the context of the project of "bestowing Turkism to Dersim" the state presented a three-stage scenario: In the first stage, the landlords in Dersim were to be exiled and, in parallel, the whole region would be cleared of weapons. The subsequent opening of schools would draw the public to Turkism. In the last stage (at the third year of the plan), the roads were to be opened and reforms would be made in areas such as commerce and agriculture.

The second and more effective method was the introduction of the Tunceli Law (1935) that stipulated downright disinhabitation of the Dersim area (van Bruinessen, 1994: 141-170). Although some logistic problems prevented the realization of the law, according to the testimony of the survivors, "massacres, exiles, and assimilations attempts based on violence continued at full speed" in many places of the Southeast (McDowall, 1992: 207). In particular, the massacre that took place in the Alevi-Kurdish town Dersim, later renamed Tunceli (meaning "bronz hand"), and cost 40,000 people their lives was going to make history as the most tragic example of this situation (Jacoby, 2004: 101).

The Dersim rebellion differed in certain aspects from the two previous rebellions. The fact that it was a rebellion in which organizations such as *Azadi* and *Xoybun* did not appear in the background, the traces of "national identity" were weak, and a general "independence program" regarding Turkey Kurds was lacking kept the 1938 Dersim rebellion at the perimeter of the Kurdish resistance (Yeğen, 2011: 11-12). The character of the rebellion with regards to the practicing of the state violence was that it staged the most violent of the massacres towards civilians among the Kurdish riots during the time of the Republic. The main strategy of the Presidency of General Staff, which explained the objective of the operation as the cleaning of the region from tribes and the termination of pillage and brigandance, was to get rid of the autochthonous frame; in this context, the Dersim incident shall be read in a frame of "non-security" (Aslan, 2011: 172). In conclusion, the Kurdish independence struggle that started with the 1920 Hozat Memorandum in Dersim was also defeated in Dersim after 18 years.

The Dersim Kurdish disciplining that was the peak point of the systematic monopolization of the state violence, especially in places were the Kurds lived, prevented the organization of a resistance against the central government for about twenty years. The Kurds were codified as "an extortionist and feudal ethnic group whose sole intention consisted of the extermination of the Turks as an ethnic community and a victim class" (Bozarslan, 2000: 361). Therefore, from that point on, a symbolic understanding of violence would accompany the force practices. The Kurdish political movement provided the modernist nationalists, who searched for a domain where they could put an internal-war fantasy in action, with an enemy that could be defined politically, ethnically, and culturally (Bozarslan, 2009c).

RELIGION-BASED COLLECTIVE ACTIONS

Due to the lack of an awareness of nationalistic cohesion, the founding elites searched for ways to instrumentalise Islamic motifs and solidarity practices from the Struggle for Independence to the establishment of the Republic (Tunçay, 2006: 92) and were very successful in this endeavor. However, after the military victory, a serious maneuver amendment was made in the relationship of the state with religion. Even though the process of decontamination from Islam that appeared as a state strategy did not take place as an obvious refutation of Islam, religion was made an important tool of the state. One of the first moves in putting this strategy into practice was the establishment of the Presidency of Religious Affairs (1924). The regime that aimed for the secularization of the societal in the long term targeted confining Islam to a specific area via this institution. The establishment of İmam Hatip Schools that would later replace madrasas in the formation of the "Republican Clergy" was the complementary element of this aim (Bilici, 2009: 295-296).

Another strategy was related to the domestication of religion by *nationalization* and designing religious references and institutions as legitimacy and control mechanisms. The *national religion* was regarded as an important factor in the restoration of order by the state; since a religion independent from the state was accepted as a barrier against the civilization goals of the state, a religious area was made the prioritized action area of Kemalists. For this reason, although *the Islamist doctrine* became independent by turning into a political subject, it transformed into being the safety valve of "regime-stabilizing" inner war doctrines specific to Turkey and especially was kept in reserve as an important weapon, although it remained in the second plan against "the leftist politics" that they could never completely abandon (Bozarslan, 2000: 61-73). The most radical attempt regarding the issue of nationalization of Islam was without a doubt the "language revolution". The change of the alphabet implied such a fundamental change that it almost proved that the Single Party embarked upon being the "governess of the nation," and they attempted to clear the cultural area completely of Islamic references. According to the sociologist Kadir Cangızbay,

> Both the nationalism and laicism of the Single Part/bureaucrat Republic were instrumental regulations that were politically preferred and enforced in line with class incentives, rather than being the manifestations of the conception of a modernist society. For example, the laicism of the state, at least the principle that the state does not have an official religion, is nothing other than an administrative tool for both directly escaping from Islam that was on the basis of legitimacy of the ancient regime as much as possible and sterilizing whole aspects of the social life in a way to be regulated and controlled by laws through bureaucracy. It is not at all a leap of dignity of French Enlightenment that liberates human philosophically against divine and politically against operators of divinity. (2008-2009: 148)

From the mid-1920s, the obstruction of the public and political expression of religion in this way resulted in the appearance of religion-based collective actions in different forms. Local riots emerged, especially against the "Hat Act" in provinces such as Erzurum, Rize, Sivas, Maraş, Giresun, Kırşehir, Kayseri, Tokat, Amasya, Samsun, Trabzon, and Gümüşhane (Gologlu, 1972: 157). In 1930, the breaking out of the *Menemen uprising*, named the "revolutionary wave" by Hikmet Kıvılcımlı, would function as a signal in showing the limits of the autonomy of the regime. Therefore, this incident was transformed into a dual strategy with regards to the state elites. First, the Menemen incident was made a tool for the legitimization of the suppression of any religious attempt from that point on. Second, the elites agreed to the forceful substitution of Republican reforms (Kadıoğlu, 1999: 47). At the same time, this event directed the regime towards taking oppressive precautions against the religious orders; however, despite everything, religious associations isolated from the cult environment found a place for themselves within the urban society.

> Although these associations refused to face the government directly, they were not holding off building social relationship and internal support networks and responding with a regime that maintained the monopoly of the whole visibility area through a "social relations map" [Şerif Mardin]. This way, the Nurcu movement that was established in 1930s by a Kurdish clergy, Said-i Kurdî, and collected the religious sensitivity around middle classes of the city imposed itself as a real parallel society that the government never managed to dissipate. (Bozarslan, 2004: 69)

As a result, the elites of the new nation-state either pushed all opposing variants that resided within its ruling field to the underground or decreased their strength substantially through their actions between the years of 1923 and 1938. While the governing class evolved into a more uniform govern-mentality, religious, ethnic, and political opposition was suppressed for the most part until the 1960s. With the multi-party period, although corrosions surfaced in the CHP's political monopoly, the DP developed a practice that polarized the political field through a *right Kemalist* discourse. A dual political field was designed comprised of the ones who advocated for a Westernized and laicist method of governing and the ones who used conservative discourses but were not all that different from their adversary. Despite the rapidly changing socioeconomic environment and the appearance of different social positions within the field, *two characteristics survived*. The first one was the crystallization that was located in the center of the political capital at risk, also called the "Republican Cosmology." Namely, the cult of Mustafa Kemal, his statist principles, the will to become one of the "modern civilizations," and the invention of the Turk as a super-identity that connected the citizens. Symbolized by the conservative cadres of our day, even Adnan Menderes created a policy within this cosmology. Since this *doxa* element that mobilized public support did not involve the political actors as a whole, it would result in prospective *fundamental challenges* (Islamist and Kurdist politizations) within the structure of the field.

The second characteristic in the field concerns the surviving position of the military that perpetuates its authority on *civil control* via the utilization of political capital in the most traditional ways (Akdeniz and Göker, 2011: 22). The position of the military in the political field was institutionalized, and this situation gave rise to two important results prospectively: First, the political class was squeezed into a cartel to which the military subjected itself by losing blood; second, the fact that politics started to be perceived as a "field that concerns internal security" (Cizre, 2005: 57-79).

CHAPTER THREE

Building of Capitalist Militarism: Paramilitarism and Moment of Birth of Radical-Constitutive Violence

The 1960s is literally the milestone of Turkish political history. Along with many actors who left their marks on history, actors who instituted the relationality of history of political violence in the ensuing years also emerged in this era. Since this study is not a study of political history, we are going to focus on the formations and transformations that stand out on the structural level, instead of the cyclical formations and conjunctions materialized in elections. We would like to remind you that our key issue is to illuminate the causal relationship between state coercion and political violence.

The phenomenon, generally known as "being capitalized," is the most distinctive characteristic of this era. The process of capital accumulation generated by the Marshall Plan, in other words industrialisation and rural-urban migration, in other words urbanisation, are objective causes. The Turkish economy, which transformed to an import substitution character similar to Latin America's, grew at 9% on average every year between 1963 and 1971.[26] In the same period of time, the population living in cities increased to 14 million from 9 million in a general population that increased to 35 million from 27 million. The demographical projection of this increase appeared as the geometrical increase in the number of workers and students.[27]

However, approaching being capitalized only from the point of its macro-economic and demographic extent would mean ignoring an essential basis of transformation: completion of state making and rebuilding of militarism with a capitalistic content. In the words of Mann, we define militarism as "an

---

26 For an overall study on the relation of economic processes with political processes in Turkey see Keyder, 1987.

27 The number of workers included in the labour act was near 755,000 in 1959; this number constantly increased during ten years and came near 1,406,000 in 1970 (see Işıklı, 1987: 316). Likewise, the number of university students in the country was 44,461 in 1960-61; it increased to 55,583 in 1965-66 and to 73,228 in 1970. With the addition of colleges and training colleges to this sum, the number of students in higher education in 1970 reached 153,358 (see Landau, 1974: 31).

attitude and a set of institutions which regard war and the preparation for war as a normal and desirable social activity" (Jacoby, 2005a: 127). Tilly's (1985) illustrative relationship between "state-making" and "war-making" shows that this militaristic character that played a key role in the Turkish state-making process transformed beginning from the 1960s. The situation, which appears as the militarization of capitalism in most countries, occurred as the *capitalization of militarism* in Turkey on several counts: This corresponds to the question of how the military is incorporated with incipient capitalistic benefits. Mann's four variants classification of "domestic militarism" indicate that the course of the '60s in Turkey was the transition course from "autocratical militarism" to "semiauthoritarian incorporation."[28] The most essential dynamic that created this transition was the tension created by the founders of the Republic who positioned the military-state above politics and classes and also carried a capitalistic class goal that helped reach the level of "contemporary civilization."[29] Capitalistic class factions that started to rise through the multi-party period demanded their political worth from this rise.

Going into details of this incorporation process would miss the focus of this study.[30] To sum up, the 1960s witnessed the sufferings of the Turkish state during the process of its incorporation with the capitalistic world on both international and domestic platforms.[31] Hence, the point of our discussion is "[i]n terms of political expediency, the growing capitalist-military coalition" for the next periods of Turkey (Jacoby, 2005a: 137). Although this coalition refers to "an uneasy accommodation" (Jacoby, 2005a: 178), the attitudes and benefits of capitalistic classes in the state compound as an area come into existence as an essential component. Solid clues of this matter are seen through economic policies applied and rapidly increasing paramilitary practices.

---

28 See Mann, 1993: 682-686. For an analytical transference of this and other variants see Jacoby, 2005a: 129-133.

29 The projection of this tension on policies level is: "Kemalism is simultaneously an authoritarian reformism and an aspiration at a Western-style liberal democracy" (Vaner, 1987: 238).

30 For a highly detailed analyisis on embourgeoisement of military elite through OYAK (Army Mutual Assistance Association) and bureaucratic logic in military giving its place to capitalist logic gradually see Akça, 2006.

31 Naturally, it should not be supposed that this tendency appearing in economical and social platforms would result in smooth state politics. For instance, following the cancellation of the intervention plan in Cyprus, which was supposed to happen in June 1964, as a result of USA President Johnson's letter to İsmet İnönü, matters such as Turkey's withdrawing from multinational armament led by NATO and engaging with the Soviet Union even for a short period of time were being discussed. For detailed information see Eroğul, 1987: 127-128. Thus, the Turkish state's approach to Cyprus issue has kept its anomalistic stand.

I. "CIVIL" HAND OF THE STATE COERCION: TURKISH ULTRANATIONALISTIC RIGHT-WING AS A GENUINE PARAMILITARIZATION PRACTICE

"Over one thousand youngsters have been trained at camps in various parts of the country. In coming years, these activities will spread throughout the land, and tens of thousands of youths will be readied for the day feared by communists and freemason-capitalist collaborators." [Alparslan Türkeş][32]

The transformation that appeared in state coercion and organizaton of militarism together with the 1960s introduced a *systematic* paramilitary organization to Turkish political history. This case is that the first paramilitarization seeds of the Turkish ultranationalistic right-wing, which had been existing ideologically since the incubation periods of the state coercion and had been continuining its existence in an uneven relationship with Republic elites, spread, and an ultranationalistic ideology was formulated step by step as a "civil war doctrine" (Jacoby, 2005a: 156, footnote 54) starting from these years. The systematic and full-fledged paramilitary structuring that rose from here kept its presence until recent periods by undergoing several transformations.

The essential political actor of paramilitary practices in Turkey was the political party named the MHP (National Action Party) in 1969, led by Alparslan Türkeş who was a pro-junta military officer in the 1960s Coup d'état. Several international factors certainly affected the creation of this party. That the sequence of military coup d'états between 1960 and 1980 presented a quite similar pattern in many countries where socialist and communist movements emerged clearly shows the effect of international counter guerilla doctrines. The field manual enacted in Turkey on 25 May 1964 according to the order of Land Forces Command (which was taken over from the USA Armed Forces), "ST 31-15 Land Forces Sahra Field Manual –Operation Against Irregular Forces," was effective as a riot suppressing strategy. Both the AP (Justice Party) and the MHP played the lead in taking "civil" steps required by this strategy.[33] The critical point here is that counter-guerilla operations started *before* radical-constitutive violence: This point is significant for the creation of the *civil war concept* since 1969 in particular.

---

32 Ağaoğulları, 1987: 214, footnote 113.
33 For detailed information see Kürkçü, 2007: 494-495.

The second international factor was the archaic German effect on the Turkish ultranationalistic right-wing. We already discussed obligatory relations of the ITC with Germany in the World War I years without making a profound political history analysis. In the World War II era, the ultranationalistic right-wing welcomed the indecisive yet close relationship between National Chief İnönü and Nazi Germany with enthusiasm, and pro-Nazi ultranationalistic views gained wide currency by both Turanist intellectuals and by middle and high-ranking military officers, one of whom was Türkeş.[34] The special care that Türkeş gave to youth branches and action in the belately founded MHP is certainly reminiscent of national-socialist youth branch practices. On the other hand, Ağaoğulları (1987: 193) pointed out a much more specific connection and stated that during his exile, discussed later, Türkeş and his friends were influenced by the "Army-Church-Party" triad that the Franco dictatorship in Spain was based on.[35] In any case, it is obvious that fascist party experiences in Europe had a serious impact on the MHP's organizational efforts.

However, the similarities of paramilitary practice in Turkey with its international equivalents should not detract from aspects of the militarism-paramilitarism relationship peculiar to Turkey. Although there had been several liquidations during the creation process of the violence monopoly, the gang/resistance tradition as real owners of the state that came from Union and Progress was included by the state as a field. Turkish militarism, even in the autocratic militarism period where it had absolute power, never liquidated "civil" gangs completely and protected their semi-organic connections with the Special Organization. As Tilly (1985) stated, an absolute *demilitarization* in the state-making period did not happen in Turkey; "civil" aspects, which were weakened and controlled up to a degree that did not require liquidation, were used systematically for ethnic criminal cleaning of Armenians and individually for incidents like killing Mustafa Suphi, who was the founder of the Turkey Communist Party, and his friends. This pro-resistance tradition "has left its print to the side of MHP/Idealist Movement 'that did not care about legality much' " (Can, 2009: 663).

---

34   Hence, Jacoby (2011: 912) stated that Türkeş was a liaison officer between the Turkish Armed Forces and Nazi *Wehrmacht.*

35   Hence, Ağaoğulları (1987: 211, footnote 73) considered that this influence had an important place in reconciliation efforts that Türkeş and his friends made with İslamist circles after they returned to the country.

There was also an ideological continuity in this sense. In the illustrative relationship that Tilly made between "state-making" and "war-making," the "Wars of Liberation/Foundation [that] accompany the formation of citizen-armies and compulsory military service accompanies the birth of nationalism and nation states"; but "in addition to this, [the] military in Turkey has functioned as a weighted actor for reproduction of modern nation construction, national-socialization and nationalistic ideology" (Altınay and Bora, 2009: 153). The increasing role of the military, let alone decreasing, in the political history of Turkey after state-making, corresponded to the homogenization of Turkish nationalism ideologies on the ideological level and the transformation of nationalism to a hegemonical ideology. The critical point here is "the fact that the military-nation myth, which is an important part of the nationalist ideology, keeps the marriage between militarism and nationalism alive" (Altınay and Bora, 2009: 154). In other words, a genuine ideological transformation from "citizen-army" to "army-nation" is at stake. That military-nation myth that has been kept alive by Turkish militarism[36] has become one of the main ideological vessels of Turkish paramilitarism. The "Turkish State is conceived as an organic existence that has its historical personality and continuity in idealist ideology" (Can, 2009: 682).[37]

In that case, this is a general thesis: Turkish militarism and paramilitarism, during the transition from autocratic militarism to semiauthoritarian incorporation, has been capitalized by preserving its organizational and ideological genuinesses.

In spite of that thesis, it would be wrong to think of the political actor of Turkish paramilitarism as a solid and consistent formation in terms of organization and ideology. The biggest difference of Turkish paramilitarism from especially its equivalents in Latin America is that it depends upon a political actor that was highly massified, and it acquired a political influence many times more than its massiveness. We will annotate step by step the

---

36   See Ağaoğulları, 1987: 191.
37   As a final genuineness, it is also possible to attach a romantic vision remaining from Turanism (see Ağaoğulları, 1987: 190). In addition to the anti-communist indoctrination that we have met in international cases of paramilitarism, the fact that the Turan dreamed by idealists was in Soviet territories has included a powerful Russian hostility to anti-communism. Althought the Turkish ultranationalistic right-wing gave up its Turan dreams and retreated to Turkish borders ideologically and organizationally starting from the 1950s, "Muscovy" hostility has kept its presence as a powerful source of motivation. It should also be noted that Ottoman-Russia wars for decades have been a cultural motive that incites this hostility. "Communists to Moskow," a slogan of the Turkish ultranationalistic right-wing in that period, has an ideological and cultural background in this sense.

role of the Turkish bourgeoisie in the creation of this political influence, but it would be wrong to reduce the reason to only this: Under this consistent massification, as well as open support of the bourgeoisie and military-nation myth being kept alive constantly by militarism, there is also a genuine ideological-organizational attitude:

The idealist movement (MHP and Hearts of Ideal) has been a "devotion" movement that has defined its main goal as massification and has built its strength with the power of massification since its foundation. Despite the fact that it had founders coming from Republic elites and a pro-coup-"pro-resistance" tradition, both its organizational form and its ideological grounding presents a loose and eclectic structure (Can, 2009: 663).

Therefore, the MHP should be seen not as a legal-front party that helped to cover paramilitary practices, but as a party that gained a political existence in the Turkish right-wing especially by its leader's "charisma" and a party that postponed its showdown with other components of the Turkish right-wing due to *urgent needs of state* and thus the *duties* that it accepted. A constant swinging is at stake here, and the leadership myth, which is apparent in similar parties, is the one that holds this party together despite this swinging:

On the one hand, there is an obdurate stance which has the slogan of "The address of idealism is obvious" and intended to break the influence of not-MHP nationalist powers; on the other hand, there is a pragmatical stance intended to contain not-MHP organizations by presenting the idealism as a main impartial ideology and mostly overlapped with clientelist relationship networks. There is a cyclical, pragmatical swinging between these two ends. (Can, 2009: 682)

After presenting the similarities between the essential political actor of paramilitary practices in Turkey and its international equivalents, and its different genuinesses, we now focus on the process of political formation. An examination of the 27 May 1960 coup d'état is required specifically to analyze the political atmosphere that created the MHP because Türkeş was one of the members of the Committee of National Unity who executed the coup d'etat.

A general opinion about the Turkish army having two wings as "moderates" and "radicals" since the 1960s does exist. Certainly, the tension between authoritarian reformism and West-style liberal democracy seeking is one of the points that emphasizes this opinion; it appears as a distinction between officers who wish to deliver the administration to electees as soon as possible and officers who wish to prolong the coup d'état and insist that long-term and vertical regulations need to be done. On the other hand, it would be quite troubling to compress the issue into only political understandings of officers. This would compress the era into the pure political history. Second and most importantly, the opinion frequently seen in Turkey even today of the 1960 coup d'état being "progressive" politically originates from this absolutization of the two wings distinction.[38] Türkeş and his friends ("The Fourteen") were dismissed from the Committee of National Unity but were never *liquidated* by the committee.

Türkeş, who was sentenced by a racism lawsuit in 1944 but returned to military service later after being found innocent, was the leader of the committee's so-called "radical" wing. Colonel Türkeş's proposals for prolonging the coup d'état and creating a centralized "Culture Super-Ministry" free from political effect were met by the Committee's high-ranking commanders with apprehension.[39] These types of proposals were not acceptable in terms of the capitalist-military coalition and national and international political balances; therefore, the demands of Türkeş were perceived as a "threat of dictatorship" in the given circumstances. As a result, Türkeş and his 13 lower-ranking friends were dismissed from the Committee on 13 November 1960 and appointed to foreign duties.[40]

This dismissal was not a liquidation. Although there is not an agreement about this matter, some researchers claim that Adnan Menderes, Fatin Rüştü Zorlu and Hasan Polatkan were put to death to quiet the inside military factors

---

38   For instance, Işıklı (1987), by accepting this distinction as given, thinks that the rights of the union and the strike were given according to the progressive characteristic of the 1961 Constitution. However, active industrialisation moves in the capital accumulation strategy of that period caused an increase in the worker population. A certain capital accumulation strategy was been realized in harmony with the worker accumulation strategy in cities which caused an increase in the political struggle. Many protests that occurred in 1960 in mostly İstanbul demanded strikes and collective agreements. The Kavel resistance in January 1963 represented a very important threshold. After these developments, laws numbered 274 and 275 of the union, collective agreement and strikes, were enacted on 24 July 1963. As a result of both a return to liberal democracy and the rapid industrialization process in Europe after World War II, there was a difference between the inclusion of "employees" and "workers" clauses in the 1961 Constitution together with their notional rights and the actual enactment of related laws in 1963. Instead of defining an implicit *freedom telos* in the 1960 coup d'état, it would be appropriate to focus on social and political processes.

39   See Weiker, 1967: 133-134; Jacoby, 2005a: 134-135.

40   For a detailed examination of Committee of National Unity's general structure and dismissal see Eroğul, 1987: 119-121.

who reacted to The Fourteen's dismissal.[41] In any case, the clearest evidence of this occurrence is the return of Türkeş to the country at the beginning of 1963 to go into politics by taking advantage of political opportunities in given circumstances. After all, Türkeş is "great and wealthy."[42]

Türkeş initally attempted to enter the AP, but since the leaders of the AP were not open to his participation, he searched for a party to put the political doctrines he developed during the period abroad into practice, and he did not have any difficulties finding one. The fact that Türkeş and his friends entered the CKMP (Republican Peasant National Party) and took control of its administration in a short time indicates a successful operation; the CKMP was fully open to this type of operation after its charismatic leader Osman Bölükbaşı resigned from the party along with his supporters.[43] The process that started in June 1965 with 10 people of The Fourteen becoming members of the party, proceeded with Türkeş electing himself as commissar and building indirect relationships with local organizations of the party. Separations and disputes within the party rose from this situation and ended with Türkeş being elected as party leader in the extraordinary congress in same year (see Ağaoğulları, 1987: 193). Following the separation of objector groups within the CKMP, the party went to a rapid transformation period and the name of the party was changed to the MHP in the Adana congress on 8 February 1969, according to this four-year transformation. In this four-year period, the MHP completed the transformation appropriate to the civil war concept both organizationally and doctrinally.

On the other hand, the 1964-65 momentum was a critical point for concentration of anti-left emotions in military and capital circles. Aside from the socio-cultural reasons created by the huge gap between high growth rates and employment rates in that period, one of the main reasons for these anti-left emotions is the withdrawal from NATO in that period by the coalition government, under the leadership of the CHP, as well as the circumstances in which USA President Johnson tried to prevent the intervention in Cyprus. Fresh off the withdrawal from NATO, the CHP build tactical relationships with the USSR. This situation "caused considerable anger and alarm within

---

41   See Ahmad, 1977: 171-172. Jacoby (2005a) also supports this opinion.
42   Yet more, according to Jacoby "Türkeş was *persuaded* to resign his commission and enter politics" (Jacoby, 2011: 912, italics added).
43   For a brief background of CKMP see Ağaoğulları, 1987: 212, footnote 74.

the military, particularly from those influenced by Türkeş who was himself a Turkish Cypriot" (Jacoby, 2005a: 136).

However, the main reason is, as we will discuss in detail, the constantly growing organizational and political capacity of the left wing. The fact that the TİP (Workers Party of Turkey) in particular was elected with 15 congressman in 1965 alarmed the related circles. In the same period, an old employee of USA-based Morrison company, Süleyman Demirel, took charge of the AP, and the AP started to spread an intense anti-communist propaganda. Kemal Karpat states that "rising middle classes would use nationationalism to protect themselves against social movements" (cited by Taşkın, 2009: 622). We can certainly add not only rational decision intended to "using," but an actual "mass fear" (Taşkın, 2009: 626) to that. If we ignore some small-scaled attempts before 1960, the TKMD (Anti-Communist Fighters Association of Turkey), initially established in 1963, became a semi-official identity after the AP came to power alone in 1965, and a "number of KMDs which set an offensive course increased fifteen times more between 1963-1965, raised to 110 at 1965, to 141 at 1968" (Bora and Can, 2004: 57). The KMDs also actively supported taking the CKMP plan of Türkeş.

It is possible to handle this transformation in three dimensions. First is the transformation that occurred from the "movement" that materialized in small radical ("above politics") intellectual groups towards the political "motion" that brought various ideational and ideological aspects together and massified gradually (see Bora and Can, 2004: 52). The CKMP/MHP, which was in close contact with other nationalist associations as well as the KMDs, spread youth organizations in this period and the ÜOD (Associations of Hearths of Ideal), whose relation with the party became more obscure, was reestablished in this period.[44] "Commando camps," established in the summer of 1968, were added to the quickly growing Hearts of Ideal.[45] That summer was an important crossroad for the history of the radical left wing. The objective of the MHP was to raise anti-communist "militia personnel" (*bozkurtlar*).[46] The sociological meaning is *consolidation* of current anti-communist street power, which existed in a disorderly manner in various associations and party,

---

44 "Dündar Taşer was one of the founders of Hearts of Ideal and of educational camps lately known as commando camps. In a sense he served as the mastermind of idealism" (Yılmaz, 2009: 668).
45 In the late 1970s, Hearts of Ideal had almost 100 thousand members. See Ağaoğulları, 1987: 199.
46 For an opinion about whether those camps were not functional as opposed to popular belief, this belief was produced by the MHP in a form of legend, and the left wing tended to expand its "enemy," see Bora and Can, 2004: 58d, 63d.

around a single "Party." Türkeş, who was excluded from military organization, in other words from state as an actor would return to state with a paramilitary organization.

> In the period of 1969-1971 where the political environment became tense, anti-communist terror of "bozkurtlar" has been accepted and supported widely by dominant community, state and [...] "civil war apparatus" in particular. It is known that the President of the Republic Cevdet Sunay told to CHP leader İnönü, who called attention to the terror of Hearts of Ideal, "no big deal, they are kids who fight against communism." (Bora and Can, 2004: 59)

One essential reflection of this transformation placed on an ideological/discursive level and shown directly parallel with this organizational transformation is "the corporatist, developmentalist-modernist Kemalist restoration design" (Bora and Can, 2004: 53), which was dominant between 1963 and 1966, giving its place to a fanatical and offensive anti-communist discourse. The natural result of this transformation was the rapid regression of " 'anti-capitalist,' 'anti-mason' discourse that disturbs grand bourgeoisie" in the CKMP/MHP ideology, which stands up for an "idealist way" (Bora and Can, 2004: 55) apart from capitalist and communist ways which were seen as a product of foreign ideologies initially.[47] Finally, as evident in the famous "Turkish as much as Mount God, Muslim as much as Mount Hira" expression in 1969, what was at stake here was that ideological discourse, which had dominant Turkist-Turanist characteristics and the laicism emphasis, was being instrumentally Islamized. Consequently, the ideological discourse was to resolve the doubts of capitalist-military coalition and embrace Muslim groups that were opened to anti-communist provocation.[48]

Changing the name and bylaw of the party in the Adana Congress in 1969 was actually the official statement of these essential transformations. Through the party bylaw accepted at this congress, a hierarchial association reminiscent of a military organization that absolutized the authority of central managing bodies but actually of a general president became official. This party managing style, in which Türkeş was elected on consensus at each general

---

47 Similarly, Türkeş swiftly left his "land reform" demand that he mentioned in the early 1960s. See Bora and Can, 2004: 53.
48 For a more extensive information about MHP ideology see Ağaoğulları, 1987: 195-198.

assembly and in which lists of executives for various stages were generated, survived until the death of Türkeş (see Ağaoğulları, 1987: 193-194). On the other hand, this type of centralization brought liquidation within the party forward. Türkeş brought street power that was initially distributed together under a single party roof and then he liquidated or intimidated both those who defended the racist-Turanist view remaining from the 1940s and "socialist nationalists" who gravely carried an anti-capitalist resonance (see Bora and Can, 2004: 55-56). In this way, ideological purification was completed after organizational siding.

After the KMDs reached a serious number in 1965, the first paramilitary attacks against left wing university youth started but there had not been any use of firearms yet.[49] After the establishment of Hearts of Ideal and educational camps named "commando camps" in 1968, idealist youngsters were exposed to both doctrinaire education and martial arts and weapon training. The MHP executives frankly accepted and announced commando camps when they were first established, hence the Türkeş quote presented in the epigraph at the start of this chapter in this period of time. But starting from 1969, the MHP refused its organic relation with commando camps after the increasing number and systematic murderous attacks on worker and student organizations. This is an important pattern that left its imprint on ensuing years regarding the relationship between the MHP and Hearts of Ideal; thus, the mind and body of MHP were different from each other in the 1970s, the party center dealt with *bigger politics* while the idealist youth struggled with *street politics*. We will see that this was not a mere cover either.

The replacement of the *bozkurtlar*, who were blessed by Türkeş with "protecting the country from communism" and "conserving the state" mission, as "civil power partaking next to the state" (Bora and Can, 2004: 59) gives a clear definition of paramilitarism and defines the inclusive way of this paramilitary organization to state field. It is important to notice that idealism and anti-communism became an *occupation* rather than a political identity[50] and the morality, employment period and source of income of this occupation is defined within the civil war concept (and the partial similarity between this and the definition of "professional revolutionist" is remarkable). After

---

49   To learn more about the AP-MHP competition that occurred in the KMDs in the 1967-68 period and
      MHPs winning this competition see Bora and Can, 2004: 58.
50   See Bora and Can, 2004: 56.

the coup d'état deactivated them, the *bozkurtlar* were "unemployed" until the 1973-74 momentum.

II. RADICALIZATION PROCESS OF THE TURKISH LEFT WING: RADICAL-CONSTITUTIVE VIOLENCE AS A SYNTHESIS

"The Proletariat party is a fighter organization that brings up any type of protests from the smallest reformist movement to revolutionist terrorism in the right place at the right time." [Mahir Çayan][51]

This section of the study is based on an essential assertion: Although self-positioning ways and strategies of actors are important in the effort to explain the ways of political violence, they cannot be the starting point. Our emphasis on historical relationality gains an original meaning here. The radicalization process of the Turkish left wing had a context in which friend-enemy differences were sharpened within multiple *collective* relationships. Within the political atmosphere of that period, for the most part, a transformation from agonistic political attitudes towards antagonistic political attitudes happened.

We will also challenge a *doxa* frequently encountered in Turkey as in several European countries: The *doxa* of '68's "innocent" student movements "deviated from the aim" by extreme left factors. The liberal argument, which alleges that social actors were driven away from politics from the moment of resorting to violence, certainly is a very important factor for the creation of this *doxa*. The historical and political construction process of radical-constitutive violence in Turkey reveals the incorrectness of this understanding, which is willful-romantic at best.

Radical-constitutive violence as a phenomenon in a social and political junction point is a product of several original dynamics. Four essential dynamics exist behind the radicalization process where the fact of radical-constitutive violence occurred in Turkey: (i) contra-movement, (ii) ideological siding, (iii) rivalry within the left wing, and (iv) the revolutionist conjuncture of the world.

The most important factor affecting the radicalization processes was certainly the compulsory mechanisms that political actors encountered. Political condensations occurring from the pushing of oppression mechanisms produced

---

51   See Çayan, 2004: 301.

a mutual oppression-violence cycle. On the other hand, explaining the physical practice, which caused the political movement to use radical-constitutive violence as an essential instrument with only routine state compulsory left the unanswered question of why related actors started to organize radical-constitutive violence in the late 1960s and early 1970s and not in the early 1960s. Here, we borrow Isabelle Sommier's "contra-movement" concept. Sommier uses the "contra-movement"[52] concept to define right wing masses used as paramilitary forces by the state and actively organized in coordination with oppression instruments. A relational understanding that will be formed based on this concept,

> in a sense, would invite to examine the constant interactions between the starting movement, which usually feeds activation cycles, and contra-movement. The occurrence of a contra-movement would create opposite effects on the starting movement; may contribute to wake it up under the perception of shock and menace or put it together; also it would influence the radicalization of movement as it did in precedent. 'Dual dynamic' following this situation would influence both values, objectives and tactics, ways of action of two groups. This perspective reminds the fact that social movements would create political opportunities and a sense of menace as well, on the other hand it also obliges to accept the essential place of emotions (fear, anger) in activity processes. (Sommier, 2012: 60)[53]

In that case, contra-movement practices would activate the rivalry within the left wing. Oppressions and attacks that both state personnel and paramilitary forces in the fermentation period applied caused the problem of the "revolutionist subject" in the left wing youth movement, and discussions about this issue brought an agonistic attitude among the opponent factors within the left. The climax of the process was the transformation of "rival" to "enemy" as a result of ideological siding. Ways of "armed struggle" action

---

52 One of the important reasons why we preferred this conceptualization is the fact that Türkeş emphasized "movement" and "action" frequently. According to Ağaoğulları (1987: 193, 212 footnote 77), the effect of the Franco regime on Türkeş had a hand in this. Another name for the Spanish Falangist party was *Partido de Movimiento Nacional*.

53 The Turkish translation of related reference (Sommier, 2012) is used. For the genuine study in French see Sommier, 2008.

coming from the problem of political struggle action formed the *separating lines* in strategy discussions of the left.

Ideological siding emerged as the rationality of the collective actor of radical-constitutive violence. The cognitive level of the issue is important at this point because there are two important factors during the transformation of a social movement to a political violence movement: "On the one hand, existence of an ideology or ethics that acknowledges the violence as a rule, in other words justify the resorting to violence [...] On the other hand, the creation of an environment that acknowledges the violence (historical activity of violence, marginalization sense of the group), namely enlargement of the belief – based on previous experiences – for violence's practical activity" (Sommier, 2012: 17). As we are going to see, belief for both theoretical and practical inevitability of violence in the late 1960s was dominant to a great extent, especially within the left youth movement. The last dynamic of the radicalization process is the revolutionist conjuncture of the world: "International context has fed up a warlike imagination" (Sommier, 2012: 31). In the international context, different types of armed struggles that people gave against imperialism and acquired successes spread the idea of an international civil war happening. Left wing actors of that period followed closely the actions, experiences, and knowledge of a global revolutionist movement and all political and military moves of the "archenemy," the USA. The series of coup d'états perceived as an international phenomenon of the 1960-80 era has a general characteristic, and it points to an original moment that intertwines the local and the universal.

Oppressions and attacks of state personnel and paramilitary groups appeared physically in two different ways of political violence during the radicalization process: (i) *violence as a defence practice* against paramilitary constitutions and (ii) *violence as an offence practice* against the state. These two types of violence occurred diachronically in the 1960s, became synchronical in the 1970s, and play an important role in the understanding of the 1975-80 political violence momentum.

It is possible to see the radical-constitutive violence, which left its mark on the political history of Turkey for years starting in the late '60s, as a product of a synthesis. Thesis and antithesis showed up in 1961: The TİP (Workers Party of Turkey) established by a group of unionists on 13 February

1961 and the *Direction* journal that began publication on 20 December 1961.[54] Physical locations where thesis and antithesis confront each other and come to synthesis are Thought Clubs that were actually student youth branches.[55]

The first Thought Club was established at Ankara University's Faculty of Political Sciences in the end of 1950s. The importance of this first club, which was under the influence of the CHP, is that it organized the 29 April student upheavals that *summon* 27 May so to speak. The upheaval happened at the Cebeci campus of Ankara University on 29 April 1960 and broke out when the students of the Faculty of Law came together and stood in silence for a student killed in Istanbul. In this memorial where CHP was an important factor in organizing the process, the direct target of the students was the Democratic Party of that period. Slogans against the Democratic Party increased after the memorial and upheaval escalated due to the university management calling the police to the campus. Police intervention pushed students to a more radical threshold, and resistance by students escalated the police violence. Police could not control the upheaval and attacked students with troopers leading the incident to chaos on a micro level. The upheaval was so big so that the Minister of Internal Affairs, the Governor, the Martial Law Commander, and the Chief of Police came. The cost of this upheaval was tens of wounded students, and 58 students in the Political Sciences were sent to jail. The political importance of this upheaval, registered as "29 April Resistance," is that it created a pattern for next MDD (National Democratic Revolution) line which might be called the Kemalist left.

The rapid increase of the TİP after a couple of years of its establishment matched the increase of anti-left emotions within military and capitalist elites.[56] The fact that the TİP (Workers Party of Turkey) was elected with almost 300,000 votes and 15 congressmen in council in 1965 was the starting point of the first paramilitary attacks. The response to this situation in the micro-cosmos of students was not delayed: During the sale of the Transformation journal at Kızılay Ankara, which published its first issue on 22 April 1965, for the first time, the contra-movement and the police joined in alliance to intervene in

---

54 Discussion about the socialist revolution-national democratic revolution that originated here has influenced Turkish socialist movement in different ways for years.
55 It may be necessary to make a methodological warning here. We use the notorious thesis-antithesis-synthesis trio as an expression instrument only to help classify similarities and differences. Therefore, we definitely do not think that the synthesis position is an implicit *thelos* for thesis and antithesis, which by the way is a mistake frequently used by Turkey's left wing actors.
56 See Jacoby, 2005a: 136.

the youth sellers making a tremendous impact. The political importance of this incident is the encountering of the student movement with an anti-fascist agenda for the first time. Secondly, the occurence of a contra-movement directly influenced the form of starting a movement. The left student activists who were in "need of recuperation" against "fascist attacks" founded the FKF (Federation of Thought Clubs) on 17 December 1965, and they gathered current clubs under a single roof.[57] Therefore, clubs obtained an institutional qualification and became the "socialist organization of student youth."

The FKF acted actively as the TIP's youth organization until 1968. The FKF, since its beginning, rather than being a mere student movement, had a literal *partisan* character. Socialist students, who were organized under the name of Thought Clubs, learned union struggle within the TİP, acting together with other union movements, organizations and mass relationships, preparing protests, preparing banners and many more experiences. The institutionalization of the FKF as the TIP's youth organization in that period caused an organic association of student activity and masses under the party roof.

We already described *Direction* as an antithesis. The political importance of this journal is its being the place where the MDD strategy, which created a huge powerful force in 1968 especially, was formulated for the first time: "a left Kemalist substitutionalism which projected that the elite, technocrats, and officers would lead Turkey 'indepedently' on behalf of the workers and peasants – 'for the people, in spite of the people'" (Samim, 1987: 155). But the youth's demand for *more radicalism*, which increased starting from 1967-68, certainly swallowed the TIP and *Direction* together. Its circulation dropped fast and *Direction* was shut down in 1967. The *Turkish Left* journal, which was the defender of a radicalized MDD formulation, took its place. This journal was under the influence of Mihri Belli who had a long-standing past in the history of Turkish socialism. Mihri Belli included student youth among the actors of the MDD strategy: "students would agitate, officers would strike, and a national junta would take power" (Samim, 1987: 157).

The first confrontation between the TİP and the MDD happened in the 1st Congress of the FKF on 22 January 1967. Although TIP's students took over the administration at the end of the congress, the MDD's steps started to come close. The most concrete appearance was that the first important memorial of 29 April happened in 1967. On the one hand, 29 April was a symbol of

---

57   Yıldırım, 2008 is generally used for incidents related to the history of FKF.

radicalism from the viewpoint of youngsters in the FKF, which began to expand and diversify. On the other hand, the MDD strategy referenced 29 April as the *yearning of 27 May*, therefore the demand of the left junta. This ambivalent situation directly reflected the pronouncement that the FKF administration published. The pronouncement, titled "Not New 28-29 April, New Turkey," welcomed 29 April as a "resistance" and dissociated the "Youth of 29 April" and the "Youth of FKF" by using socialist terminology: "Yearnings of '60s youth were symptoms of classical bourgeois liberty such as two chamber, right of proof, liberty of press etc. *Conscious youth* of 1967 understood the country's salvation problem to the core and reached to true liberty and the people's wish to obtain infinite growing and developing" (Yıldırım 2008: 121, italics added). The criticism of the FKF about 29 April was that the "Youth of 29 April" were under the CHP's guidance. The TIP and FKF logic conducted a strategy of separating their own political logic by taking into account that the yearning of 27 May was the political motivation under the memorial of 29 April. The TİP is the will of disengagement from 27 May and the political forms it represents (pro-junta and jacobinic government strategies); it gave the government strategies from below prominence by emphasizing political channels of public and socialism and enabled a disengagement contact on this level: The FKF "has played an important role for youth, who appears with its offical organizations in Kemalist corporative state structure, 'to be disengaged from state completely and in mass' " (Sarısözen, 1988: 2070).

However, the TİP started to come loose politically in this period for various reasons. Firstly, after the TİP was elected with 15 congressmen in council in 1965, a representative of military-capitalist elite group, the AP government changed election laws in such a manner that prevented the success of small parties. Secondly, the Czechoslovakian invasion of the Soviet Union caused a grave crack within the TİP. Third and most importantly, the TİP did not respond to the students' energy of protest created in Paris in 1968. The "lack of protest" assignation made at the FKF congress in this period transformed to a "pacifism" accusation in a short time.[58] The basic criterion of radicalism within left wing rivalry was *anti-imperialism* now, and the Vietnam War certainly had an absolute role.

---

58   The concept of "pacifism" is used for "antiwar" in Europe but it is used for "running from protest" in Turkey's left-wing jargon.

After 1961 and 1965, the critical turning point in Turkish left wing history was the year 1968. Everything progressed rapidly in 1968. Doğu Perinçek was elected president at the 2nd Congress of the FKF on 23-24 March 1968 and left Kemalist discourse directly became prominent: Front politics against "obscurantism and bigotry," "enemies of science," and "feudalism."[59] In this period of a couple of months, the FKF joined the *Dev-Güç* (Union of Revolutionary Forces), which was a union comprised of leftist-pro-junta associations, and myths such as "Second War of Independence," "Glorious 29 April Resistance" entered into political rhetoric. After a couple of months, May 1968 in Europe made an impact in Turkey as the June Occupations; heroic anti-imperialism expressions gave their place rapidly to substantial demands of students. There were no responses to demands of "educational reform" and "educational revolution" in the MDD strategy and self-management practices occurring from occupations undermined the MDD. Finally, anti-imperialist protests that burst out against the 6th fleet in July terminated the TİP's influence over student youth once and for all. Here are Veysi Sarısözen's words from the TİP, who was the president of the FKF for a short period of time:

> In the previous period youngsters read a lot, know a lot, speak well, were the example of socialist youngsters. But these were displaced by physically strong people who know how to fight. Scales of being "radical" have changed unbelievably fast in one year. In early 1968, being "radical," being "extreme," was equal to being from TİP of being socialist, but at the end of 1968 being from TİP stood for staying behind in both theoretical and practical protest. (Sarısözen, 1988: 2082)

When the synthesis position explained below emerged in Doğu Perinçek's relegation to the presidency of the FKF, the theoretical equivalent of this synthesis appeared in a bulletin dated 20 January 1969. Expressions like "establishing organic bonds with nationalist class and layers" and "progressive revolution" in the bulletin show parallelism with the MDD logic in general. However, expressions like "proletariat organization" and "proletariat leadership" in the bulletin clearly show the disintegration in the MDD, which previously broke its connections with the TİP. The practice repertoire of the FKF in that

---

59   "Feudalism" is defined as a *cultural deficiency status* in left Kemalist jargon.

period clearly presents this situation: On the one hand, students of the left wing participated in anti-imperialist protests (the peak of those was the burning of USA Ambassador R. Commer's car at Middle East Technical University); on the other hand, they participated in the protests of workers and peasants. The political assignation of imperialism being an "internal fact," not an external enemy, witnessed the birth of a political mind that transformed the anti-imperialist struggle into a civil war concept. Books telling the experiences of Leninism's 3rd World adaptations were quickly translated into Turkish and were read widely. The heresiological jargon acquired from Leninism rapidly came into circulation in that period: revisionists, reformists, opportunists, in short equivalents of Kautsky, Bernstein etc.

Another intensifying factor in the 1968-70 momentum was the attacks by the contra-movement. The left opposition, particularly the youth struggle, was exposed to paramilitary attacks where firearms were systematically used and murders occurred. Therefore, the contra-movement both secured its political ground and became professional in that period. Oppression created by the contra-movement directed the youth movement to "collecting together," i.e., *condensation* once again: the FKF's name was changed to *Dev-Genç* (Federation of Revolutionary Youth of Turkey) in the 4th Congress of the FKF on 9-10 October 1969. This was not only a name change but a new mission definition. Thus, the student organization left campus after a mass of students. In the words of its own actors, the mission of *Dev-Genç* was "to collect organizations, which contain masses of workers and peasants in particular and fulfil the duty of revolutionists bravely not only in universities but nationwide, under our roof" (Yıldırım, 2008: 371).

On the other hand, the working class wanting a "proletariat organization" soon confronted the young revolutionists. The separation of the DİSK (The Confederation of Revolutionary Trade Unions) from the *Türk-İş* (The Confederation of Turkish Trade Unions) in 1967 caused an increased number of protests such as occupations, strikes, and marches. The intense conflict in which 100,000 workers engaged with security forces on 15-16 June 1970 at the İstanbul-Kocaeli line became the climax of the class movement:[60] "A class movement within a society persistently called the 'unprivileged classless' by Kemalizm! A movement that overcomes the police, even military barricades!" (Laçiner, 1976: 19). Both professionalized and systematized paramilitary

---

60   For detailed information see Öztürk, 2001 and Işıklı, 1987.

attacks and this massive radical protest of working class were interpreted as *reveille of civil war* by *Dev-Genç*. But this new mission incapacitated *Dev-Genç*; starting from early 1971, as the final condensation stage, three leader figures of the youth movement (Deniz Gezmiş, Mahir Çayan and İbrahim Kaypakkaya) established the revolutionist "parties" who undertook this mission. A condensation like the molecules that come closer and activate as the boiling point approaches occurred from Thought Clubs to *Dev-Genç* and from there to revolutionist "parties." The seekings named "the process/stage of becoming party" later and nearly transformed to a fetish in the history of the left will always take this pattern as an example:[61]

> The meaning of these cores is the fact that youngsters with all of their inexperiences now step up into a relationship area defined by a morality depending on a life or death war and by new human relationships within a highly specific cooperation mechanism that is different than traditional student companionship. A starting point that all "underground organizations," "revolutionist movements" established in ensuing years can rely on has been formed within these relationships inseminated at 1968. Established at 1971 and became the womb of all revolutionist "policies," THKP-C, THKO and TİKKO[62] have risen from these "cores" [...] When evolutional lines of these groups are considered, it is not a coincidence that even a single person who did not come from these first "professional revolutionist" cores of 1968 do not exist in their leadership. (Kürkçü, 1998: 2107)

There is an important matter here that separates the radical-constitutive political violence actors of Turkey from their equivalents in Europe: Armed struggle in Turkey evolved not as a product of taking over the government, who foresaw civil war, the strategy of revolutionist struggle, but it developed against the attacks within mass struggle in universities, factories, street protests,

---

61 Although the establishment style of the text may seem biased, we would like to stress that we do not have an evaluative attitude against policy implications and strategies developed by left wing actors of this period. Our goal is to determine the moment of birth of radical-constitutive violence actors who will keep their presence for long years in political history of Turkey.

62 THKP-C (People's Liberation Party-Front of Turkey), THKO (People's Liberation Army of Turkey). TİKKO (Workers' and Peasants' Liberation Army of Turkey) is in fact the name of TKP-ML's (Communist Party of Turkey-Marxist Leninist) military organization.

occupations, and briefly in cities. In other words, the starting of armed struggle and the use of violence instruments such as firearms have not been a product of *a priori* thought that existed before experience: "As a matter of fact, in Turkey's recent history arms showed up before 'the armed revolution idea' " (Kürkçü, 2007: 494).

An aspect of ideological siding developed at this point, and the emphasis on the working class concentrated in *a lá* Third World Leninism caused different violence strategies within the practical struggle to be framed by revolutionist party programs. When both parliamentarian and left-junta roads came to an end on 12 March, the birth of the "public war" strategy had already materialized through *armed struggle organizing from below*. This strategy, by its Leninist character that dogmatically separates it from 1968 Europe, depended not on an anti-authoritarian and anti-organizational motivation but on a political mind intended to build contra-authority and contra-organizations. In that case, it is possible to formulate a thesis, anti-thesis and synthesis:

Thesis: The basic approach of the first position depends on the *priority of politics to the military structure*. The political party established in a legal area, which finds a place within civil society, is seen as a political unit that carries social-political demands to the parliament. Representative of this line, which has "Socialist Turkey" as its political goal, is the TİP. The non-governmental organization in which the TİP is grounded for mass organization is unions, but it is grounded in parliament in political society. It is possible to define the first position, which connects to parliamentarian political channels through mass study and political party, as in establishment, pacifistic.

Anti-Thesis: The second position that depends on the *priority of military structure to politics* supports a left-junta strategy organized within the military. This strategy that sees political parties and student-worker-peasant movements as potential means of parliament suspension is the logic of the MDD, and its political representatives are the *Direction* journal, Mihri Belli and Doğu Perinçek. The organization in which it is grounded is oppression instruments of political society and basically the military. Mass movement are seen as instruments to wear out the government by invalidating parliamentarian forms to pave the way for a military coup d'état. It is possible to briefly define the second position, which depends on the "revolutionist" wing of armed forces taking over the government through coup d'état, as not-parliamentarian but in an establishment position.

Synthesis: The basic approach of the third synthesis position is *armed struggle under the decisiveness of the political.* The political representatives of the synthesis position, which defends public war strategy based on armed struggle under the leadership of a party established within people, are the THKO, THKP-C, TKP-ML. Mass struggle formed by petite-bourgeois movements besides movements of workers and peasants constitutes the social movement moment of a radical disengagement (political movement). The third position is not based on given organizations unlike the first two positions; it tries to demolish them and to create its own political and military contra-organizations. Mass struggle connects to armed struggle through a political party. It is possible to briefly define the third position, which acknowledges violence as a form of political struggle, as non-parliamentarist, anti-establishment, uncompromising.[63]

In analyses on this era, there is a tendency to see the second and third position as identical or continuations of each other.[64] Putting aside the philosophico-political conservative understandings that categorically equate coup d'état and revolution or the liberal approaches about politics-violence relationship, this tendency has an understandable part in the sense of history: There is a short period of time between the creation of the third position and the death of its initiators.[65] Therefore, although the "synthesis position" did completely separate theoretically from the MDD logic, the armed practices that started shortly before the 12 March Coup D'état was perceived as if they were the coup d'état preparatory practices.

On the other hand, in a state-centric analysis framework, in a study that examines the evolvement and organizational forms of militarism in Turkey

---

63 This formulation was presented before in another study. See Öğütle and Etil, 2014.
64 For example, see Samim, 1987.
65 For instance, all leader militias of THKP-C that completely broke off their relations with MDD logic through an open letter in January 1971 were murdered in March 1972.

for instance, the margin between second and third positions would not make a big difference. Therefore, Jacoby (2005a: 137-138) giving his essential attention to *MDD/radical officer conspiracy* is totally understandable and consistent. However, very important empirical and methodological results of this margin exist in the sense of this type of study oriented to examine the relationality between state coercion and collective political violence and the actors occurring from this relationality.

The first empirical results are related to the transformation within the context of used concepts. We already stressed that *anti-imperialism* is an essential criteria in the process of disengagement from TİP. However, a transformation occurring within the context of the imperialism concept exists in the difference between second and third positions. Imperialism from the point of the second position, which is called left Kemalist, is an *external* fact that has *political* collaborators in the country, and the expression of this in terms of action is "driving the enemy into the sea" as seen in the 6th Fleet protests.[66] The third position defines the imperialism as an *internal* fact that has *class* collaborators in the country, and the expression of this in terms of action appears as a civil war concept that takes on a dominant class structure. A similar transformation is applied to the concept of "fascism." Emphasis on fascism from the point of the third position has shifted from the "ideological" analyses focusing on micro basics out of the state body to political analyses related to the state structure itself. The concrete meaning of this is the term fascist getting rid of cultural meanings such as "obscurantist," "bigot," "enemy of science," and becoming an adjective that directly describes the state. This also means a disengagement from the "tyrant state vs. civil society" understanding that directs the TİP to parliament and the MDD to the military. The importance of those conceptual transformations regarding our subject results from that the behaviour of taking the state on with all of its organizations by making "fascist" the adjective of the state will be the essential starting point of guerilla strategies. The behaviour of making an anti-imperialist theme a part of the civil war concept by defining "imperialism" as an internal fact, an aspect composed by dominant classes, will directly affect the definition of "complicitous civilians" (Goodwin, 2006). Therefore, ignoring the transformation of these concepts obscures the constitutive aspect

---

66   "Driving the enemy into the sea" directly refers to the revocation of İzmir from Greek occupation at 1922.

of political violence, the definition of "enemy," and makes a political mind of radical-constitutive left violence in the 1970s and its violent strategies largely incomprehensible and inexplicable.

The second empirical result, which comes from not setting a margin between the second and third positions, is that this will seriously injure the explanation efforts devoted to the political violence moment of 1975-80 and most importantly to the Kurdish radical-constitutive political violence movement. Although there is a short period of time between the creation of the third position and the death of its initiators, the strategic rationality in theory and practice here has played an important role in the practices of followers. The Kurdish movement, as a whole, has been formed by discussions and its relationships with radical left groups during the 1970s in particular.

Finally, there is also a methodological mistake, which could be called a *teleological mistake*, in naming radical-constitutive violence actors as "preparatories of coup d'état" as a result of ignoring the margin. This means attributing the intent to actors based on conclusion, which is the trademark of conspiratorial approaches. These approaches read the political history of Turkey through a concept of "coup d'état" purified from its historicity, and transform the political sphere into a theater stage for the over-history struggle of civil society and military forces. It is not possible that these types of approaches, which consider coup d'états as sinister interventions not having any social relations, coming from outside, can properly understand the mechanisms of state coercion, let alone political violence movements.

CHAPTER FOUR
Chronic Political Crisis and Civil War Status

There are several opinions about what the essential objectives of the military coup on 12 March 1971 actually were. Certain writers such as İhsan Sabri Çağlayangil, Ali Gevgilili, and İsmail Cem draw attention to matters like the discomfort of the USA for the AP's relative independence policies (the poppy issue in particular) and defend the opinion that the coup was staged against the AP;[67] on the other hand, Bülent Ecevit thinks that the military coup's essential objective was to prevent the development of the "left of center" movement (see Aydınoğlu, 2007: 242-243). Although all of these are partly correct, we believe that these factors did not have a determining role in the timing and reason for the military coup. On the other hand, even though military and police interventions realized after the military coup against the socialist left made an impression that the essential target of the military coup was the socialist left, it is good to be prudent in this matter. Although the pressure created by the radical left and social movements with proletariat movements particularly is obvious, it is hard to say that this pressure required the urgency of a military coup. The upheaval of social movements (e.g., the confrontation of workers against soldiers on 15-16 June as the first instance) surely worried the bourgeoisie, but the socialist left was not able to provide political mobilisation of those social movements in that period of time due to its fragmented structure. The more urgent issue worrying the capitalist-military coalition was that officers in the high command who were under the influence of the MDD were preparing a "Nationalist Revolutionist" military coup (Aydınoğlu, 2007: 242): The eradication of the Madanoglu junta just three days before 12 March clearly reveals the reason for the military coup's urgency. Radicalized aspects of the military were rapidly dismissed right after the military coup, and at first pro-MDD left Kemalist officers and then many Marxist officers

---

67   Keyder (1987: 51-52) also put into this the discontent of the Turkish bourgeoisie against the AP government towards the end of the 1960s.

were discharged between 1971 and 1973.[68] As a result of this systematic discharge, "[p]urged of its leftist sentiments, the military elite took on what Mann identifies as the conservative-constitutionalist/ rightist-authoritarian split apparent in Germany" (Jacoby, 2005a: 139).

> Any other opposition movement questioning the strategical relations with USA will never show up in Turkey after 1971. Besides, the military will continue to be implicit in politics but its effect and control will always be conducted in accordance with military hierarchy. (Aydınoğlu, 2007: 251)

Vaner remarks that this discharge process also matched with the process including the protection of radical rightist officers connected to the MHP and paved the way for their activities.[69] This means that the military coup did not have an objective to discharge *all* radical aspects, and certain causes and effects can be determined on a structural level. The first is the military returning to its conventional status as an active actor, but this return occurred under the decisiveness of a capitalist-military coalition and resulted in trimming the rights acquired in the 1960s: "The politically decentralising effects of a relatively liberal constitution had been considerably allayed by an elite strategy that had absorbed bourgeois calls for greater representation without surrendering to a full party democracy" (Jacoby, 2005a: 138). There was definitely an oscillation between the military, which lost its political autonomy following the gradual bourgeoisification of superiors, and the *absolute* autonomy illusion of mainstream political parties that presumed that this *relative* loss of military's autonomy was a non-return transformation; this oscillation was one of the many causes of the chronic political crisis in

---

68   In the military, it is also possible to trace the above-mentioned dissolution between secondary and tertiary positions of left. Contrary to what is believed, it is not possible to say that young Marxist officers and superior Kemalist "radicals" in the military got on with each other (see Vaner, 1987: 261-262, footnote 10; Samim, 1987: 159-160). As Aydınoğlu claims, the essential target of generals who staged the 12 March military coup "was not young communist officers who had relation with leftist organizations of that time, rather it was the officers who made preparations for a radically programmed military coup a few days before 12 March 1971" (Aydınoğlu, 2007: 243). Thus, juntaist radical officers' political programs directed to the post-coup period were not a social transformation program defined in a Marxist manner, rather "in many ways they had major similarities with anti-Western military junta movements occurred in Egypt, Iraq or Syria at 1950-60s. They had schedules that recall the transformations of Nasır at Egypt (1953-1970), General Kasım at Iraq (1958-1963), Emin Hafız at Syria (1963-1966)" (Aydınoğlu, 2007: 246).
69   See Vaner, 1987: 240.

the 1970s. What is really important in the sense of our study's focus is the implicit yet organic complicity that the capitalist-military coalition made with paramilitary forces, as well as the bourgeoisification of superiors and the bourgeoisie becoming rightist.

The military coup government that removed the AP from the administration intended to provide consistency with a "civil" technocrats' administration under the presidency of Nihat Erim and to carry out projected reforms. The Erim administration, which could not provide the desired consistency and delegated to Ferit Melen on 22 May 1972, in an economic sense, evidently took a stand next to the metropolitan capital. In a political sense, the Erim administration conducted practices such as the limitation of the 1961 Constitution articles related to individual freedoms and the formation of State Security Courts.[70] The Erim period between March 1971 and May 1972 was also the first time that Turkey became acquainted with systematic tortures and massacres.[71] In conclusion, the technocrat government practice under direct military guidance, which remained until the Presidential election in 1973 and substantially failed to put projected reforms into practice, came to an end through the parliament's persistent denial of the presidential bid nominated by the military (Chief of Defence Staff Faruk Gürler) and Fahri Korutürk (although a retired soldier, he was approved by parties in the parliament) being elected president.[72] This approach by the parliament played an important role in developing the absolute autonomy illusion.

Another important reason for the chronic political crisis in the 1970s was the unstoppable rise of the CHP beginning from the 1973 elections. The CHP, which received 33.3% of the votes and increased its numbers more than one million compared to the 1969 elections, won first place despite not having the majority required to form the government alone. This acceleration let the CHP have a 41.4% vote in the 1977 elections. Following the short-termed

---

70   See Schick and Tonak, 1987: 366-367.
71   Erim was assassinated in July 1980, which was the peak point of winding violence that we will discuss later. The organization called the Revolutionary Left, which defined itself as a follower of the THKP-C, claimed responsibility for the attack.
72   The most significant progress during the period of the technocrat administrations was the foundation of TÜSİAD (Turkish Industrialists' and Businessmen's Association) on 20 May 1971 which still plays a central role in conveying political demands and discontents of the bourgeoisie to administrations. According to Keyder, this period of technocrat administrations was "a period of transformation when industry went through a purge, and new concentrations of capital, organized in holding companies, appeared on the scene" (Keyder, 1987: 53).

CHP-MSP coalition formed by the CHP after the 1963 elections,[73] the main goal of the political complex led by Demirel was to keep the CHP out of government, because the CHP being in power in the 1970s meant that the radical left's radius of action would increase.

At this point, it is necessary to closely examine the reflection of keeping the CHP out of goverment strategy onto the capitalist-military coalition. An important part of the bourgeoisie in that period felt uncomfortable with the statist and reformist rhetoric materialized by the "left of center" formulation of the CHP. In addition, it is also possible to include the sympathy raised in Third Worldist circles of the CHP by the anti-Western rhetoric of the MSP. Hence, "it is hard to underestimate the impact of such a convergence of views on a modernized urban bourgeoisie dependent on the West for credit, know-how, and energy" (Schick and Tonak, 1987: 368). The military part of the coalition revealed that the "moderate" superiors of the military, who found their representation in a reformist CHP line on 27 May, approached the AP, which received 52.9% of votes in the 1965 elections and searched for a political reconciliation with superiors as a result of bourgeoisification perceptibly corresponded by OYAK investments. The emphasis in relation to the military losing its political autonomy gradually found its physical correspondence in this clear dependence of the military towards a certain economic and political system:[74] The military, beginning from 12 March in particular, became the explicit guardian of capitalist restoration.

I. POLITICAL CONTEXT AND SPECIFIC POLITICAL RATIONALITY OF PARAMILITARY VIOLENCE

It would not be a prophecy if anyone had said that the CHP-MSP coalition founded after the 1973 elections would not last long. Although there were common grounds in party alignments taking form around themes such as opposition against economic and cultural hegemony, the sociocultural histo-incompatibility between two parties was very obvious. This coalition, which was largely based on an obligation from the viewpoint of the CHP (aside from

---

73   The MSP (National Salvation Party) was an Anti-Kemalist political party under the presidency of Necmettin Erbakan with its class antagonism corresponding to the petit bourgeoisie of small Anatolian cities, and it used an intense religious rhetoric. For further information see Toprak, 1987: 227-230.
74   For more detailed analysis on this sociopolitical transformation of "Moderates" see Vaner, 1987: 248-257.

the AP who would never ally with the CHP, the MSP was the third party who took nearly 12% of votes) and based on pure pragmatism from the viewpoint of the MSP, caused practices that often made parties contradict themselves. One of the most clear examples of this is that Bülent Ecevit, who took the lead of the CHP with a left of center motto, accomplished a plea for political detainees of the 12 March period despite the MSP and only with the help of the Constitutional Court. However, this short-lived government had a mark on one of the most important incidents in Turkish political history, which is the Turkish invasion of Cyprus on 20 July 1974 after obtaining a vote of confidence on 7 February 1974. Ecevit, who looked to public support and political wind raised by the Turkish invasion of Cyprus took a major political risk and resigned the prime ministry in September. Ecevit's move, aimed at coming to power alone, resulted in a coalition with four different political parties led by the AP after a cabinet crisis that lasted for three months. The wind obtained from Cyprus produced a paradoxical result and swelled the MHP's sails: "The new coalition soon came to be referred as the Nationalist Front (*Milliyetçi Cephe*), and its actions and policies bear testimony to the fact that this name, with all its historical connotations, was not incidental" (Schick and Tonak, 1987: 368).

One of the most important distinguishing features of that period is that the bureaucracy was captured to a large extent by extreme Right cadres. The reason why the MHP acquired two ministries although it had only three members in the parliament was its bargaining power and the key role it gained in the coalition which kept the CHP out of power as its *raison d'être*. The MHP, by making this chance count, activated a certain type of *grassroots power strategy*, which provided a direct relationality with the rise of the left and the social opposition movement beginning from 1974, which we will discuss subsequently.

The AP, representative of the capitalist-military coalition, supported or at least overlooked this rise of the MHP: "[AP], representing the big bourgeoisie, protected and supported the MHP as it used the idealist youths as a strike force against democratic and leftist sectors" (Ağaoğulları, 1987: 200-201). The most significant indicators of this support are AP leader Demirel's famous words "you cannot make me say that rightists commit murder" and that the MHP's striking power on the street was barely prosecuted during the 1970s. On the other hand, this should not lead us to mistake the right political complex led by

Demirel as a compact complex. Without a doubt, one of the obvious reasons for this is the objections made from the AP that were against the MHP's street activities and increasingly raised during the '70s.[75] However, the main reason for this mistake is related to a perception that dominated the Turkish left to a large extent, which is that the MHP is not a real actor, rather only a "tool," and the MHP's practical-political rationality should be examined to produce counter arguments.

Consolidation of the right wing's mass grassroots level *on the street* was at the heart of the MHP's grassroots power strategy. The slogan as "The Turk has no friend but the Turk" which gained currency after the Cyprus Operation and hence the USA embargo, and the nationalist climate created by these event, provided a very fertile environment for MHP's goals to increase its striking power capacity and to take over street hegemony: "The strategy, which has had a purpose to include AP-MSP grassroots into MHP direction through increased political tension and agency, has been performed successfully by means of mass provocations and making anti-communist terror a part of daily life" (Bora and Can, 2004a: 61). In fact, there is a bipedal strategy here. The first goal of the MHP was to staff in the state mechanism by taking advantage of the sensitive balance that the Nationalist Front was based on, and thereby to obtain *state experience* by developing its communication and relation opportunities with a capitalist-military coalition. As a sociopolitical basis of this strategy, the secondary goal was to transform the anti-communist front union, which it was trying to obtain through its *street experience*, into an acceptable reputation and vote on a parliamentary level.[76] In that case, in particular, the main objective of the strategy pursued by the MHP until 1977 was to increase its parliamentarian power and if possible, to come into power in this way. Clear indicators were the MHP's striking power on the street that followed a parallel course with the activity of the left between 1974 and 1977 and efforts devoted to organizing masses where Turk-Sunni sensibility was high. As a matter of fact, both the quantity and the scale of the MHP's act of violence practices withstood a dramatic change after 1977.

This political strategy of the MHP brought a critical vote increase in terms of voting rates. In Middle and Eastern Anatolia, some factors were determined that affected the increase in votes stolen from MSP grassroots.

---

75   See Ağaoğulları, 1987: 201.
76   See Bora and Can, 2004a: 61-62.

Although it is difficult to say that the social base, which MHP was based upon, did not have a homogenous quality, it found most of its correspondence in the countryside's traditional petit bourgeoisie (middle provinciality, few craftsmen and tradesmen communities) who showed a significant tendency to dispossession beginning from the second half of the 1970s. Petit bourgeoisie factions, who began to worry about not being able to create a life space for themselves and being blocked, become susceptible to radical ideologies; and it is an manifestation of the *petit bourgeoisie radicalism* as a supporting fact not just for the right, but for the left too.[77] The MHP promised economic order for those classes that brought them to their old secure status. "Although MHP have not embodied that promise, it has represented the reaction to current change, a 'sincerity' to conserve the whole cultural-ideological heritage of 'the old order' with a revanchist agency" (Bora and Can, 2004a: 64). The conclusion that the MHP completely consolidated the factions of petit bourgeoisie in question under its own political schedule should not be drawn here. On the contrary, dependence on the AP in the sense of country petit bourgeoisie was still essential. On the other hand, components of country petit bourgeoisie which were uninvolved in the MHP circle showed a "minimal sincerity" to the MHP similarly to Demirel's relation with the MHP in upper politics.[78]

The Sunni-Alevi faultline is a determining factor in Middle and Eastern Anatolia where the MHP lifted its effectiveness. An important part of cities where the party received 10% or more votes in the 1977 elections are the cities where Sunni and Alevi communities live together.[79] The MHP had an offensive Turk-Islamist ideology with powerful religious timbres and displayed the power, dynamism, and radicalism required by this ideology more intensely than the MSP, and it was no doubt a factor that increased the

---

77 "Between 1970 and 1975, the proportion of 'self-employed' small entrepreneurs in the nonagricultural labor force declined from 23 to 21 percent, and their numbers in the manufacturing sector alone decreased by 9,3 percent" (Keyder, 1987: 55).

78 As an example supporting this determination, Bora and Can quote from an idealist teacher who worked in the country during the 1980s: "In those extremely political days where everyone was a party member, citizens have mostly considered that fire of circle as a propaganda, those who were religious have appreciated MHP but have voted for their own party. The religious section in the country (in general, rightists) have considered idealist youths as a barrier against communism and assumed them as saviors in current conditions. But you should pay attention to this: Countrymen have considered the idealist a savior but have not adopted his ideals" (Bora and Can, 2004a: 66n).

79 Yozgat (22,9% -1 congressman), Erzincan (18,8%), Elazığ (18,7% -1 congressman), Kahramanmaraş (15,5% - 1 congressman), Sivas (13,2% - 1 congressman), Erzurum (12,8% - 1 congressman), Çorum (12,7% - 1 congressman), Gaziantep (11,1% -1 congressman), Tokat (10,6% -1 congressman), Malatya (9,2%). Other cities where MHP received similar vote rates in the 1977 elections are in Middle and Eastern Anatolia or nearby cities.

effect of anti-Alevi agitation and propaganda. On the other hand, there was a class reason under the reaction in those regions against the Alevi population. Since the Sunni petit bourgeoisie factions, which regressed economically, were underdeveloped in the sense of capital stock, they had a special grudge against the Alevi population, which was oriented towards labour and public service, and they considered these professions as more stable and elevated careers. The rival presence of the Alevi population who engaged in small-scale production and traded in related cities enhanced this grudge even more.[80] MHP's Turkist-Islamist agitation and propaganda had a great impact and functioned by equaling "Alevi" with "communist" and "heretic."

The majority of the MHP's grassroots in metropolises and cities was comprised of people who came to those metropolises and cities by social migration from Anatolia's related regions. The "'reflexes' of this mass were conservative and depended on tradition, but their value systems severely suffered from erosion in their environments and in themselves; their Islamic origins became weak and blurred" (Bora and Can, 2004a: 67). It is possible to interpret this as a cultural shock. According to Bora and Can (2004a: 67-68), the fact that this mass, which took over the previous generation's, mostly their parents' reactions against proletarianization, is not leftist, but rather idealist depends almost always on environmental impacts or random events.

This mostly explains the character of this mass with a rather weak ideological power and a highly striking power that expands on declassed positions. On an ideological level, "[r]ejecting socialism as well as capitalism, they could hardly remain indifferent to an ideology which held that the complex process of change was the result of a conscious conspiracy by enemies of society, which should be opposed by violent means" (Ağaoğulları, 1987: 192). What is in front of us as a socio-psychological type is a figure who mostly determines daily political practice by acting independently, holds on to congregational relationship in the jungle called the city, glorifies machist values with a spirit of adventure arising from being rootless: "the satisfaction provided by daily life which is dominated by violence has been keeping a unique 'real man/gang' culture alive, and in guise of 'man of cause' mystifying it even more" (Bora and Can, 2004a: 68). We need to emphasize that paramilitary factors who organized bloody mass murders after 1977 emerged from these urbanized/partisan networks. Hence, the country folk

---

80   See Bora and Can, 2004a: 85-86.

who were transformed into professional organizations quickly took these forms. There is an open continuity with the pro-resistance movement form that took a supralegal position during the state-making period both in the sense of current class positions and in the sense of the logic of organization and action despite the fact that they were results of very different social conditions. This continuity had its formal identity through the figure becoming uniformed and semi-uniformed during the 1990s in particular; this paramilitary figure transformed into a foundational human resource of counter-guerilla practices through the nihilism he took over from a gangster who could not adopt himself to the regular army.

We mentioned before that the MHP adopted the construction of an anti-communist front union through its "street experience" as a basic strategy and implemented it with a monopoly both on the street and in the elections. The MHP really expected to succeed in the 1977 elections. However, although there was a meaningful increase in its own right (from 3.4% to 6.4%), the increase in the MHP's votes was only limited to Middle and Eastern Anatolia, and reached its maximum in those regions. The MHP could only steal a certain amount of votes from the MSP's grassroots. However, the MHP provided an important increase in its cadres in the state bureaucracy and on the street.

When we put the CHP, which increased its vote rate in the June 1977 elections by 8 points compared to the 1973 elections and reached the maximum of its history (41,4%), into its essential place in the big picture, it is possible to interpret this election as a clear expression of polarization. On the other hand, the "civil" strategy of the MHP followed until the 1977 elections has no continuity at all. Adding an explicit oppositeness of capitalist-military coalition against the CHP government into this picture shows the reason why the administration, scarcely founded by Ecevit in January 1978 and intensely attacked by the right complex, becomes clear. In this environment where the AP's "flag rallies" and efforts to increase the anti-communist delusion provided an important swing, the MHP abandoned its civil strategy and tended towards a *civil war* strategy. By means of this terror strategy, having a purpose to force the Ecevit administration into declare a martial law, the MHP worked its way into power through its partisans in the military. In November of 1978, Türkeş said that "authority and responsibility should be transferred to military government" (narrated by Bora and Can, 2004a: 92).

This transformation of the MHP in its practical rationality could be taken together with the transformation of its repertory for acts of violence and of targeted goals through those acts. The state of mutual conflict, which included the MHP's *bozkurtlar* who left campus as revolutionists and materalized with the objective to prevent revolutionist youth to make policy in universities, gave its place to mass attacks in 1978; the first example of this new form of violence was the 16 March massacre.[81] [82] This type of mass attack with a purpose of suppression and creating intimidation was performed many times in large cities, and after losing its selectivity, it completely started to go against random crowds. It seems that attacks against coffee shops, bus stations, cinema exits where the left population was high became routine in 1978.[83]

Another component of the violence repertory that materialized in 1978 was selective assassinations of dignitaries or well-known people. In the scope of those attacks, many scientists, journalists, government officers, unionists, and managers of democratic mass organizations were murdered.[84] This component of paramilitary repertory with a violent momentum was faced again in the 1990s, and representatives, intellectuals, literati, and businessmen of the Kurdish political movement were added as targets.

The third component of the paramilitary violence repertory was the attempts of mass provocations and pogroms applied in the provinces. The MHP, which pursued the goal of disabling the left wing from engaging in politics in large cities, had a main goal in the provinces. The goal was to make mass support permanent and put the rising right wing into its own direction because the MHP was well aware that it could be easily expendable by the prevailing coalition if it could not show that it had the necessary power to compose anti-communist reaction potential. The MHP performed these mass provocations and pogroms in most of the cities where it received 10% or more of the votes. The first example is the Malatya incident:

---

81 "At 16 March 1978, 7 students were murdered and a great number of students got injured due to the bomb tossed at students coming out of Istanbul University. This has caused a powerful, nationwide resistance wave (...) The tension increased by the great reaction shown has revealed that this 'move' was a successful exit regarding the strategy of idealist movement" (Bora and Can, 2004a: 88n).

82 Commandos of MHP also carried out some small-scale attacks such as intruding rallies and meetings by weapons between 1975 and 1978. However, implementation of the civil war strategy with its structure referring to "categorical terrorism" resulted in those attacks reaching *massacre* dimension.

83 Only in various districts of Istanbul, there were 48 attacks to coffee shops on the books between 1975 and 1979 (Keleş and Ünsal, 1982: 69). Compared to attacks against other places, attacks made against coffee shops have a separate symbolic value on the grounds that they were paramilitary attack types stimulating Gazi Quarter Riots in 1995.

84 For a detailed study on those murders and the way they have been prosecuted see Sezgin, 1987.

The Malatya municipality mayor, AP member Hamit Fendoğlu (Hamido) who was considered as "close to MHP" was murdered at 17 April 1978 when opening the package sent to his name from Ankara including a bomb. After this murder, idealists provoked right Sunni population in the city against the Alevi population and left in general to carry out a mass attack. In the following months, the fascist movement has performed similar provocations in many cities and towns of Middle-Eastern Anatolia, with the greatest of those attacks being carried out in Sivas and Elazığ. In the Elazığ case, provocations acquired an ethnical dimension too due to attacks against Kurdish population. (Bora and Can, 2004a: 90n)

The most important reason why these ethnic-denominational provocations, which found the appropriate environment in the provinces to a certain degree, could not be implemented in large cities (particularly in slum areas where similar social conflicts happen) was that these attempts confronted a powerful resistance in large cities. The first repertory component was therefore a result of the incapacity for passing from mass attack to mass provocation.

The Ecevit administration persistently resisted the declaration of a martial law despite that this paramilitary violence repertory was implemented with all of its components and led to an increase of violence by the MHP on a level that caused public indignation. In this environment where selective assassinations were increasingly made against objective and respected people, a pogrom in the provinces reached a mass slaughter level. The most terrifying example of this was the Kahramanmaraş massacre in December 1978:

The chain of provocations, which was started by an idealist who planted a bomb in a movie theater playing an anti-communist film and declared this bombing as a "communist attack," was upgraded by an attack organized against the funeral of two Alevi and leftist teachers murdered next day and became a mass massacre via anti-communist "jihad" expressions. As far as confirmed, 111 people were murdered, hundreds of people got injured in the Kahramanmaraş massacre and the greater part of Alevi society has had to leave Kahramanmaraş. (Bora and Can, 2004a: 93n)

After the Ecevit government became obliged to declare martial law following the Kahramanmaraş massacre, the MHP made a decision to "bury weapons" through a tactical move determined by its headquarters. Although some people considered this as the first phase of the MHP's current power strategy that became successful, it would be wiser to interpret this as a result of a critical legitimacy loss after the massacre. In this environment where general public opinion accused the MHP's cadres as mainly responsible for the Kahramanmaraş massacre, there was a practice here out of hand that frightened pro-MHP officers in the military, not to mention the capitalist-military coalition and the AP. The MHP's executive staff considered that the martial law was declared against them and anticipated to both lead the state coercion, which rose after martial law towards the left[85] and to enforce internal discipline by putting out of hand lower levels in order. These attempts by the MHP, however, remained inconclusive. The embodiment of this is that the AP, who got first place in the 14 October 1979 elections, rejected the MHP in its minority government. Against the impossibility of taking the military's support as whole, the last remedy of the MHP to provide active partnership of authoritarian and fascistic aspects in the military was to escalate blind terrorist attacks to strengthen the perception of an "authority gap" in public opinion and efface itself while doing so. Illegal shell organizations such as ETKO (Army to Liberate Captive Turks) and TİT (Turkish Revenge Brigade) were founded during this period and undertook paramilitary violence practices.

In the same period, some components of the radical left shifted from a defence position to an attack strategy against the MHP's organizations and cadres, which was another factor playing a key role in the extraction of buried weapons. The assassination of Gün Sazak in May 1980, one of the leaders of the MHP, by the organization called the Revolutionary Left resulted in the MHP mounting a nationwide counterattack, and the Çorum massacre, which was planned as a second Kahramanmaraş incident, was attempted in that period (July 1980). Thus, Çorum, in which the massacre was prevented with a powerful anti-fascist resistance, "has become the den where MHP and idealist movement have completely lost their move initiative" (Bora and

---

85 "According to the *Başbuğ*, martial law was declared against us. If we continue our actions, we could collapse. For this reason, all actions have been categorically prohibited. You will make sure of it. Thus, the martial law, which targeted us, will be forced to crush the communists. All weapons and similar material must be immediately eliminated, even buried" [quoted from the that period's President of ÜGD (Association of Idealist Youth) Şevket Çetin, narrated by Ağaoğulları, 1987: 205].

Can, 2004a: 96). The MHP exposed itself to an absolute isolation from the dominant complex and a shock created by being an open target due to the 12 September military coup.

It is possible to trace the MHP's transformation in its practical rationality from civil strategy to civil war strategy as a common ground for the three components of the paramilitary violence repertory and as the targets of paramilitary attacks expanding from revolutionary-socialists to the left and increasingly to all social sections in social mobility. This transformation means that the MHP added to its strategic targets all people and even government officers such as prosecutors investigating its actions, except for the capitalist-military coalition and the political complex around it.

We believe that it would be right to define the characteristics of this organization, which materialized these paramilitary practices, as some sort of "timar holder" model (Bora and Can, 2004a: 100). Unlike an often shared view, the relationship between high politics and street politics in the MHP did not present a military model in which the chain of command was established in a strict hierarchy. One of the most important reasons for this is, as we mentioned above, the fact that the MHP, which had been the essential bearer of Turkish paramilitarism in the 1960s and '70s was massified in comparison with its global equivalents and obtained a political influence far greater than its massification. This rapid massification formed a structuring that had a *disciplined central context* image but, in practice, involved disjointed authority relations and groups drawn together in an eclectic and pragmatic manner. Thus, this was the reason for a powerful tendency to become a mafia that revealed itself in cadres who were not *real cadres*. From the point of the MHP's administrative level dealing with high politics, this pragmatic approach referred to both a sense of lack of control and an unwillingness to control. Depending on the goal to keep an extended striking power alive in an anti-communist action, this timar holder model that left the job of creating resources, required for economic necessities, to local and regional gang leaders created its own political death and isolation through "lumpen crowds, violence prone swordsmen, murderers who get bored and search a man to kill" (Bora and Can, 2004a: 99). All in all, the MHP created an anti-political grudge machine in the late 1970s that constantly produced itself on a nihilistic existential ground once its most general strategy and targets were ambiguously formulated and its machinery activated.

II. VARIANT OF RADICAL-CONSTITUTIVE VIOLENCE AS A RADICAL SOCIETY CONSTRUCTION STRATEGY

The 1970s represented a momentum in which left thought and practice placed on Turkey's political agenda. This means an extremely large data stack and field of study ranging from union practices to occupation of workplaces and resistances, from practices devoted to establish associations spreading in many aspects of social life to activities of political publications and of literature, from legal mass parties built around socialist thought to illegal organizations. We will not discuss the left activity in general, which is a subject of a completely different study per se, rather the relationality and its theoretical and practical contexts that generate the left variant of radical-constitutive violence.

The most striking political fact of the 1970s was the unrestrainable rise of the CHP. The departure of its founding figure, İsmet İnönü, due to ideological reasons, proves that in the 1970s, which could be described as an *ideologies era*, the CHP became a party of ideology, at least loosely, via a "left of center" formulation and a gap that occurred between itself and the government domain despite the fact that the CHP was "the party that found a state." We already explained how the government domain was formed around the interests of the capitalist-military coalition after the 12th of March. Following the alienation of the new policy, which Ecevit's CHP had been working to structure around a "left of center" formulation, from a conventional member of state characteristic, in major cities it found its correspondence in slums and among organized or marginalized proletariat, in the provinces it found its correspondence among poor people and the Alevi population in particular. The new and additional support caused an increase of votes on behalf of the CHP that came from those places.[86] This has also brought, even though not in major cities definitely in the provinces, the construction of a – certainly not guided – symbiotic relationship between the CHP and left political organizations, and the MHP's mass provocations in the provinces are the main factors that tightened this relationship.[87]

---

86 See Keyder, 1987: 55-56.
87 As Melih Pekdemir, in the leading cadre of one of the most mass radical left organizations (Revolutionary Path) of that period, said "there were warm relationships with CHP's grassroots. Particularly in the provinces, revolutionary youth had a close contact with "elders" of CHP in the struggle against fascists" (Pekdemir, 2007: 774).

On the other hand, the most basic social fact that made its mark on the 1970s was the rapid revival of social movements by themselves. After the relative peace in 1971 and 1972, the movements of the proletariat, which accelerated through legal and illegal strikes (these illegal strikes were named "resistance" in that period) during 1973 in which martial law was still in progress, started to rise in 1974 (Aydınoğlu, 2007: 282-283). Another social movement dynamic was the rapid politicization of university youth in particular. Following the physical destruction of student organizations in the 1960s and radical left organizations that evolved out of them through 12 March, student agglomerations that originally started as unorganized, small groups were important because leaders of settlements of both left radical-constitutive violence and the Kurdish movement, which were oriented towards armed struggle, were *fermented* within these groups, so to speak. These small student groups *recovered* quickly by themselves through the pressure created by social movements and the low-density state of conflict created by the MHP on campuses.

The physical equivalent of these political and social processes regarding the left was rapid *massification*. Unlike the TİP, which had worked to build its local organizations patiently and energetically by visiting cities and counties one by one in the early 1960s, political actors who were released by the 1974 amnesty were welcomed enthusiastically. From 1974 forward, "socialists coming from center were not the ones who have looked for local militants, rather it was the exact opposite. In other words, people politicizing rapidly search a left organization, party, movement, circle etc. to establish a relationship" (Aydınoğlu, 2007: 283-284). It is possible to connect the speed of national urbanization and industrialization with general reasons for this mass tendency to the left. However, the fact that organizations that were actors of left radical-constitutive violence became essential components of the left requires looking for other reasons.

The emphasis made by Keleş and Ünsal (1982: 41) to define "unplanned urbanization" as not the main reason for political violence, but as a "facilitating variable," is significant yet inadequate by itself to explain this fact. Even so, other and more dominant reasons should be discussed. The primary reason is that class and also Turk-Kurd and Sunni-Alevi fault lines repressed in the first years of the foundation of the republic started to move via violence, and the role of the state's military and paramilitary practices are determinative on this.

Therefore, we must determine that the state coercion is a relational element accelerating political violence. Second, and related to this element, Turkey is one of the active and intense execution areas in which counter-guerilla activities operating internationally and systematically (sometimes coordinated) happen, and Turkey's geopolitical character during the Cold War is decisive here. The last reason is that the radical left, which was intensely assaulted, could not break with the Leninist burden it obtained in the later 1960s while radicalizing and turned in upon Leninist orthodoxies with several variations. Thus, the lines of radical-constitutive political violences in Turkey have shown, unlike 1968 in Europe, a tendency toward not marginalization but massification and should be considered together with these reasons. All in all, Turkey settled into the global conjuncture of the 1970s not as a European country, but as a Latin American country, so to speak.

When Turkey's radical left is considered in the general sense, we confront a picture that maintains the Marxist-Leninist characteristics and diversifies according to ideological developments in the world. The Soviet-China disintegration, which became a keen contradiction in the international context of the 1970s, immediately made an impact in Turkey and corresponding positions were swiftly formed.[88] Since the groups deployed at either side of this disintegration avoided radical-constitutive violence strategies, we will not discuss them here.[89] The majority of cadres in the THKO, another radical-constitutive violence actor before 12 March, experienced a "self-criticism" process, in their own words, following the release from prison by amnesty and completely broke its connections with armed struggle strategies by installing itself first into a Maoist, then pro-Enver Hoca line and taking the

---

88 Soviet-China disintegration, which caused entangled balance policies and temporary alliances in international relations, actually started before the 1970s in terms of ideology. The fact that the Soviets invaded Czechoslovakia in 1968 and that the dispute at the Soviet-China border became a military border clash in 1969 is a critical twist transforming disintegration into split. Across Turkey, it should be noted that the invasion of Czechoslovakia created a critical dispute and fracture within the TİP. The PDA (Proletarian Revolutionary Enlightenment), which consisted of Maoism's main frame under the presidency of Doğu Perinçek in that period in Turkey, beginning from 1969-70 started to process the "social imperialism" thesis that got into circulation against the Soviets. The authenticity of the 1970s is that international Stalinist/communist poles independent of each other came into existence across the world and that equivalent of this existence in Turkey got the edge in this open polarization to commit violence against each other. For detailed information on the effects of international Stalinist polarization in Turkey, see Samim, 1987: 164-167; Aydınoğlu, 2007: 330-335.

89 Although the PDA has constantly kept "public war" discourse on the agenda as propaganda, it never took steps in that direction. The only exception in the Maoist flank was a small group named TİKKO that separated from the PDA (Karş. Bozarslan, 2007a).

name of the HK (People's Liberation).[90] Setting aside the TKP-ML/TİKKO, which carried out highly limited guerilla activity in some local countryside regions of Eastern and Southeastern Anatolia, *strategical* bearers of the left radical-constitutive violence in the 1970s were successors of the THKP-C, particularly the Revolutionary Path that comprised the main frame.[91]

A fundamental characteristic of the period regarding the socialist left is that even groups that did not stand for armed struggle strategies started to bear arms, beginning from 1975-76 in particular and that *firearms became a part of daily life*. It is possible to talk about a cultural-psychological reason here: In the psychological and ideological climate that can be considered as a follow-up to the 1969-72 momentum and fed by an international context, the formulation of "revolutionary violence" has a very high legitimacy level.[92] Masculine codes, characterized by males between 20 and 30 years of age becoming dominant can also be added into this formulation. However, paramilitary attacks, which sustained a change of form and content in parallel with revolutionary students leaving campuses and going towards slums in major cities, particularly beginning from 1976,[93] were essential determinants in this progress: "Attacks of idealist militants turned defence against armed assaults into a contemporary problem in a short time for entire left wing" (Aydınoğlu, 2007: 343). The MHP militants who expanded their target ranges towards the entire left including the CHP did not differentiate between left groups that did or did not uphold armed struggle. What was essential regarding the MHP's political rationality was to restrain every left actor from getting power and effectiveness on local levels. In conjunction with this local conflict environment becoming systematized, *local deployments* occurred that were called "liberated zones" by actors of that period. This practice in which leftist actors were withdrawn with the intent of self-defence and "keeping the mass"

---

90   For the narration of Aydın Çubukçu, one of the HK's leading cadres, see Çubukçu, 2007. Although it was comprised of THKO cadres, a small group named THKO-MB (Unity in Struggle) under the presidency of Teslim Töre did not embrace THKO's practice either.

91   According to Murat Belge, except for Sovietist and Maoist groups, motivations of the "independent left" subsequent to THKP-C were based not on a "nationalistic reflex, rather on (1) the belief including the necessity for socialist movement of every society being able to act independently and (2) a tendency such as avoiding using discourses of conflicted parties on existing and conflicting different socialist conceptions in the world, which could not be miscounted. However, grassroots mainly getting together here could be based on an uncertainty of a separating line between socialism and nationalism" (Belge, 2007: 39-40).

92   The notion of taking political power by force was the common vision of all socialist actors in that period, and the only discussion was made about timing. However, using tools of violence is the subject of an *intra-left* discussion.

93   See Pekdemir, 2007.

canalized the left in general to *"predominantly defensive, but necessarily combative armed struggle* (Samim, 1987: 163), which is called "active defence" in leftist literature.

An important byproduct of this process where firearms became a part of daily life was "intra-left violence."[94] Common characteristics of intra-left violence, namely that left groups directed tools of violence at each other, provides a clear image about organizational and ideological formulation of left actors of that period. In fact, intra-left violence began as a result of the exact dissolution within the youth movement in late 1969 from the violence that militants of the *Dev-Genç* following the MDD committed against members of the TİP. However, these early outbreaks, as distinct from systematical practices after 1974, could never reach a volume to conclude ideological discussions within the left, and firearms were never used in these conflicts. As of 1974, this practice that started by fights and hussles in rallies and meetings, and became routine by being naturalized under the title of "ideological struggle" in publications of certain left organizations, caused conflicts resulting in deaths because firearms had become a part of daily life.

There are two attitudes on the discursive level here. Groups identifying themselves with the socialist approaches of the Soviet Union, China, or Albania appropriated those conflicts as an inevitable result of political struggle and flagged their ideological opponents clearly in the "enemy" category. The linguistic correspondence of being flagged as the enemy was from Sovietists being called "social fascist" by supporters of the Albanian Labour Party and Maoists, and their being called "Maoist fascist" by Sovietists. In intra-left violence practices that the "independent left" following the THKP-C got involved in, a dialect referring to "provocation" and calling for "sobriety" was mobilized and local supremacy struggles ruled over these conflicts. A comprehensive perspective of this issue indicates that rare breed orthodoxies that increasingly became distant from practical politics and produced books and publications not in "theoretical" but in the "ideological reproduction" category (Belge, 2007: 42) were formed. Intra-left violence was a result of intra-left competition along with claims of those orthodoxies over "truth" and the distortion of the "enemy" definition created by orthodox blinders. Intra-left competition created the effect of a dose of rising violence, especially in groups

---

94   For a detailed documentation about intra-left violence, see Öznur, 2004 and Köse, 2014.

that were close to each other territorially.[95] Therefore, we call these practices, which intensified in line with the MHP shifting to a civil war strategy in 1978 and aimed at wiping left political opponents away, *state-making practices on a local level.* Speaking the state's language, in other words *acting as state,* even the cases in which the organization or the movement comprised of a handful of people, both refers to an obvious effect of Marxist-Leninist ideological burden and a result of civil war status created virtually.

The concept of civil war, which was actualized by paramilitary structuring in the late 1970s, increased the emphasis on the THKP-C's revolution strategies in organizations' statements that were subsequent to the THKP-C, the strategical bearer of left radical-constitutive violence in particular:[96] "Under such conditions it was impossible to shake off the legacy of focoism" (Samim, 1987: 163). Related actors in that period, particularly the Revolutionary Path, made a "civil war" observation and tried to express this observation through Çayan's terms ("pioneer's war," "artificial balance" etc.) (see Pekdemir, 2007: 757-758). However, we must stress that the emphasis made on the related strategy did not mean that this strategy had been made applicable. The reason is not because left radical-constitutive violence actors did not intend to implement it, but systematic paramilitary attacks did not allow the complete and systematic materialization of any political strategy. So not only public war strategies, but any type of leftist strategy was not materialized systematically in this period of time, and this can be considered as a success of the anti-political grudge machine created by the MHP. A radical left that asked for the government but failed in its early state-making steps, is in question here. One of the reasons that radical-constitutive violence strategies had a remarkable influence in Kurdistan was because the mass of people necessary for this paramilitary practice did not exist in this geography.

In spite of that influence, especially after the Kahramanmaraş massacre, those actors made an "active defence" as well as some attacks. Because the

---

95 It has been claimed that ideological closeness, rather than ideological polarization had an important role in the increase of intra-left violence, and that rivalry and competition between "groups which were in the same league" due to a "leadership" cult (Belge, 2007: 40) became more intense and harsh. Although this claim seems to depend on violence incidents between the Revolutionary Path and Liberation, two organizations subsequent to the THKP-C, we think that not ideological but spatial closeness was decisive.

96 For the strategical formulation called "politicized military war strategy" by THKP-C leader Mahir Çayan and seriously influenced by revolution strategies that occurred in Latin America, especially the theses written by Brazilian revolutionist Carlos Marighella, see Çayan, 2004. A distinguishing feature of this strategy is that it gave priority to a "pioneer's war" that urban guerilla units entered in the path to public war.

number of security guards murdered between January 1980 and July 1980 was 93 (Keleş and Ünsal, 1982: 57), it is also possible to take this as a sign of the transition from "active defence" to attack. In the 1978-80 momentum, the Revolutionary Path was in a struggle to organize guerilla units (Pekdemir, 2007: 774). On the other hand, many large and small groups and organizations, which accused the Revolutionary Path for not being radical enough and/or for not saving the Bolshevist party as promised, and declaring themselves as the true heir of the THKP-C, were established in the same period. The most efficient of them was the Revolutionary Left that was formed through the disassociation of the main body of the Revolutionary Path's İstanbul office and left its mark on the left radical violence campaign in the 1990s. The assassination of Gün Sazak, who was the vice president of the MHP and the previous minister for customs and monopolies, was executed by this organization on 27 May 1980 and caused a revenge campaign that continued until the 12 September military coup. The climax of this campaign was the Çorum incidents that were planned as a secondary "Kahramanmaraş" but prevented by armed defence, which, by the way was a result from absolute isolation of the MHP from the dominant complex.

Taking into account these incidents, if we have to draw a typology on the radical left militant, then it is the male typology between the ages of 18 and 30 who provide the dominant characteristic for movements that are systematical bearers of radical-constitutive violence. Although there are minor differences among empirical studies made on this subject, the age range in question covers more than 75% of related left organizations and movements.[97] On the other hand, there is a significant difference between left radical members and leaders regarding data on the distribution of jobs. The jobs of those who were captured after 12 September were: 22.6% student, 20.7% unemployed, 15.4% self-employment and 14.0% employee;[98] the distribution of jobs of left movement's leaders who were captured and wanted was 61.2% student, 13.3% teacher, 4.1% unemployed and 3.1% self-employment, and did not include employees (Keleş and Ünsal, 1982: 59-60).[99] This data, on the one hand, supports our argument about the decisive character of the first student

---

97   See Ergil, 1980: 113; Keleş and Ünsal, 1982: 62-63.
98   Other percentages are: 9.9% civil servant, 6.6% teacher, 1.2% housewife and 9.6% others.
99   Other percentages are: 5.1% civil servant, 4.1% engineer, 1,0% academic member, 1.0% unionist, 1.0% driver and 6.1% others.

agglomerations after 12 March on the development of organizations and movements; on the other hand, it also helps us to deepen militant typology.

The actors who were bearers of radical-constitutive violence actually represented the politization of students and country youth, which is very obvious in the case of the Revolutionary Path. The symbiotic relation that radical left organizations and movements made with CHP's grassroots in the provinces is apparent in the cultural formation of revolutionary youth in the provinces; it is possible to trace this in revolutionary "martyr" figures stepping in narratives of Alevi messianism.[100] "Martyrdom," which gradually became popular dating from 1968-69 in radical left jargon as a fidelity-making expression standing in the junction point of theology and politics, created a very powerful motivation for the engagement of militants in that period.

This symbiotic relation that occurred in the provinces gave its place to a more independent radical left in cities. An important reason for this is undoubtedly the large room for maneuvering possessed by the gradually radical left in university campuses. However, a more typical and more important reason for breaking from the CHP in cities lies in, to a large extent, a contradiction that came from those living in slums who supported members of the CHP for mayoral elections:

> The conflict between mayors who took up the position directly by vox populi and small-scaled entrepreneurship settled in city councils has caused a discomfort in local organizations of CHP. This class conflict is undoubtedly different than the essential conflict that the left has defined thus far. Heretofore, the dominant contradiction has been defined between "imperialism, its local collaborationists and public masses," now a conflict of interests is in question which has arisen between large-scaled proletariat and microentrepreneur who is considered as a natural ally of "democratical revolution" in cities. (Batuman, 2013: 81)

As a result of this conflict, the slum movement gradually started to gain a radical left vision because the CHP did not nominate "its mayors who were in the position of leaders of new municipalism movement" in

---

100 For a detailed analysis on this transformation which found its most clear correspondence on ballads composed by Alevi poets in the name of "revolution martyrs", see Küçük, 2007 and 2013.

the 1977 elections. The demolition of slums beginning from the 12 March regime already constituted a natural ground for the relation of slum-dwellers with the radical left, which brought "organized construction of districts" in the late '70s (Batuman, 2013: 83). Another determinant was the increasing pressure and control of mafiatic groups in districts. Seeking a remedy for this: "embellishment associations, which [have been] reopened three years after being shut down by military regime,[101] [have been] considered by young squatters as an organizational tool against this type of mafiatic groups and have been captured" (Batuman, 2013: 77). The physical equivalent of this regarding our subject is that "active defence" tools were directed to mafiatic groups as well as paramilitary groups. The process of organized district constructions also appeared as the decontamination process of the district from the mafia. Therefore, it is not coincidental that one of the main areas of state-making practices on the local level was slums.

According to Murat Belge, "most [of radical leftist cadres] were students from petty-bourgeois families and expressed the traditions of that sector. A militant from a working-class background would soon conform to the dominant pattern, in so far as he became a militant, and would thereby behave differently from his working-class friends" (Samim, 1987: 168-169). Although this description is correct to a certain degree, we consider it as a result of limited observation because encounters in both slums and the provinces caused a hybrid typology to appear that obtained certain features of each component. Unlike the universal figure embodied in Mahir Çayan before 12 March, the actor of the left radical-constitutive violence implemented after 1975 was a far more *localized* figure who tried to found origins for itself, which should be taken as a result of fast and unexpected massification. The typological transformation created by these encounters and massification appeared in the form of a disintegrating experience. According to Bozarslan (2007b: 1172), the disintegration between movements established by intellectuals such as the TKP-TİP-TSİP and movements depending on "action" that mobilized both student youth and youth in slums and the provinces such as the *Revolutionary Path*, the Revolutionary Left, the TKP-ML, and the HK was founded on the

---

101 "One of the first things that has been done in newly formed slum areas was to build 'associations for district embellishment' in order to provide legitimacy of the settlement before authority and to bring infrastructure services to the settlement. For example, the number of associations for district embellishment was 853 at 1960, but this number increased to 2142 at 1964, and to 4644 at 1968" (Batuman, 2013: 76).

increasing distance between "organical" intellectuals with the capacity of forming an ideological expression and declassed layers that were mobilized as *a social movement*. Therefore, it is not a coincidence that movements within the second group were more inclined to violence instruments than the first group.

On the other hand, as a pattern characterized by those movements in the second group, especially by the Revolutionary Path, it is not a coincidence again that they built the collective actor as a "political movement", rather than an "organization."[102] The main difference of "political movement" from "organization" is that it has not a regulation (an "organizational law") and that it does not consolidate regular congresses. Due to the absence of regulation, the distribution of work and hierarchy was determined arbitrarily; consequently, there were ambiguities about the differentiation between cadres and sympathisers and about who was responsible for which job. This form, comprised of a lot of people who believed that they were members of the organization but actually were not, was the source of "an interesting combination of leadership authority and spontaneism" (Aydınoğlu, 2007: 351) and a culture of organization shaped by this way. There are three possible reasons for this combination: Firstly, in these political movements, which welcomed youth in the provinces and slums and trailed a major social movement in localities in which it displayed activity, there was an intuition with a powerful sociological content regarding the fact that this ground would fall apart if it were organized hierarchically. Secondly, the allergy of bureaucratism taken over from the *Dev-Genç* and deep mistrust against big chiefs in the late 1960s dominated this second group's movements entirely. However, it would be wrong to say that a political movement in the form of a "movement-party combination" like the German Green Party (Aydınoğlu, 2007: 355), which intended to increase initatives of individuals and grassroots and to cover new social movements, emerged here. What emerged in practice was the belief that the "leadership" would be generated within "action," and young chiefs followed the rejection of the big chief. This belief leads to the third factor. This second group's movements, just like those who had "organization" character, claimed that they would build up a conventional Stalinist organization: "[post-1972] there was an eagerness directed to structurings in the form of classical communist party, rather than frontial organizations" (Ünüvar, 2013: 40). However, this

---

102 For a detailed evaluation of organization-political movement differentiation, see Aydınoğlu, 2007: 351-386.

"eagerness" appeared as an understanding of a revolutionary organization that was described "in a perfection worth of a future that has not been known when to reach" (Aydınoğlu, 2007: 366) and in the form of an "organization fetichism" that constantly delayed *perfect* construction of the "party" or "organization" to an indefinite future within political movements of this second group.

There was an entirely blind violence spiral just before 12 September. One of the main reasons behind it was the proliferation of nihilism within the second group movements that increasingly lost its political character due to failure in implementing the strategy, and was the reflection of an anti-political grudge that increasingly became dominant in the radical left, especially in small groups who declared themselves as subsequents of the THKP-C and did not shoulder any responsibility. The spontaneism that had a part in the characterization of the "political movement" caused gang practices similar to the MHP's autonomous gangs in certain extreme conditions (it is therefore not a coincidence that some elements of those small groups showed a tendency to become mafia). The momentum of 1979-80 in which a great deal of idealists, security guards, and revolutionists (including those who died as a result of intra-left violence) lost their lives and became routine news of daily newspapers was a momentum that all sides of civil war lost reference points of their political strategies as well as their political rationalities: the MHP dragged itself and an entire political area into nothingness.

CHAPTER FIVE

Kurdish Radical-Constitutive Violence Variant as Independent State-Making Project: Parallel Universe?

I. THE TRANSITION FROM THE CIVIL-REACTIONAL TO RADICAL-CONSTITUTIVE VIOLENCE

At first glance, there was a quiet period in the Kurdish political movement between mass uprisings in the 1920s and 1930s and the increasing radical-constitutive violence campaigns since the 1970s. After uprisings that were realized with a civil-reactional content against the Republic's founding paradigm were suppressed in the hardest way, the Turkish State completed its state-making process gradually by extinguishing any type of ethnic, religious, and class objections. However, with regard to the Kurdish movement, it would be terribly wrong to define the 1940-1970 period, standing between the transformation from civil-reactional violence into radical-constitutive violence, as some sort of vacuum because there were movements providing the continuity between these two periods, including violence but not offering a clear political quality and not showing a tendency to violence despite their clear political contents. Kurdish political violence in the 1970s received many symbolic aspects of its *violence* content from the first kind of movements. Its *political* content took shape by discussions and disintegrations between the second kind of movements.

Movements of the first kind materialized within "Kurdish banditry." Kurdish banditry which mostly appeared as a massive fact in the 1950s, reached its peak in the 1960s and *suddenly* disappeared through the rise of radical-constitutive violence in the 1970s. According to Özcan (2014), Kurdish banditry was perceived as a state threat due to two reasons. The first was Kurdish nomadism that posed a critical obstacle against a settling and recording policy, which was the foundation of the nation-state making process and constituted the essential human resource of Kurdish banditry.[103] The second reason for the Turkish State to consider Kurdish banditry as more than a simple public security problem was the concern felt against potential reflections of a process developing towards building a Kurdish state in Northern Iraq. The state had a purpose to demilitarize the region during the creation process of the monopoly of violence. Therefore, both the objective of suppressing Kurdish national consciousness and the objective of disarmament lie under commando operations (raids on villages, searching people collectively and tortures) which started from the late 1960s and continued until spring 1970, and were directed to the region by becoming "manoeuvres." The state fighting against the "bandit" was interwined with its fighting against the political Kurdish movement of that period in many ways. This found its equivalent in mutual political memory. That the Turkish State defined the first Kurdish guerillas as "bandits" for a considerable time manifested itself as the most clear projection of this memory (Özcan, 2014: 166). On the other hand, the presence of "PKK militants who selected their code names by taking from names of famous bandits" (Özcan, 2014: 204) is proof that this conception of the state had a correspondence in the Kurdish political violence movement.

To obtain a genealogy of the second kind movements, i.e., movements which had a clear political content but did not show a tendency to violence, we should look at the fact of Kurdish nationalism of which its core is dated, according to Bozarslan (2009a), as the Sheikh Ubeydullah Revolt at 1880.[104] The politicization process of Kurdish nationalism starting from 1914 in particular (Bitlis, Barzan and Soran uprisings) was paused temporarily by the alliance made with the state during the War of Independence and became the source of civil-reactional violence in the 1920s and '30s. The objective of the Kurdish communities in that period was to participate in the state-making process from which they were excluded by state coercion and to tend towards a Kurdist governing structure within the Republic which was founded collaboratively. When we focus on the fermentation process of Kurdish radical-constitutive

---

103 "Law enforcement violence of the state over measurements taken against brigandage has aimed to discharge nomadic Kurdish communities as 'last remains of reactionary Ottoman society.' Nomads with their social structure including marginal features, particularly their elemental organization and Êzidilik, smuggling, and honour killing in terms of the nation-state-making project and who resist every regulation of central administration have become social rebels without having to be bandits." (Özcan, 2014: 166).

104 A helpful definition of Kurdish nationalism is: "Kurdish nationalism is a movement that has aimed for building a governing structure based on Kurdishness (autonomy, federation, or a separate state) with specific symbols and a political expression" (Bozarslan, 2009a: 841).

violence in the 1970s concordantly to the periodization we made, the "Kurdish Left" is at the center of analysis: the "Kurdish movement and Kurdish left almost arise as equivalent words after World War II, particularly after military coups in Iraq at 1958 and in Turkey at 1960" (Bozarslan, 2007: 1169). In other words, the energy that helped Kurdish political actors to move towards radical-constitutive violence appeared through Kurdish nationalism being termed within a leftist perspective. It is wrong to classify the period between 1959-1974 in particular under the title of "Kurdish nationalism."[105]

Kurdish uprisings against the *Turkish state* that started just after the foundation of the Republic and continued until 1938 were supplied with two separate oppositions (Bozarslan, 2009a: 848-850): On the one hand, tribes and sects, provincialism in general against a *state* which was opposite of Ottoman,[106] and on the other hand, the Kurdish nationalist intelligentia which had a western orientation, was opposed to the state not because it was modern, but because it was *Turkish*, and was organized in *Azadi* (Freedom) and *Xoybun* (Maintenance of being self) committees. This process, which made the Kurdish nationalist movement tribe-based and nationalized Kurdish tribes as a result of mutual interaction, was the basis of a certain political Kurdish typology (a nationalist but also traditionist and even conservative typology) until the period where the "Kurdish movement" identified with the "Kurdish left." In the "years of tiredness" beginning from the Dersim Rebellion in 1938 to 1959, Kurdish intellectuals made publications in which Kurdish culture was protected or memories were cited. The importance of these activities regarding our subject is that they are the source of nationalist historiography, a vital point of the Kurdish movement's memory and nation consciousness that is still in existence. These culture-literature circles that act as a group of friends rather than an organization entered into the process of politicization again in the late 1950s, but this time the process included both left and right timbres. The climax of this politicization process was the

---

105 For an argument about the thesis that the period between 1959 and 1974 should be considered as an "ethnoregional movement", see Alış, 2009 and 2012.

106 "The fact that the Kemalist government has attempted to break traditional social structures, enforced compulsory military service, "nationalized" the economy, militarized borders that did not exist before or did not aim a disengagement among Kurds, abolished the caliphate, has been a resource of legitimacy during War of Independence, made impositions in terms of religion acknowledged as interference in private life, has made way for these layers to move into an anti-state violence-based opposition" (Bozarslan, 2009a: 848).

arrest of Kurdish intellectuals known as the 49s just before the 1960 military coup, i.e., the last roundup of the DP government.[107]

The junta administration considered Kurdishness after the 1960 military coup as a clear threat against the state. One of its first practices was to gather 485 Kurdish "landlords and masters" in a camp at Sivas and then to exile 55 of them; the general amnesty granted after the junta did not cover the 49s and Kurdish nationalists known as the 23s in 1963 also were arrested (Akkaya, 2013: 92; Bozarslan, 2009a: 853).[108] However, on the other hand, the constitution enacted after the military coup enlarged freedoms of speech and organization, and consequently magazines such as *Barış Dünyası* (World of Peace), *Dicle-Fırat* (Tigris-Euphrates), *Deng* (Voice), *Yeni Akış* (New Flow), *Doğu* (East) benefited from this, despite the fact that they were exposed to enclosure and oppression even though they used a timid language. Issues previously discussed under the title of the "East" problem started to be called the "Kurdish" problem in the late 1960s. The Kurdish problem was discussed intensively in socialist magazines such as *Ant* (Vow), *Türk Solu* (Turkish Left), *Aydınlık* (Bright). In the 1960s, there was a shift from "Kurdish nationalism to Kurdish movement as a social opposition" (Bozarslan, 2009a: 852), a period in which the main actors gave form to the Kurdish political arena in the 1970s, and it refers to a crucial twist about our subject.

We mentioned before that there were right-oriented people among the 49s. The first steps were taken in the period of the DP administration: "transition to a multi-party system (...) has ensured tribes and cults to build center-privileged boss-client relations by being integrated into political system" (Bozarslan, 2009a: 850-851). For instance, the fact that the DP elected Melik Fırat, the grandchild of Sheikh Said, as congressman was a significant gesture in this regard. Hence, "when the late 1950s is considered, members of all tribes, cults and big families in Kurdistan have either entered the service of the state or waited in line for this to happen. Some of them have become a part of Turkish intelligence service" (Gündoğan, 2012: 105). The AP, which entered politics under the title of the DP's heir, increased its vote rates in the

---

107 Among the 49s who got arrested in 1959 were names playing important roles later in the political arena, such as Said Elçi, Şerafettin Elçi, Nurettin Yılmaz, Medet Serhat, Sait Kırmızıtoprak, Canip Yıldırım, Musa Anter, Yaşar Kaya, and Naci Kutlay (Bozarslan, 2009a: 852). For a complete list of those who were arrested, see Alış, 2012: 64n.

108 The leader of the junta, Cemal Gürsel, made the following statements in speeches he gave at Kurdish cities a few months after the military coup: "In this country and in the entire East, there is no Kurdish nation whatsoever... Spit in faces of those who mislead us by whispering. Say no, the essence of this country is Turk" (Akkaya, 2013: 92).

region during the 1960s (40% of votes that the CHP received in 14 Kurdish cities in the 1961 elections decreased to 20% in the 1969 elections; on the other hand, in the same cities, the AP increased its percentage from 10% to 30%),[109] which clearly refers to the center right core that continues its existence in the region even today. The YTP (New Turkey Party), which was founded in 1961 by mostly old members of the DP and claimed the title of the DP's main heir, was described in general as "the first legal party who is identified with a 'Kurdishness-oriented' politics" (Akkaya, 2013: 93). The reason why this party was accused of "Kurdism," which did not include the cultural and political demands of Kurdish people in its manifest and stood for integration into Turkish society and voluntary assimilation, was that Yusuf Azizoğlu, the Minister of Health in the coalition government in 1963 had close relations with rich people in Kurdish cities, raised many health care centers in the region, and helped many association in the region financially (Alış, 2012: 68; Akkaya, 2013: 93-94). However, over 30% of the votes that this party received from 14 Kurdish cities in the 1961 elections decreased to 10% in 1969 (Alış, 2012: 80) and the party soon faded from the political scene.

Aside from the presence of the YTP that faded in a short span of time not in terms of a political mentality, but of a *political party*, the roots of the Kurdish left and the radical-constitutive violence movement that left their mark on the 1970s had formed two origins in the 1960s (Bozarslan, 2007b and Gündoğan, 2012). The first was the TKDP (Turkey's Kurdistan Democratic Party) that was the first Kurdish political organization after *Xoybun* and was founded in Diyarbakır in 1965 as an extension of the KDP (Kurdistan Democratic Party) in Iraq. Şakir Epözdemir, one of the founding fathers of the party, stated that founders of the party comprised of "two attorneys, two public servants, and two public accountants" (2005: 8). The TKDP, which was governed by Said Elçi after the first president of the party, Faik Bucak, was assassinated, was based mostly on a social ground comprised of local rich people, i.e. traditional social faces such as landlords, masters, clan leaders, of artisans, and of *"meles"* (religious scholars) from madrassas, and it had a conservative and traditional political perception (Gündoğan, 2012: 112; Bozarslan, 2007b: 1176). One of the important indicators showing that the TKDP had had a traditional perspective was that it did not bother to make use of modern struggle tools such as publishing a newspaper and magazine, founding an association, or

---

109   See Alış, 2012: 80.

distributing leaflets (Gündoğan, 2012: 113). Despite its explicit traditionalist and conservative nature, the TKDP was not able to prevent a part of its grassroots moving towards the left.[110] The reason why the TKDP is important to our subject is that the TKDP was one of the organizers of the East Rallies, which we will discuss later. Also, some radical-constitutive violence actors in the 1970s came from this party. Finally, the Kurdish movement in Turkey gained a *cross-border* qualification together with the TKDP. The course and the result of the pro-Barzani movement in Iraq directly influenced political developments in Turkish Kurdistan and were effective in the prominence of violence instruments.

The second origin of the Kurdish radical-constitutive violence movement was the Turkish left that became concrete in the TİP and FKF/*Dev-Genç* and took shape in disintegrations within these organizations. However, before illustrating certain milestones of encounters of the Kurdish movement with the Turkish left starting within the TİP, it will be helpful to evaluate political and intellectual context of the relationship between the Kurdish and socialist movements in Turkey.

The routine political channels opened by the DP, although it had pragmatic concerns, was complete by the 1960 military coup and was an important factor for Kurdish activism to go towards a socialist movement. The first critical indications for the orientation of Turkey's Kurds to a socialist movement was in the left-right differentiation among the 49s (Alış, 2012: 64-65; Bozarslan, 2007b: 1175). The reason why Turkey's Kurds met leftism later than those in Iraq and Syria was, according to Bozarslan (2007b: 1175), because the left movement in Turkey, which approached the USA during the DP administration by making opposite progress toward radical dynamics in the Middle East, was weak and that anti-DP opposition was actually managed by Kemalist ideology.[111] Kurdish intellectuals, who accused Kemalism for being the reason for both "national cruelty" and "underdevelopment," started to consider socialism as an exit from these two disasters. The main characteristic of the Kurdish movement that identified it with the socialist left and directly left its mark on the 1970s is its unconditional dependence on Marxism-Leninism, which was defined as "universality of the poor" by Tuğrul Artunkal (narrated by Bozarslan,

---

110 In the words of Epözdemir, one of founding fathers of TKDP, the Kurdish youth "has immersed itself into leftist flow (…) could not pull through the leftism illness" (2005: 8-9, 10).

111 In return, the Kurds in the Middle East had already started to build relationships with the Soviets, although it was based on pragmatic concerns rather than an ideological or political closeness.

2007b: 1170): "Starting from the late 1960s, this ideology made it possible for Kurdishness as 'the subjective' to be legitimized by 'the universal' and consequently to explain its own state of being suppressed through humankind, and to become a part of the 'universality' including Turks, Arabs, Iranians and to consider the 'other' as an 'enemy state' and 'friendly public' rather than a 'public enemy' " (Bozarslan, 2007b: 1170). In this sense, Kurdishness has pointed to a more *universal* national identity than "oppressing nations." The characteristic of Marxism-Leninism that acknowledged the national matter as a legitimate matter ("self-determination") and associated it with class wars fed the image of the *October Revolution as a breakthrough that started national liberation wars* predominating by both Turkish and Kurdish socialists, just as in many countries of the Third World. This was forecasted by western Marxists such as Karl Korsch in the early 1930s.

> These movements [in marginal areas] cannot seek connections with reformism, since it is inseparably tied to the expansionist and colonialist policies of the core nations of the world capitalist system today. However, they will find in Leninist Bolshevism and Communism a form of Marxist ideology, which is strongly anti-imperialist. It could be used as a transitional ideology for their own anti-imperialist class struggle. Such a process would again be analogous to the spread of Christianity among the barbarians outside the territories of the Roman Empire (Korsch, 1974: 11).

The Kurdish left, which found its presence in this political and intellectual context, operated under the umbrella of the TİP until the ideological differentiation within itself became a clear disintegration by the 1971 military coup. The group of Kurdish politicians within the TİP in the name of "Easterners" contributed to the TİP and the Turkish left in general, which considered the Kurdish problem in an economical-developmental framework, to gradually change this perspective. It is possible to see this change, which was caused by Kurdish groups adopting a particular attitude towards Mehmet Ali Aybar in a schism within the TİP, in programmes and notices written in the TİP congresses during the 1960s. Along with the emphasis made on economic and social underdevelopment of the region, ethnic and denominational discrimination was also emphasized in the manifesto which was penned by

Aybar with a prudent approach due to being a legal party and accepted in the 1964 congress.[112] In the 2nd Congress organized in Malatya in 1966 (in which pro-Aybar Kurdish groups clearly became influential), the TİP was supported as the one and only political organization in which "our working society, our socialist intellectuals (…) could come together to solve problems of the East that has been exploited materially and morally" (narrated by Yeğen, 2007: 1217). "Psychosociological factors" were directly emphasized after this point of view developed more in the third congress organized in Ankara in November 1968 (narrated by Alış, 2012: 74). It is quite ironic that the fourth congress in October 1970 in which "the facts that Kurdish people live in the East of Turkey, that fascist administrations dominant over Kurdish people from the beginning have implemented oppression, terror and assimilation policies which sometimes became bloody cruelties" (narrated by Yeğen, 2007: 1218) were declared publicly caused both the closure of the TİP and Easterners becoming distant from the party due to inner conflicts.[113]

Historical and ideological reasons for the Kurdish movement in Turkey becoming independent from both the Turkish left and the Barzani effect through the foundation of the DDKO (Revolutionary Eastern Cultural Hearths) in 1969-1970 are obvious. On the other hand, Alış (2012: 76-80) suggested that the disintegration within the Kurdish movement has roots in the TİP and therefore it would be wrong to consider Easterners as a whole, and he based his claim on the voting attitude of Kurdish voters in the general elections during the 1960s.[114] According to Alış, three different factions came together among Easterners that contained many contradictions and points of conflict: The socialist group comprised of those who studied in university, had a profession, and helped the TİP to become a party in the region;[115] the group engaged in politics under the umbrella of the TİP and were comprised

---

112 "One of the services that Turkish Labor Party prodives immediately and studiously in the course of realizing development of the country is East Problem (…) Citizens here are underdeveloped socially and culturally in parallel with economical underdevelopment of the region. Furthermore, people who speak Kurdish and Arabic or are a member of Alevi sect within those citizens have been exposed to discrimination due to these facts. We confront with vexed issues created by this situation (…) Turkish Labor Party will approach these citizens as fellow countrymen" (narrated by Yeğen, 2007: 1217 and Alış, 2012: 74).
113 For a detailed analysis of the relation between Easterners and TİP, see Alış, 2009: 99-144.
114 In view of Alış, clientelism and tribalism are essential for the votes given to the TIP in this region, just like other political parties.
115 Tarık Ziya Ekinci, Naci Kutlay, Mehment Ali Aslan, Kemal Burkay, Tahsin Ekinci, Edip Karahan, Canip Yıldırım, Örfi Akkoyunlu, Yaşar Kaya, Enver Aytekin and Musa Anter were connected with this group.

of pro-TKDP people or those who did not show their true party colors;[116] and the group was made up of Kurdish youth who helped election campaigns of the party, distributed its publications, studied in universities at major cities, and played an active role later in the foundation of the DDKO. The active effort of various Kurdish groups, the DDKO in particular pushing the TİP administration, lay behind the declaration in TİP's 1970 congress in which the presence of Kurdish people and national oppression were acknowledged (Akkaya, 2013: 96).

We believe it is important to discuss behaviours of those who took sides with the MDD ("antithesis position") on the Kurdish problem in the polarization between the TİP and the MDD, although they did not really influence Kurdish political actors to formalise their own policies in this period. Mihri Belli, the founder of the MDD understanding, argued that the Kurdish problem could only be solved within national pact borders and through the discharge of feudalism and that the Sheikh Said rebellion in particular, and rebellions breaking out in the first years of the Republic, were "reactionary movements in line with interests of English imperialism" (Yeğen, 2007: 1219), and therefore assumed Kemalism as progressive. Doğu Perinçek, who was a party in the disintegration within the MDD in 1970, has followed this nationalist-leftist or leftist Kemalist line until today and even solidified it. However, Mahir Çayan, who was the founder of the line, which we called the "synthesis position" in a previous chapter, also targeted Belli's approach to the Kurdish problem and criticized Belli's emphasis on the "National Pact" severely by accusing him with "petit bourgeoisie nationalism" in the separation process from the MDD (Yeğen, 2007: 1219-1220). The main reference point here is the Marxism-Leninism's sense of "self-determination."[117] It was not possible for Kurdish youth gathering around the DDKO to show interest and sympathy in a political framework which, although it denied nationalism in theory and in practice, assigned a progressive role to Kemalism of the 1919-24 period, because the main issue regarding autonomous Kurdish politics represented in the DDKO was Kemalism itself (Akkaya, 2013: 97). However, we will outline the clear traces of this "synthesis position" in the political climate

---

116 Said Elçi, Abdülkerim Ceylan (Mele Abdülkerim), Mahmut Okutucu (Mele Mahmut), Sait Kırmızıtoprak, Mehmet Emin Bozarslan, Mehdi Zana, Nazmi Balkaş were connected with this group.
117 "…revolutionary proletariat […] clearly reveals the question of when and under which circumstances resolution processes such as separation, autonomy, federation etc. prescribed by the self-determination right of nations be valid" (Çayan, 2004: 258).

created by the PKK (Kurdistan Workers' Party) which has become the sole and prevailing party at the end of Kurdish political movement's development.

Two decisive incidents escalated the Kurdish movement to the radical phase, i.e., the transition from "cultural rights, economic investment and social justice demands expressed in the midst of the 1960s to describing Turkey as a state 'depending on imperialism and oppressing Kurdish people/nation' in the early 1970s [...] and to 'defending self-determination right of nations' " (Bozarslan, 2007b: 1176). The first incident was the East Rallies organized in 1967 and 1969.[118] Those rallies in which the TİP and TKDP played the leading roles and were organized for the purpose of protesting cultural oppression and economic problems, took place with a public participation far more than expected. Given the fact that the Kurdish movement in the 1960s was mostly based on mobilisation of students and intellectuals, those rallies surprised Kurdish political actors in a similar way that the working class protests on 15-16 June surprised the Turkish left and functioned as a wake-up signal.[119] The second incident is the commando operations performed by the Turkish state between 1969 and 1970 against the mass rallies, against the excitement of Kurdish political actors in Turkey created by "the autonomy established by Barzani movement in Iraq through 1970 Declaration" (Ergut, 2014: 219), and against the banditry movement that excelled in the same period of time. [120] The effect of these two incidents is clear on the change of expression in the TİP's 1970 Congress.

On the other hand, state coercion hardened after the 1971 military coup (raids on villages, searching people collectively and tortures which became routine during the 1990s were performed systematically in those commando operations) got a strong reaction from Kurdish people and also

---

118 Places and dates of East Rallies: 13 August 1967 Silvan, 3 September 1967 Diyarbakır, 24 September 1967 Siverek, 8 October 1967 Batman, 15 October 1967 Tunceli, 22 October 1967 Ağrı, 18 November 1967 Ankara, 13 April 1969 Diyarbakır, 17 July 1969 Suruç, 27 July 1969 Hilvan, 2 August 1969 Varto, 2 August 1969 Siverek, 24 August 1969 Lice, 3 September 1969 Diyarbakır (bkz. Akkaya, 2013: 95n).

119 For a detailed analysis of the East Rallies, see Beşikçi, 1992 and Gündoğan, 2005. On the other hand, the fact that Kurdish people were clearly belittled by *Ötüken*, one of the racist magazines in that period and that the Turkish goverment stayed silent against this is counted as one of the reasons why an unexpected crowd participated in the East Rallies (bkz. White, 2000: 132-133).

120 It should be noted here that local commando operations made within the context of "perturbation" against Kurdish bandits already started in the early 1960s. Therefore, commando operations were made to suppress the development of the Kurdish movement as well as disarm the region. For instance, in the operation made with 2000 commandos and military police officers and six helicopters in Silvan on 8 April 1970, Kurdish people were arranged in order, 3144 persons to be precise, and were addressed as: "Dogs of Kurds! Spies of Barzani! Tell us where you have hidden your arms!" (narrated by White from Kutschera, 2000: 158, footnote 9).

showed them that "the national matter has another dimension outside of socialism programme" (Bozarslan, 2009a: 856). Although armed struggle strategies were discussed within the Turkish left and caused a radicalization of Kurdish youth, those "synthesis positions" were embedded into their own agendas and attributed a progressivist role to the Kemalism of the 1919-1924 period. Self-determination as a post-revolution problem already kept Kurdish youth, who did not show a tendency to armed struggle, from participating in these movements. Along with the TİP increasingly fading from the political arena after the 1969 elections, the first stage of the Kurdish left gaining its independence from Turkish left started. On the other hand, radicalization, which was neck and neck with state coercion, caused Kurdish political actors in Turkey to be "denied to perceive themselves as a simple extension of Iraqi Kurdistan" (Bozarslan, 2009a: 856). For sure, the ideological histoincompatibility between conservative TKDP and Kurdish youth who "universalized" the "subjective" by force of Marxist-Leninist ideology had a great role in this radicalization. This *dual autonomization* of the Kurdish movement was addressed by the DDKO. Another turning point with regard to the Kurdish left passed. The Kurdish parallel universe was built through the first steps of the transition to an autonomous and increasingly independent Kurdish left movement following "the transformation from Kurdish nationalism into a Kurdish movement as a social opposition": *DDKO Bulletins* "show that the Kurdish left changed in a considerable extent to find its raison d'être not in Turkishness, but Kurdishness and to search for the salvation of this Kurdishness in a universally left ideology" (Bozarslan, 2007b: 1176). Clear statements about the disintegration from the Turkish left on the grounds of a national matter were expressed in common pleas made by different groups that were arrested due to the DDKO case.

Despite its short-dated presence, a formation was formed that was important in the process of the Kurdish movement gaining autonomy and in the development of its statement on armed struggle. Sait Kırmızıtoprak (Dr. Şıvan) who was one of the 49s, wrote about the Kurdish problem in the *Direction* magazine in the early 1960s and conducted pro-TKDP activities within Eastern organizations. He formed a new organization called the T-KDP (Kurdistan Democratic Party in Turkey) in 1968. Although some researchers evaluate this organization, which was very close to the TKDP and yet in a fierce competition with it, as the left wing of the TKDP, it is best defined as a separate organization. Dr. Şıvan, who compared the Iraq Kurdish movement to the Viet-Kong resistance, is the person to take steps to reconstruct the Kurdish left on national matters by accusing the Turkish left of being under the influence of Kemalism as a whole. Dr. Şıvan argues (and therefore, perhaps Kurdifies the left-Kemalist ideology by this way) that the driving motor of history regarding Kurdish people is the transition from feudalism to nationalism rather than from feudalism to socialism by explaining that "the primary contradiction" to be solved is not class contradiction but "national contradiction." The importance of Dr. Şıvan regarding our subject is that he is the prototype of many features that gave shape to the Kurdish movement after 1974. Those features are that it gave the first signals of radical disintegration from the Turkish left by clearly expressing the national resistance theme underlying the transition to left, that it demonstrated clear indications of the disintegration from traditionalist and conservative Kurdish nationalism despite its organic relation with the Barzani movement, that it gravitated towards an approach based on a party organization foreseeing armed struggle, and that it symbolized a powerful leader figure for the first time apart from Barzani. Dr. Şıvan was murdered in 1971 by the KDP led by Barzani himself on the grounds that he killed Said Elçi and two of his friends.[121]

II. THE BIRTH OF KURDISH RADICAL-CONSTITUTIVE VIOLENCE

Following the 12 March 1971 military coup, almost 100 Kurdish people were arrested within the scope of the DDKO and TKDP hearings in Diyarbakır. The period in which the Diyarbakır prison transformed into a university for Kurdish political actors until the 1974 general amnesty was the period during which new disintegrations started. The group, which was comprised of components of the DDKO who did not support the TİP but gave shape to it and gathered around Mümtaz Kotan, took steps for an organization that was later called *Rizgarî* (Liberation). In a subsequent period, *Rizgarî* was considered a direct extension of the DDKO (Gündoğan, 2012: 117-118). While supporters of Said Elçi preserved the TKDP, followers of Dr. Şıvan's theses started an organization that was called the DDKD (Revolutionary Eastern Cultural Associations).

---

121 For further information see Bozarslan, 2007b: 1177-1178; Akkaya, 2013: 97-98; Gündoğan, 2012: 113-116.

The team of Kemal Burkay that completely disconnected itself from the TİP formed the TKSP (Kurdistan Socialist Party of Turkey).[122]

While the DDKD and the TKSP had a pro-Soviet line, the TKDP and *Rizgarî* located themselves outside of the Soviet-China conflict, but what they shared in common is important regarding our subject. The first common ground was that all four organizations excluded violence as an *urgent* political instrument, although they were illegal organizations due to mandatory conditions of that period. Therefore, the Kurdish radical-constitutive violence practices beginning from 1977 became the main topic through an intense "pacifism" accusation to those "big brothers."

The second and most important common ground was that the argument suggested in publications and pleadings of these four organizations to acknowledge Kurdistan as a separate country from Turkey and as a *colony* shared by four states was the common ground of all Kurdish organizations founded after 1974 (Bozarslan, 2007b: 1180).[123] This caused the "national salvation" statement to become prominent as a result of Kurdish national demands re-expressed within a Marxist-Leninist perspective. However, this radicalization within the Marxist-Leninist universe did not follow the formulations of the Turkish left anymore, and the formation of the Kurdish problem "through a socialist and Marxist perspective" (Alış, 2012: 86) took place by Kurdish political actors and on the grounds of a dyad composed of two perspectives, namely the colony thesis and the illegal independent organization. The fact that "publishing houses managed by Kurdish intellectualists such as Koral and Yöntem have published articles about armed struggles of colony countries such as Guinea and Mozambique" (Bozarslan, 2007b: 1181-1182) in a period when publishing houses managed by actors of the Turkish left published books about Latin America guerilla wars and partisan resistance against fascism in the Soviets and the Balkans is a clear indicator of this situation.[124] Another development that occurred based on this "national agitation" phase of the Kurdish left movement (Alış, 2012: 59) is that the *Newroz* mythos and *Kawa* legends were built as an *origin mythos* starting from the midst of the 1970s to take the

---

122 These were main separation points. Note that the DDKO supported almost all Kurdish organizations by its cadre.

123 Although there were some exceptions in the late 1960s, Bozarslan (2007b: 1204, footnote 56) states that "the colony thesis" was *theoretically* developed for the first time by Kemal Burkay and then by the *Rizgarî* magazine in the early 1970s.

124 Kurdish political actors in that period have also shown a particular attention towards colonialism and anti-colonialism practices in Eritrea, Angola, Algeria, and Palestine (Akkaya, 2013: 101, 103).

origins of Kurdish people back to the Medes (Gunes, 2012), and therefore to generate a historiography that questions the legitimacy of Turkey itself beyond Kemalism. Thus, the Kurdish left movement as a whole focused, on the one hand, on international colonialism experiences and on the other, started to build modern "Kurdishness" as a political *topos* completely independent from "Turkish people," in its move to connect "subjective" to "universal."

The colony thesis also led to a perception that made armed struggle a salvation from colonialism, even if theoretically. It was true that no Kurdish organization after 1974 "has responded armed struggle categorically in theory" (Akkaya, 2013: 102). The main discussion from the point of Kurdish left political actors who excluded violence in that period was not about the categorical denial of armed struggle, but the timing of it, as in the case of the Turkish left. However, political actors, who were engaged in armed struggle and underlined its "urgency," embodied not only a certain political rationality but also a certain set of *affects*.[125]

This type of sociological investigation had a cross-border dimension regarding the Kurdish movement because the recovery process of Kurdish political actors starting from the 1974 general amnesty overlapped with Barzani's decision to stop the struggle in 1975. According to Bozarslan (2009a: 857), the defeat of Barzani caused significant political effects on the Kurdish movement in Turkey as a whole. The Kurdish movement in Turkey, which lost its reference point with this defeat that it would use as its base, was faced with the responsibility of becoming a referential Kurdish actor of the Middle East. Another fact that deepened the fragmentation of the Kurdish movement in Turkey during this *transition period from discipleship to mastery* was that Barzani, who was supported by the USA and also defeated through the "betrayal" of the USA and the Soviets who supported the Bagdad regime caused both *radicalization* and *searches for new perspectives*. To achieve the goals of our study, we will not discuss organizations that kept being pro-Soviet, the TKSP in particular, because Kurdish radical-constitutive violence appeared *in spite of* these organizations. As a result of searches for new perspectives that have created radical-constitutive violence actors since 1977, a Maoist organization called *Kawa* arose under the influence of the Soviet-China conflict that occurred in the Turkish left at the midst of the 1970s.

---

125 For a study about this type of sociological investigation oriented towards the 1970-73 violence momentum of the Turkish left, see Öğütle and Etil, 2014: 300-312.

However, organizations constituting the mainstream of armed struggle; i.e., the KUK (Kurdistan National Liberationists) and the PKK were in a position independent from the Turkish left as well as the agenda of the Turkish left.[126]

Behind radicalization was the structuring of the political arena narrowed down under the custody of the capitalist-military coalition that made legal Kurdish parties and access to symbolic sources about Kurdishness impossible. Another important reason for this radicalization was the concept of civil war, which was a part of the Turkish left, and consequently a massive provocation and pogrom component of the MHP's paramilitary violence repertory that emerged in certain cities with the majority of Kurdish people. Most of the 18 cities in which martial law was declared after the Kahramanmaraş massacre were Kurdish cities. Another reason for radicalization, which was as decisive, was that the Kurdishness cause became ownerless after the Barzani defeat and gained an "eschatological quality" (Bozarslan, 2009a: 859) in the form of a matter of life or death. Insecurity and anger were deeply felt due to the defeat of Barzani. This situation, which appeared as an "intergenerational crisis" (Bozarslan, 2007b: 1184), found its correspondence in Kurdish youth by a separation and an ideological/biographical refinement similar to the experience in the Turkish left in the late 1960s. The accusation set by the *Dev-Genç* in the late 1960s towards the TİP and the MDD ("pacifism," "reformism," "bourgeoisie nationalist" etc.) was possessed by Kurdish youth and was directed to old school political actors who were considered responsible for the Barzani defeat. The actors of the Kurdish radical-constitutive violence that were in action after 1977 were targeted to become the main actors of the Kurdish political arena in the Middle East. The theme of "resurrection," by laying claim to national pride through violence and ideological/biographical refinement from any type of tradition, was now dominant over a secondary socialization processes that Kurdish youth mostly from the provinces had to endure. The class determinative about this process of tendency towards violence was "the rise of low classes" (Bozarslan, 2009a: 858).

The year of 1977 when the independent candidate of the TKSP, Mehdi Zana, was elected as mayor of Diyarbakır witnessed both massification and

---

126 There were seven principal organizations in the Kurdish left that arose from three main origins after 1975. The TKDP-based KUK, DDKO-based *Rizgarî*, *Kawa* and DDKP-KİP (Kurdish Workers' Party), and the TKSP, PKK and *Têkoşin* (Struggle) originated from all three the Turkish left. If we separate them according to Soviet-China conflict in that period, the TKSP and the DDKP-KİP were in the Soviet line, and the *Kawa* was on the Maoist line; other movements located themselves independently from this conflict. For further information see Akkaya, 2013: 103-108 and Ercan, 2010.

fragmentation, and also the birth of actors who carried radical-constitutive violence. However, as this fragmentation appeared as precise separations in the level of cadres, it would be wrong to consider that it happened as precisely in the general view of militants and sympathisers. On the contrary, people were constantly moving from one place to another in search of something. This intra-organizational mobilization was mostly based on kinship and tribalism rather than ideological impulses, and naivety appeared sometimes in the choices made. An important, even if not principle, reason for intra-violence in the Kurdish political arena can be found within the competition to capture mobilized masses.

In this multiple organization context, organizations put armed struggle into practice and started the socialization process based on violence were actually the KUK and PKK. However, a strong tendency towards this direction in *Kawa*, which entered the Kurdish political arena by a namesake publishing house and magazine after important cadre disintegrated from the DDKD in 1976, should also be discussed. The main reason why *Kawa*, which attempted to take local steps to move into armed struggle by 1978, could not "go to war all together" despite its clear tendency to, is that it first split into two and then soon after into four within the scope of discussions about the three world theory. After the separations, attempts by the pro-Albania group to build a professional cadre organization and to start a guerilla war remained inconclusive because its leading cadres were murdered in Qamishli, Syria on 12 December 1980 by the intelligence service of Turkey, just after the 12 September miltiary coup. This is an historically important incident because it was the first cross-border operation of the Turkish state against Kurdish organizations.[127]

The KUK, one implementer of Kurdish radical-constitutive violence, emerged as a result of the TKDP's separation. Discussions on reasons for the Barzani movement's defeat within the TKDP started in 1977 and resulted in separation. The left wing, which was mostly comprised of young militants, took the party administration over and named it KDP-KUK following the notice published on 1 May 1978. Hence, in the same period, socialist (sometimes Maoist) wings arose in Iraq's and Iran's KDPs, and there was a general tendency to "become leftist" (Bozarslan, 2007b: 1189-1190). Although a defacto dual structuring occurred as a result of the traditional wing continuing operations

---

127 For details see Gündoğan, 2007 and Kısacık, 2010.

under the name of TKDP, the KUK mostly marginalized the TKDP. The KUK, which declared that "the party is possessed by Marxists" and that "the urgent task is to rebuild the party in ideological, political and organization fields and on Marxism-Leninism grounds" (narrated by Bozarslan, 2007b: 1191), gave a start to armed struggle by making this statement to "Turkish revolutionists" that "the national matter could not be postponed until after revolution." The concept of intra-left violence that had appeared within the Turkish left since 1979 was also experienced to an even more devastating extent within Kurdish organizations; conflicts between the KUK and the PKK, which led to hundreds of deaths, played a key role here. Rather than an ideological enemy label based on the Soviet-China conflict, struggles for hegemony, namely *state-making practices on local level* were much more decisive.[128] There were great similarities and common grounds between the KUK and the PKK in terms of both political expression (a shallow, instrumentalized for armed struggle, symbolized, standard form of Kurdified Marxism-Leninism) and of the grassroots they were based on (first generation urban youth and rural youth) that caused an impact potentiating this intra-violence. On the other hand, the PKK was a systematical implementer of this intra-violence (the PKK has attacked not only the KUK, but all Kurdish organizations, tribes and families of rangers lived in its domain) and had a unique motivational dimension. Although the KUK, which was losing its efficiency in this intense internal conflict environment, entered into a front organization together with the TKSP and the DDKD-KİP in the same period, this attempt remained inconclusive. It faded from politics by transforming into an exile movement because its cadres, who were able to go abroad after 12 September, split into many pieces.

In the course of radical-constitutive violence's occurence in the 1970s, we explained the importance of student agglomerations rising in the form of small groups after 12 March. The roots of the PKK who had become the dominant actor of the post-1980 Kurdish movement were actually based on these student agglomerations. The PKK was founded by Abdullah Öcalan ("Apo") who operated within the "synthesis position" before 12 March and

---

128 This concept of intra-violence does not only pertain to the Kurdish left in Turkey. Major battles between the YNK (Patriotic Union of Kurdistan), which was under the leadership of Celal Talabani, and the KDP resulted in hundreds of people's deaths in Hakkâri beginning from May 1978. The Kurdish left organizations in Turkey such as the DDKD-KİP and *Rizgarî* were active in those battles (Akkaya, 2013: 105).

participated in the process of founding the ADYÖD (Ankara Democratic Association of Higher Education) in 1974 after being imprisoned for several months during the military coup period. Within this association, some Kurdish students who were under the influence of Öcalan entered into a separate socialization process by being a distinct political-ideological group. The "Apoists" who had their first meetings in Ankara with the goal to form a distinct Kurdish left organization expanded their organizational network through face-to-face communications by moving their meeting places to Kurdish cities such as Gaziantep, Diyarbakır and Elazığ from 1975 until 1977. This group, which was at first named "Kurdistan Revolutionaries" and then the UKO (National Liberation Army), declared its name as the PKK after becoming a party through a congress held on 26-27 November 1978 in Fis, a village in the Lice district of Diyarbakır.[129]

Çayan's revolutionary strategy, i.e., a politicized military war strategy based on the idea that awakening and organizing are only possible through armed struggle, could be found in the PKK, which was going simultaneously into the development of armed struggle and the process of political construction beginning from 1978. However, the first acts of violence were headed not towards government agencies and the military, but towards tribes dominant in the region and other Kurdish left organizations. These actions give clues about another understanding within the PKK, which will be explained later. Armed struggles that the PKK performed against the Süleyman tribe in 1978 at Hilvan and against the Bucak tribe in 1979 at Siverek implied the declaration of the establishment of the PKK and were also considered as the preparation period to guerilla war (Akkaya, 2013: 107).[130] Following the armed conflicts against tribes of which Bozarslan described as (2009a: 860) "they have not weakened the state and have been conceived as a violence between Kurdish people," the PKK took steps to enter guerilla war by sending nearly 50 militants to Palestine camps in Lebanon in late 1979. Although the return of these trained militants to Turkey was interrupted by the 12 September military

---

129 For a non-objective but detailed description, see Marcus, 2007: 23-40. Also see Jongerden and Akkaya, 2010: 126-130; White, 2000: 134-136.
130 On the other hand, Gündoğan underscores that the violence directed by the PKK towards certain tribes, the Bucak tribe in particular, did not mean that the PKK took on all tribes in the region: "PKK has explicitly carried out its armed struggle in 1979 against Bucak tribe at Siverek, with the cooperation of Kırvar tribe, the archenemy of Bucak tribe. As a result of this relationship, militants of PKK and some members of Kırvar tribe who have partaken in armed conflicts have been put on the same trial together after 12 September" (Gündoğan, 2012: 122). The PKK adopted the same manner at Hilvan while taking support of shareholders against members of the Süleyman tribe.

coup, the PKK who had "exploited opportunities created by Turkey-Syria tension and 1982 Lebanon War" (Bozarslan, 2009a: 861) reorganized on a military basis by preserving an important part of its executive and trained cadres. The guerilla section of the PKK, which was named the HRK (Kurdistan Liberation Forces) in this reorganization, fired "the first bullet" and officially initiated guerilla war on 15 August 1984 by assaulting government agencies in Eruh and Şemdinli.[131]

In the post-12 September conditions where no Kurdish organization except the TKSP managed to keep its presence, Akkaya (2013: 107-108) arranged the ideological and organizational reasons enabling this progress of the PKK into four groups. Firstly, the PKK was not based on original groups of the Kurdish movement, namely the TKDP and the DDKO, and this situation protected it from the chequered developments in the Barzani movement and the negative effects of the YNK-KDP conflict. Secondly, the PKK stayed out of the Soviet-China conflict, keeping it away from the discussion about who represents the real socialism, which shattered leftist movements in that period. The third reason is that the PKK had already started preparations for guerilla war before 12 September, unlike other Kurdish organizations. Lastly, the PKK managed to protect its devoted and trained militant cadre and its firm organizational structure, although they were damaged severely after 12 September. As an additional reason, it is possible that the paramilitary organization could not find a Turkish-Sunni ground open to be provoked in most Kurdish cities, which provided advantages to the PKK as it was something that other Kurdish organizations could not exploit due to crises and separations within themselves. On the one hand, this means that the PKK got rid of a foundational obstacle which disrupted the Turkish left's state-making practices on the local level at the very beginning. On the other hand, the energy that was created by the confrontation with the state's physical and symbolic violence mechanisms (instead of the "civil" hand of state coercion) after the declaration of martial law in particular and flowed directly into radical-constitutive violence channels was enormous.

However, although the reasons listed by Akkaya are correct to a certain degree, it is useful to present some oppositional annotations. There are other Kurdish organizations that met the first two criteria, and *Tekoşin* is the most

---

[131] See Marcus, 2007: 40-86; Jongerden and Akkaya, 2010: 130-135; White, 2000: 142-143.

important of those.[132] However, bloody battles erupted between the PKK and *Tekoşin* and resulted in the physical destruction of *Tekoşin*. On the other hand, the discharge of internal opposition through violence and the construction of "leadership" based on a leader cult played a foundation role in providing the fourth criterion.[133] The guerilla war that started in 1984 was executed after this discharge and construction. Gündoğan (2012: 119n) listed the PKK's originalities in a helpful way: To use violence instruments quite easily not only against Turkish government agencies, but also introvertedly (Kurdish tribes, Kurdish organizations and intra-organizational adversaries); to act not ideological but as *pragmatical* as far as possible while searching for allies outside; to be born as a leader's organization since the very beginning; to feel free to benefit from traditional foundations such as conflicts and blood feuds among tribes in the rural area; and to be based on, particularly in the beginning, the social layer who lived in cities and were defined as the "lumpen proletariat" by Marxist literature.

In a period of time where Kurdish left organizations were attached to the Kurdish diaspora either by becoming politically ineffective or by becoming social-democrat, as in the TKSP case, the atmosphere that helped the PKK start a guerilla war by gravitating towards an even more radical line that left its mark on the 1990s had also mental and motivational reasons, as well as the aforementioned ideological, political and organizational reasons.

According to Bozarslan, Kurdish movements, as is evident within the PKK, have been mentally connected with symbols of radical left movements formed in the Middle East power culture, rather than leftist thinking itself, and "[s]ince their emergence, they have in fact been impregnated by mottoes such as 'Party discipline,' 'leadership,' 'armed struggle,' 'revolutionary justice and violence'" (Bozarslan, 2000: 25-26). These types of ideas belonging to the vocabulary of the Middle Eastern power culture were and still are reproduced constantly through statements and textbooks of most Middle East countries. "Authoritarian regimes usually give birth to authoritarian oppositions" (Bozarslan, 2000: 26), and this is an important reason why the PKK survived in the changing world of the 1980s and 90s. Within this mentality in the PKK was some sort of *Kurdified Kemalism* (see Bozarslan, 2009a: 862-864). The state's symbols of power ("leader," "flag," "national ideal" etc.), which were

---

132 *Tekoşin* was founded by being detached from *Salvation*, the only THKP-C rooted organization defending the colony thesis within the Turkish left.
133 For details see White, 2000: 136-138 and 144-146.

fought against, were reproduced by being Kurdified and, by going beyond a symbol over time, became essential elements of a "national independence war" that produced internal cohesion as well as power structurings within Kurdish society. In that case, the concept of pretending to be a state, which is a result of the Marxist-Leninist ideological burden evident in other elements of both the Turkish left and the Kurdish left, was carried out by the PKK to its logical conclusions in total harmony with Middle Eastern political culture.

The motivational dimension supporting this mentality first materialized in the attitude against "tradition." As a matter of fact, heavily criticizing traditionally dominant classes and "tradition" itself as a whole and rejecting it are common features of all Kurdish organizations after 1975 (including those originating from the TKDP). The originality of PKK is that it transformed this rejection into "some kind of a hate speech and has expanded it in order to embrace Kurdish people" (Gündoğan, 2012: 120). The PKK, unlike classical Marxist-Leninist guerrilla movements dignifying *the people*, developed a linguistic that defined Kurdish people as a "dehumanized" and "degraded" public: the PKK, which departed from the idea that "you can only hate an existing Kurd, considered armed struggle as a condition to *homo kurdicus*" (Bozarslan, 2009a: 863). This linguistic of the PKK, which was clearly expressed beginning from its foundation in 1978, will become sharper and be articulated in a "resurrection" narrative:

> Subservient and submissive history of Kurdish dominant classes has become the slavery history of Kurdish people. Dominant classes have contaminated their non-national features to people and even attempted to voluntarily dehumanize the public. (narrated by Gündoğan, 2012: 121)

> [PKK] accepts resurrection with and in the war as a principle, rather than nationally being pined away in a peaceful atmosphere every day." (narrated by Akkaya, 2013: 103)

In this clear Fanonist motivation,[134] violence is inevitable, which will resurrect the "Kurdish nation" with no past except the prehistoric Golden

---

134 "According to Fanon, colonialism does not only cause an economical, political and military weakening in the colonized one only, but it also brings a psychological weakening with itself" (Ünlü, 2011: 17). See Fanon, 2008: 64-88 and 1963: 1-62.

Age, to go towards "existing Kurdish people" first. The violence against tribes was the first appearance of this and showed its face in assaults made against ranger tribes during the 1980s and partial 1990s. On the other hand, although the PKK mentioned "spy organizations released by colonialists through putting a revolutionary mask on them" (narrated by Gündoğan, 2012: 121n) and featured a Stalinist jargon in the course of its violence policy against Kurdish organizations,[135] it is obvious that this intra-left violence policy had a character exceeding the struggle for regional hegemony. Ünlü, who compares colonialism practices in the cases of France/Algeria and Turkey/Kurdistan, refers to a very similar violence policy that was conducted by the FLN (*Front de Libération Nationale*) fighting against French colonialism: "In the first years, FLN has killed more Muslim than European. It has targeted *harki*s (...) which were considered as impartial and collaborator" (Ünlü, 2014: 422). The "First bullet" fired on a "colonist" in 1984 transformed into a *meta-incident* that killed the "existing Kurd" along with the "colonist" (Bozarslan, 2009a: 864) and celebrated it for years as *the beginning of the history*: "It is interpreted in Kurdish movement as a first bullet that simultaneously killed the colonist and the colonized one of which the spirit and the body have been slaved (Eruh and Şemdinli assaults in 1984). Sartre and Fanon are clearly referred to here" (Ünlü, 2014: 429).[136] As a matter of fact, this statement by Sartre, told by radicalizing Fanon's theses even more, is nearly a complete definition of this Fanonist tragic vision that the PKK intends to create: "to shoot down a European is to kill two birds with one stone, to destroy an oppressor and the man he oppresses at the same time: there remain a dead man, and a free man; the survivor, for the first time, feels a *national* soil under his foot" (Sartre, 1963: 22).

---

135   Kurdish left groups in that period have used this Stalinist jargon embodied with an "espionage" accusation against the PKK. For instance, such a statement made in *Jina Nû* (New Life), the media organ of DDKD-KİP: "It [PKK] is far more different than any spying, provocateur organization. It always hides its true intentions… struggle against Apoism today is tightly coupled with struggle against colonialism" (narrated by Akkaya, 2013: 115).

136   Ideologically, the PKK surely did not define itself as Fanonist. However, the Fanonist gesture, which kills the colonized one along with the colonist, is pretty much decisive in the motivational aspect on the disintegration of the PKK from other components of the Kurdish left. Fanon's theses are therefore useful to comprehend this motivational aspect. On the other hand, the fact that Fanon's colonized status and his writings about violence became the main topic of the Kurdish movement is due to the *Kurdistan The Inter-State Colony* study written by İsmail Beşikçi in 1991 (see Ünlü, 2011: 29). The fact that the Kurdish movement has considered Eruh-Şemdinli assaults within the context of Fanon's "first bullet theory" is therefore a result of retrospective historiography.

The origins of pro-PKK militant typology that came into existence with the tragic vision against "the human type that has internalized the colonist's linguistic, cultural, epistemological violence" (Bozarslan, 2014: 25) lie in the personal practice of Mahir Çayan who was idolized by disordered student groups, which foundational cadres of PKK fermented in, and who codified "revolutionism" not only as an ideological-political attitude, but also as a personal process of self-destruction and rebirth. This personal practice, which is actually based on the idea of a "new man" planted by Che Guevara's "pioneer guerilla arms," takes its form through a *heavy biographical disintegration* in which 'citizenship,' 'studentship,' being someone's 'son/daughter' and all identities developed before would be left behind (Sommier, 2012: 84), and includes a set of emotional motivations comprised of senses such as loyalty, honor, catharsis, and justice. Accordingly, the "new man" of Che Guevara who was engaged into an *international brotherhood* in an internationalized war has a *universal* character stylistically, despite the fact that it culturally fulfils the content. This typology was the basis of radical-constitutive violence actors from both Turkish and Kurdish left. But the pro-PKK militant materializing as a result of heavily biographical disintegration is not an international warrior figure, but a Kurdish warrior figure. Personal recreation was designed as a *Nation's being*, not as a universal human being, and the new man of Che Guevara became a Fanonist figure.

The only resort where this Fanonist figure could be tested and prove itself is as "martyrs," and the "leadership" that is both the source and the embodiment of all features belonging to them. This rare combination of Middle Eastern political culture and a guerilla leader such as Fidel Castro and the Fanonist motivation has been the source of a very powerful leadership cult and has materialized *homo kurdicus,* including his personal characteristics, within Öcalan himself. The history of the Kurdish national movement has therefore reduced the PKK, and the PKK's history has reduced Öcalan. As Öcalan said to party militants once: "Do not forget this! The real history of PKK is my life history. I wish the party's history would be your history and a renowned one too. But you cannot make it" (narrated by Bozarslan, 2009a: 870, footnote 86).

In conclusion, the Kurdish movement has four critical turning points. Firstly, Kurdish political actors became acquainted with the left through separation among the 49s, and they entered into a radicalization process through the East Rallies. Secondly, the Kurdish left became independent, on the basis of the colony thesis, from the Turkish left and gradually from the Barzani movement after the 12 March military coup. The third turning point is the appearance of various actors of Kurdish radical-constitutive violence through the fragmentation culminating in 1977. The fourth is the Fanonist disintegration of the PKK and the fact that it has become the leading actor dominating the Kurdish movement. The PKK has managed to keep this dominant position from the 1990s up to the present is due to the ideological, political, organizational, mental, and motivational reasons we addressed, and to the unique combination that subsequently arose. This combination, which was not sustainable for long, confronted a political blockage in the late 1990s. However, Öcalan, as we already know, continues to be one and only addressee of the Turkish state for solving the Kurdish problem.

CHAPTER SIX

The Depoliticization of Political Field And
The Inveteracy of Ominous Problems

The 12 September military coup not only caused important fractures within the nature of the Turkish political field, but it also passed into history by creating long range results as the most radical military coup that kept its influence up until today and penetrated into macro and micro levels of social life. It is not possible to say whether Turkey today has managed to mostly surpass the catastrophe created by 12 September. In this regard, the 80s has become an unprecedented period of time for the history of Turkey in which the dose of pressure and violence engaged by the state apparatus became so intense. While class power relations and the state's institutional architecture have been restructured in a neo-liberal framework, an enormous militarization was activated in Kurdistan. Therefore, the military coup in 1980 corresponded to excluding the social from politics completely and gave rise to the construction of new powers and variables. Those who staged this military coup applied a series of autocratic strategies by claiming that the expression of pluralism, which corresponds to the reflection of social and ideological based conflicts on politics, was a threat against "national integrity." The most prominent of these strategies were: All political bodies were closed, parliamentary system were eliminated, new political elites suitable for the system were generated. A systematic oppression that suppressed current political movements was initiated against collectivites with opposition potential (Groc, 2009: 196). Therefore, in this chapter, we will present both the state's strategies and the variety of collective political formations aimed at these strategies, and the tangled relations between two poles – without getting far from the focus of our study. The complex process as part of the continuity of state coercion between the 80s and 90s will be discussed together with new political dynamics (i.e. Islamism gaining strength or demilitarization of Kemalism) developed through this process. We will explore these 20 years through the legal field, transformations within the military's dominant structure, monopolization of the PKK, gangs within the state, government and crisis policies, and Islamic radicalism.

I. TRANSFORMATIONS, CRISES AND NEW STRUCTURINGS IN THE STATE FIELD

The new constitution enacted in November 1982 included, in the words of Barkey and Fuller, the "most totalitarian policies of modern times in the cultural sense" (1997: 73) and established the building block of a new political order.

> The execution was intensified with this constitution and placed in a position that legislation reduced to a single parliament could not reach, and it was admitted to the presidency as far as possible. Constitutional institutions that could interfere in the legislation, but remains as unaudited (cl. 89), were attached to the president who is elected for a span of seven years – it was supported with Presidency Supervisory Council, which is the civil equivalent of National Security Council and intends to measure "Kemalist and Republican" insight of motions tabled to parliament. The electoral law has covered a series of provisions such as 10% threshold that prevents minor parties to be elected, and redetermination of electoral districts for diminishing the influence of the urban vote rate. (Groc, 2009: 196)

The 1982 constitution, unlike the previous constitution (1961), caused transformations in three different fields of the state. The first transformation was to remove the supremacy of legislation, the second was to create a semi-presidential system with exceptional powers given to the presidency, and the third was jurisdiction dominated by execution (Parla, 2007: 67). Unlike the 1961 constitution, the 1982 constitution transformed Kemalism and Kemalist ideology into the official ideology (Özbudun, 2011: 138; Parla, 2007: 35). This issue, which was defined as a result of commitment to a founding ideology, laid great stress on principles such as nationalism, secularism, and a unitary state, and the statement of "indivisible integrity of the state with its territory and nation" was emphasized in the constitution 16 times (Özbudun,

2011: 139). As high interests of the state and *raison d'etat*, Kemalism was consolidated and homogenized again (Parla, 2007: 55).

Two important historical conditions legitimised this: First, domestic political struggles and street fights between radical rightist–leftist groups that occurred before 1980 caused the public to have a negative perception toward ideologies. The notion of ideology, which had a negative meaning for conservative people too, replaced the strict and nationalist interpretation of Kemalism. Second was the lack of trust that Kemalism felt for any type of *-ism*. As Parla (2001: 313) states, Kemalism illustrated itself as the only -ism by not trusting both liberalism and socialism.

One of the main features of the 1982 constitution was secularism being subject to a strict and harsh interpretation (Özbudun, 2011: 139). This principle, which is defined by Özbudun (2011: 140) as imposing secularism, was tranformed into a matter that restricted the religion's role not only in the public sphere, but also in the social sphere. On the other hand, the image of religion reached its peak, particularly with Kenan Evren's statements referring to the moral and material happiness of the Republic of Turkey (Parla, 2007: 37). In addition, a more totalitarian pluralism in which the execution was more powerful was created with the rejection of liberal and socialist thoughts by predicting a solidarist populism (Parla, 2007: 38-39).

The 1982 constitution transformed the relationship between state and citizen into a new form by restricting fundamental rights and freedoms through expressions such as duties and responsibilities towards the state (Parla, 1982: 45). Ideological control was reinforced with Islam by transforming Kemalism into an institutional monopoly (Parla, 2007: 103-104); in addition, powers of jurisdiction and legislation were weakened before execution and the idea of creating a nonideological generation was reassurred by making Kemalism the official political ideology. Consequently, pluralism and democracy stopped being a goal through actions made for stability after 1980. The state mandate and channels opened by the state paved the way for seizing a place and politically unearned incomes through these actions for stability. As a result, the approval, by being reconstructed in both state and civil fields, solidified the tendency to legitimate new rightist rhetoric. For instance, with the Building Code enacted in 1985, only municipalities were entitled to give reconstruction permits and this reconfigured the scale and relations within local politics, a channel of which Islamism took advantage later. Therefore, fields that were or were not in the charge of the state were rescaled through approval mechanisms in the eyes of civil society.

This constitution also helped the military's role to be legitimized more powerfully than ever by intensifying the position of the military within the executive power. However, the main reasons for the 12 September military coup were totally dependent on the reorganization of class relations. The discharge of the proletariat, which became gradually politicized in the 70s, from the governmental domain was calculated through acts of violence intended to protect current property relations. The absolute discharge of democratic institutions through violence paralysed the proletariat in not only an organizational sense, but also in the sense of their intellectual capacity. The dominant block, which was established as a result of the cooperation of financiers lead by TÜSİAD and the military, made the best of this opportunity to consolidate its authority through this military coup (Dilek, 2014: 366).

The state ensured the reintegration of the poor in rural areas into middle-low classes and the proletariat through economic and political reforms representing the actualization of the 24 January decisions after 1980; then the Turkish economy came under the rule of the IMF entirely and radical changes were made in the development paradigm (Kazgan, 1995: 163-164). A new funding regime transformed, as Korkut Boratav (1991: 42) said, the purpose of "creating a low-wage economy" into a main objective after the ANAP (Motherland Party) came into power in 1983.

Another development that allowed the military to consolidate its power was the Kurdish political movement using a new strategy focused on armed struggle in 1984. As we will elaborate later, following the first attack in 1984 made by the PKK against the military, the influence of the military and consequently of *state coercion* on Kurdish cities significantly increased, and thereby the military obtained a new arena by legitimating a civil war concept in the sense of political domain. This concept delivered a *nationalist doxa* to become hegemonical and also stabilized a process that reduced political apprehension to the supremacy of the state and completely detached the public sphere from political practices by subordinating it to "national interests."

The economic field was configured according to the needs of the market economy. Another important development within the political field was the rise of religious-political mobilization as an ideological and political resource, which was disguised under cover of the Turkish-Islamic mask and was a total stranger to Kemalist references. In this regard, Özal liberalism pursued a goal to create a *class* that could intervene with the economic funds of the actors, rather than directly intervene with the actors. Therefore, a *hybrid* formation ranging from the "industry" of fictitious export to Islamic holdings occurred that put the Anatolian middle-class in order (Çiğdem, 2009: 24). According to Michael Mann's conceptualization, the *military-industrial complex* intensified its own political positions by synthesizing strategies of a capitalist-liberal regime with semi-authoritarian articulation techniques that gradually developed after 1960. A number of measures ranging from reinforcement of open market mercantilism to the oppression of labour organizations started to signal tension lines generated in the current political field.

The ANAP, which came into power in 1983 with the intention of combining four fundamental political tendencies before the military coup (right, left, Islamic and radical right) activated a Western-centered economy and culture policy, and also worked to make Islamic emotions a component of the state administration. The state, in this regard, pursued a policy controlling Islam in solving both the legitimacy problem and strategy to make the market sovereign (Cizre, 2005). On the other hand, the synthesis formulated between religiosity and economic understanding focused on export appealed to a considerable part of the Anatolian petit bourgeoisie including people who achieved success by founding cooperative associations based on Islam (Özdemir, 2006). Thus, some elements of Islamic mobilization applied a policy accelerating from the periphery to the center under the custody of the state (Jacoby, 2005a: 149). However, ANAP, which had a populist and demagogic identity, was not a shelter to ideologically satisfy all different interests, despite its contradictory compound. The advantages given by Turgut Özal to technocrats to break the bureaucratic characteristic of political enforcement structures within the government, the anti-populist and Thatcheresque economic understanding, and particularly the unbending approach of the party in the matter of "cultural globalism" radicalized Islamists by drawing them close to nationalists (Kadıoğlu, 1996: 191).

Besides, military spending and consequent high reliance on debt to the USA as well as the perception that Özal had a large room to maneuver against the support of the West increased the political tension even more.

However, because Özal was elected president and then replaced by Mesut Yılmaz, who was a "faithful secularist," and Yılmaz's government supported the invasion of Iraq by the USA caused Islamists within the ANAP to move to the RP (Welfare Party), which is successor of the MSP. This made way for the RP to become the party taking the most seats in parliament after the elections in November 1995: "Following extended negotiations to return to an [ANAP] coalition, allegedly ended by the military, the RP was eventually excluded from government by an alliance between the two centre-right parties [the ANAP and the DYP (True Path Party)]" (Jacoby, 2005a: 150). The DYP, which was directed by Tansu Çiller after Demirel was elected president in 1993, involved a number of major authorities including an old chief of defence and a retired regional governor of the state of emergency. For both this reason and preventing Islamists to gain influence within the ANAP, following the dissassociation process from the ANAP in the middle of a bribery scandal three months later, the DYP was allowed to form a coalition with the RP (Jacoby, 2005a: 150).

For the first time in the history of the Republic, a politician who wanted to build an *Islamic regime*, Necmettin Erbakan became prime minister. Then, the military litigated to the Constitutional Court to close the RP because it violated the secular foundations of the Turkish state. And, as a result of high pressures and the memorandum on February 1997, it forced Erbakan to resign. The RP was closed and its leading cadre was banned from active politics for five years. Then, in the 1999 elections, the nationalist left inclined toward the DSP (Democratic Left Party) under the presidency of Ecevit came into power with 22% of the vote. On the other hand, the MHP was second with 18% of the votes, which was a high rate for a politically marginal party. The classical center-right (ANAP, DYP), which governed the country for 16 years, and traditional Islamism under the leadership of Erbakan weakened (Kazancıgil, 2009: 142-143). The DSP and nationalist right MHP came into power (1999-2002) due to the absence of the left and they was the last government of the political process that started in 1983. Between 1983 and 2002, a number of delicate socio-political facts and incidents that increasingly became chronic, ranging from revision of Kemalism to lack of a solution to the Kurdish problem, from the rise of political Islam to NGOs becoming contextlessness, took the stage as the central motives of the political arena.

CONSTANT CRISIS POLICIES

The political crises in the '90s, which we can consider as a tangible output of the 12 September process that broke the bipolar nature of the Turkish political field, caused a severe erosion on the representational levels of political parties by means of gaining continuity. This *constant crisis* situation caused parties' substances based on social/grassroots to be discharged and a *hegemony depression* ranging from party line to state apparatus by breaking the bond between the *mainstream* parties of the center left and right and the *represented citizen*. Almost all the current parties entered into a course in which they would never reach their social grounds entirely as they had in the 1950s, '60s, and '70s. Although these parties changed their own political and economic patterns, they could not give confidence to social classes and layers. Fragmentations, unifications, and re-fragmantations happened in the center right and left; changinngs of the guard between old leaders and their "caretakers"; none of them induced developments that provided stability in the political field. The fact that the scope of alternatives had a narrow representational perspective resulted in voters' preferences becoming *randomized*. Rapid but partial increases and sudden downfalls started to occur in election results. Receiving 20 percent or more of the votes became a sign of "overachievement" for many parties (Berktay, 2008: 36). This would be one of the most important social-political phenomena to make the AKP (Justice and Development Party), which came to power after 2000, remain in power for years and reach hegemonical capacity.

DEMILITARIZED KEMALISM

Establishment of a "civil" Kemalism commenced as a result that Özalism weakened Kemalism's positions within the bureaucracy. As Necmi Erdoğan stated, the official Kemalist restoration projection that reached the top through 28 February represented an autonomous reaction that developed within the state apparatus against the hegemony depression in Turkey's social formation (2006: 585). That being the case, since the metaphorical power and imaginary aspect of Kemalism were drained at the *state level*, Kemalist elites used a new strategy: "Kemalism has chosen to mobilize its hegemonical demands in civil life via a political project that provides forms of identities against religious fanatics or ethnic nationalists, and becomes evident in direct or implicit interventions of military to politics" (Çelik, 2006: 91).

A number of new political groupings started to bloom in the political arena through this development corresponding with a new political strategy for Kemalists. This new political focus, which was fundamentally motivated by "political love devoted to look after the state from the outside" (Bora and Kıvanç, 1996: 779) and had a quite heterogeneous positioning, started to show up in the political field with semi-paramilitarian organizations ranging from the ÇYDD (Association for Supporting Modern Life) to the KMD (The Association of Kuvayı Milliye). However, this movement would not have a chance to grow in the post-political period of the 2000s. The KMD, in which retired officers struck a pose in front of the Quran, flag, and weapon triad, never achieved significant power in this process. The reason for this could be that organizations like the KMD had a goal for "militarization of the people, peoplization of the military" and that the "Republican Army" emphasis made by the ÇYDD prematurely presumed that Kemalism was able to be civilized right from the start. Therefore, that an organization that could connect similar formations on the national level and toward inclusive goals did not occur made civil Kemalism rhetoric obsolete.

THE STATE WITHIN

Counter-guerilla structuring in the '60s was supported by the CIA and basically aimed to stop a "revolutionary situation." The organization formed against the PKK after 1980 became a severe oppression apparatus on local people due to its implementation of inhumane methods for the most part. Its registered military unit, The Special Warfare Department, gained enormous autonomy in Kurdish geography under the pretext of stopping a potential "civil rebellion." The deep power oligarchy of which its members mostly were obtained from radical right movements and armed forces used strategies fueling anti-Kurdishness across the country through provocative actions sometimes. These organizations which were linked with incidents such as Susurluk (which we will elaborate on shortly) were identified later as a type of organization, such as Police Operation Teams, JİTEM (Gendarmerie Intelligence and Anti-Terror Unit), that was directly connected to the Ministry of Internal Affairs and open to political infiltration (Vaner, 2009: 184-185). The projection of paramilitarism in the '90s was actually the central aspect of the reconstruction of national security understanding in Turkey and the category of "enemy" was reconstructed within a Schmittian context in the course of this construction process. The village guard system enabled by force starting from 1992[137] compelled local people to take a side between the PKK and the TSK, and "in a civil war atmosphere conducted against an ambiguous enemy without defined borders, flag and uniform, the answer of who was specifically included into the enemy category" was determined (Paker, 2010: 422).

According to Jacoby's dual militarism identification, although there were semi-autocratic attachments in Western regions in return for autocratic militarism in Kurdish cities, the personnel and practices of that autocratic-militarist organization were also mobilized to suppress political violence actors in the West. As a result, implementations such as transforming villages into outposts to "eradicate" PKK guerillas were also performed in certain quarters of Istanbul and in prisons, where political detainees and convicts stayed, surely on micro scales and various violence levels. A mutual strategy developed for *cleansing the place*. In particular, a total war in the Kurdish geography, revolutionary left groups, Alevis and their living space on "peripheries" or their "physical and social natures," i.e. Kurdistan, labour quarters-slums in major cities, prisons and newspaper buildings, were included into the enemy category (Fırat, 2014: 386-387).

According to Hamit Bozarslan, this complex process cannot be explained only by intense fragmentation in Turkey's political field; what actually happened was a shifting from routine coercive practices to a "customized" violence:

> According to many official reports written in second half of 1990s, "gangs in uniform" have not only provided service as being "death squads" at security bodies' command, but they have also become decisive actors of the system by sharing tens of billion dollars obtained from security rent and drug trafficking in political conditions of that period where PKK guerillas were suppressed. Old militants of the radical right were pioneers of

---

137 The system designed against the PKK in 1987 was composed of Kurdish militias. This organization, which was armed and financed by the state, also had the meaning for the handover of a part of state authority to non-state elements because members of this unity were armed by the state and forgiven for crimes they committed before (Bozarslan, 2009b: 240). However, this system, which was a result of an impossible effort such as military, gendarmerie, and police controlling a field covering nearly 5 thousand villages and 7 thousand mountainous terrains, could not provide any efficiency for the state consequently (Vaner, 2009: 185).

gangs. The civil war conducted by these gangs at the top of the state took the shape of kidnapping, torture, and even executing many members of rival intelligence services. The immunity that they had has given the opportunity of finding official protectors at the top level of the state or provincial level for other violence actors like militants of Islamist Hizbullah organization which has been responsible for hundreds of illegal executions. In that same period of time, it is clear that a similar fact was emerging within PKK, which has transformed some military commanders into warlords and has increasingly used customized violence. (Bozarslan, 2009b: 236-237)

However, the most important evidence that illegitimate coercion and legitimate coercion were intertwined in Turkey was the shocking *Susurluk scandal* that happened in the mid '90s. This incident, which claimed that the state had become a field in which it united with outer coercion bodies and gangs, showed that state field had clearly become "a shattered tyranny," in Charles Tilly's words. However, this incident should be considered as a 20-year process that "was started in 1970s by the MHP clearly resorting to violence, kept going through the integration of some idealists into the force apparatus of system on 12 September, and continued with the rent created by unconventional warfare performed against the PKK in the 1990s and by an informal economic field throughout the Middle East and the Balkans causing a civil war on the top of the state" (Bozarslan, 2005b).[138] Because the Turkish state attempted to immobilize the political field by making secret alliances against crises on a legal plane, and it also allowed non-state structures by giving up its right to use force through radical rightist militants, mafiaesque elements growing within security forces, and it created certain Kurdish clan leaders and socialization environments. The '90s therefore show clear evidence of how a state in the Schmittian concept of enemy within as the foundation of politics transformed into gang-like organizations.

---

138 For detailed analyses about the symbolic and organizational affect of the MHP on the Special Team and JİTEM, which were two of the main organizations of this civil war apparatus, and about the "anti-terror ideology" that the MHP established in the 1990s under the titles of "union with Turkish police" and "full loyalty to army" see Bora and Can, 2004b: 117-120, 126-142.

II. VARIANTS OF POLITICAL VIOLENCE

KURDISH REBELLION GAINING STRENGTH

The '80s and '90s were also years that the PKK seized the actual monopoly of the Kurdish movement. Although the organization, which adopted a total war strategy, did not reach a level to start an uprising ("serhildan" in Kurdish) in the Kurdistan of Turkey, which is its room for maneuver (Vaner, 2009: 182), it activated a globally remarkable guerilla war practice. A socialization environment based on violence, which was provided by the pre-'80s KUK and PKK practices for Kurdish youth, disappeared after the 12 September military coup; but on the other hand, symbolic resources that could enable a new, violence-free political socialization were completely banned. Inhuman treatment in the Diyarbakır Prison, which was embodied within the attack against Kurdishness, and the deaths of pro-PKK convicts who entered into death fasts and burned themselves in 1982 to protest those treatments, transformed Kurdish youth, who were adolescents in 1984 and forced into an illegal socialization and into being basic human resources in the guerilla war in the '90s.[139] The majority of Kurdish people supported this practice by considering it as an uprising of national pride, rather than embracing ideological goals one by one. The guerilla war, which lasted throughout the 1990s, obtained a character that mobilized tens of thousands of Kurdish young people through calls made for *serhildan* and mobilization from time to time.

Kurdish political representation in the parliament showed a narrow political field provided by the Turkish state to political parties founded after 1990 such as the HEP (People's Labor Party), the DEP (Democracy Party), the HADEP (People's Democracy Party), the DEHAP (Democratic People's Party). It follows that the Turkish state handled the issue from a limited perspective of *separatism* and *terrorism*.[140] The fact that the Kurdish movement's room to maneuver was restricted in the legal platform paved the way for the PKK to become stronger and its grassroots to become more radical because the Turkish state used a "double-headed institutional strategy" or "autocratical

---

139 "...these kids will see the conflict between the PKK and the State as both capturing and legitimizing symbolic resources via violence and throwing away the plug before their socialization. When they become teenagers, 'being guerilla' has transformed into a concept synonymous of a future full of sacred ideal, self-sacrifice and prestige" (Bozarslan, 2009a: 861).

140 The symbolic chain of events defining this is that the parliamentary immunity of DEP's deputies was lifted in 1994, the party was closed by the Constitutional Court, and deputies were taken into custody in the parliament and served years in prison.

militarism" as Michael Mann called it, comprised of social representation and local pressure from the 1980s to the 2000s. The army had been the backbone for the state's efforts to protect order and property in areas affected by the guerilla and militia activities of the Kurdish movement. Violence increased even more since initiatives based on the state's force such as planning for village evacuation, organization of ranger system etc. were not subject to control. The Kurdish political movement provided a politically, ethnically, and culturally definable enemy for modernist nationalists who searched a domain to actualize a civil war installation in Turkey (Jacoby, 2005b: 641-665).

The radical-constitutive violence practice that materialized by the PKK entered into a blocking process towards the end of the 1990s. One of the main reasons for this is that although the objective of creating *homo kurdicus* in the person of Öcalan provided an enormous militant energy, it could not offer a realistic programme for Kurds. In this period of time, the PKK formulated objectives "that [have] required an important mobilization every time but have not had any chance to come true and have been erased from the memory shortly after replaced by other objectives" (Bozarslan, 2009a: 865). On the other hand, obligatory dependence on everchanging balances of the Middle East and counter-guerilla practices that almost reached a low density war level weakened the PKK considerably. Öcalan was captured in Kenya while the PKK discussed whether abandoning armed struggle was an obligation, accelerating the process of withdrawal of "total war."[141] Following this transformation, which also refers to withdrawal of a strategic objective for independent and socialist Kurdistan ("Democratic Republic" with a new formulation of Öcalan), it is possible to name the PKK, regarding the period until today, as not a radical-constitutive but a *reformist armed movement* in essence, even though there have been and still are rhetorical and practical tides *within the borders of Turkey*.

LAST DANCE OF THE LEFT RADICAL-CONSTITUTIVE VIOLENCE VARIANT
Two basic phenomena were created by 12 September in both Turkish and Kurdish left: exile and prison literature. These fields, which were and still are experienced by tens of thousands of political detainees and convicts, deserve to be examined in their own dynamics. The relevant part of this is that

---

141 The PKK Presiding Council decided to quit armed struggle on 5 August 1999 (Bozarslan, 2009a: 865).

"resistances in prison," as its subjects are called, have a central place in the narrative integrity of radical-constitutive violence in the 1990s, as is evident from the death fasts and self-immolation protests by the PKK militants in the Diyarbakır Prison. It is possible to take death fast protests at the Metris Prison in 1984, which resulted in deaths and were led by militants of the Revolutionary Left who entered onto the stage of political violence history in the later '70s, as a constitutive meta-incident of *ressentiment* which was systematically produced by this organization in the 1990s.[142]

Following the first social movements composed of student, labour and civil servant protests in the 1988-89 momentum, what remained of the Turkish left entered into a recovery process. Attempts were made to resurrect and combine the cadre potential in the '70s, but the important part regarding our subject was the implementation of a significant "selective terrorism" (Goodwin, 2006) campaign by the Revolutionary Left.[143] The organization, which gathered its limited cadres by traditional resources of the left (student youth, young squatters, and rural youth) and aimed to implement Çayan's politicized military war strategy word for word, was named the DHKP-C (Revolutionary People's Liberation Party-Front) after 1994. In this period of time where the concept of international "terrorism" was completely adopted by the Turkish state and the relationship between the media and political violence became a fundamental political field through the increase of mass communication mediums, the year of 1996 was the year that this political violence campaign of the state reached its peak through military and paramilitary practices particularly in slums and prisons. Some essential incidents and facts belonging to this mutual violence spiral that caused the 1995-96 peak momentum are the following: The relative massification of the left radical-constitutive violence variant; the introduction of "enforced disappearance" against the Turkish left which was already applied systematically in Kurdish geography; incidents started by the barrage against four coffee shops and one bakery in the Gazi

142 The aforementioned organization has used this *ressentiment* without hesitation not only against the state, but against other left organizations who criticized its practices too. The continuous reproduction of this *ressentiment* was provided by forming a militant typology and an organizational culture with a Homeric character on the axis of organization-leader-courage-honor-sacrifice-martyrdom. For an analysis on this matter, see Sarıoğlu, 2007: 1015-1021.

143 In this terrorism campaign of which the violence gradually decreased 1990-96, there were many assassinations plotted against tens of people who were considered to play a role in the execution of state coercion such as former ministers, retired or active duty generals, members of MİT, high level constables, police officers and prosecutors who worked on anti-terror.

Quarter of Istanbul in March 1995, resulting in the deaths of 17 people; the deaths of 7 people due to a military operation conducted against the DHKP-C wards in two different prisons on September 1995 and January 1996; the assassination plot carried out by the DHKP-C with a "categorical terrorism" (Goodwin, 2006) against the Sabancı group, which was one of the leading investment groups; the deaths of three people due to fire commenced on corteges on 1 May 1996; the starting of death fasts that resulted in the deaths of 12 people on 20 May 1996.

The fact that imprisonment durations and sentences have increased enormously within the scope of the new anti-terror law enacted in 1992 following the amnesty in 1991[144] has transformed prisons into an essential component of the *counter-institutionalisation* practice, into a *micro-space* and into a *site* for all related sides by making them stop being *accommodation addresses*. In this period of time in which the PKK worked to make the Turkish state acknowledge convicts in prisons as "prisoners of war" according to the Geneva Convention, prisons were places in which "the inside" was associated with the "outside" more directly than ever before and in which "resistance" culture spread from "inside" to outside when related left political violence actors are considered. In the critical days of the death fast protest that started in 1999 and was led by people arrested and sentenced due to the DHKP-C case, the state executed a military operation, which was ironically named the "return to life" operation and started simultaneously, against revolutionary wards in prisons throughout the country. The outcome of these ward raids and massacre policy, which was tested on a local scale during the 1990s, was 122 deaths and more than 600 permanently disabled people. The reason why we are describing these prison practices in detail is the story of the left radical-constitutive violence variant that started in prisons in the 1980s and also ended in prisons at the end of '90s.[145]

The reasons why this political violence variant marginalized up to the point when it faded out in the 1990s is as follows: (1) the increasing of the dose and scope of PKK's political violence completely independent from other political violence

---

144 Within the scope of this law, organization militants have punished with sentences ranging from 15 years to death. Even today, some people convicted in that period are still in prison.
145 See Bargu, 2014 for a comprehensive analysis on the death fast and its sembolic dimension.

organizations in Turkey,[146] and the emergence of a counter-guerilla apparatus with an enormous volume and efficiency left its mark on the '90s. In military terms, this stands for a breakdown of the Clausewitzian reciprocity principle from the point of left radical-constitutive violence actors and for the huge anti-terror mechanism ("state within") organized in accordance with the concept of war against the PKK to crush, so to speak, left political violence organizations that were far away from the effectiveness of the PKK. (2) Except for the young Kurdish population who were the grassroots of the PKK, there was a fast disintegration of the atmosphere providing the legitimacy of political violence for the majority of the masses who were the grassroots of left organizations. It is possible to date this fast decline in leftist public opinion, which legitimized the violence, to the fact that the mass groups of the Turkish left such as *Revolutionary Path, Salvation* and *People's Liberation,* which were illegally organized before, founded legal parties with names of ÖDP (Freedom and Solidarity Party) and EMEP (Labor Party) in 1996.[147] The *ressentiment*, which was developed by *Revolutionary Left/* DHKP-C and found its reflection on addressees, caused a sharp fragmentation in left historiography that still exists today. Therefore, the 1995-96 period refers to a critical momentum for all related elements of the Turkish left. (3) The PKK giving up its project of building an independent state. The meaning of this change of strategy in the sense of the left political violence variant, was that the room for maneuver, which was lost politically, completely disappeared militarily too. A description made by one police commissioner, Hanefi Avcı, in a recent period about this organization is ironically striking: "These are like Japanese soldiers left on the island after World War Two" (Ongun, 2015).

BIRTH OF ISLAMIC RADICALISM

Islamic opposition that passed through a short-termed civil-reactional violence period after the foundation of the Republic pulled back to a private field following the riots suppressed through violence. This opposition avoided translating its demands into a political rhetoric starting from the beginning of the multi-party period to the late 1970s, and it has mostly stayed under the

---

146 The most symptomatic indicator of the fact that these two political violence variants separate completely from each other was the Sabancı assassination. The DHKP-C took the blame for that assassination as retaliation for "comrades" murdered in prisons. The PKK interpreted this categorical terrorism act aimed at civilians who did not fit to its own definition of "complicitous civilians" as an attack of the "state within" against an investment group that desired a democratic solution for the Kurdish problem. Discussion on this assassination still carries on today.

147 This should be considered with translation activities that increased after the second half of the 1990s and focused on leftist searches and particularly "radical democracy" discussions in the West.

dominance of the center-right and exploited this alliance as much as it could. On the other hand, it is possible that the MHP's aggressive street practices in the 1970s decreased the votes of the MSP and also marginalized radical Islamist opposition groups.

Therefore, the modernist Islamist ideology born during the collapse of the Ottoman Empire has actually become a significant political power group since the late 1970s. In this birth process triggered by many factors ranging from translations of works of ideologists and activists such as Seyyid Kutup who theorized the legitimacy of violence and as Ali Şeriati, the master mind of "Islamic revolution" to the Iranian Islamic Revolution, the mobilization of political violence is dated after 1980. Organizations that have transformed violence practices into key components of Islamist politics and strategies popped up everywhere after the military coup and reached critical effectiveness levels in the '90s (Özçetin, 2014: 318-319).

On the one hand, four developments with international influence and on the other hand, cyclical transformations on internal politics of the country played a major part in this radicalization. According to Hamit Bozarslan (2012: 144), Islamists in Turkey have closely approached the idea of revolution due to the Iran revolution as well as the Mecca incident, the Camp David accords signed by Egypt and Israel, the invasion of Afghanistan by the Soviets, and the versatile attack of 12 September. These events discharged the left wing in particular, opening a space in which radical Islamist ideology could develop. First, we will discuss – without focusing on the intellectual journey of Islamist movement in Turkey – the '80s and '90s in which militant Islamist groups gained importance in the political field, and then the legal rise of Islam-based political repertories in the parliamentary system. Whether these two levels supported each other is the subject of a different study.

The Turkey branch of Hizbüt-Tahrir, which was established in Jordan in 1952 as the extension of the Muslim Brotherhood founded in Egypt in 1928, was founded by a group of young people in METU in 1960. The ultimate goals of the organization under the leadership of Ercümend Özkan were as follows:

> The constitution of Hizbü't-Tahrir includes clauses such as cancelling the republic and reforming the caliphate; determining the source of sovereignty as shariah; termination of democratic regime; banning all parties except for Islamic ones; establishing

heavy industry; combining the whole Islamic world into a single state; forcing all women to wear religious clothes; and closing all entertainment places down. (Özçetin, 2014: 333-334)

However, this first formation organized itself around intellectual and political struggle and did not really leave a mark in the sense of influence. But it became more of an issue by preparing future illegality conditions. The number of similar structurings increased during the intense war that the PKK fought in Kurdistan. Many large and small illegal organizations started to mobilize in Kurdistan without being subjected to state abuse. Hizbullah, founded by Hüseyin Velioğlu in 1983, was the most formidable of these organizations. The organization, which chose the Iran Islam revolution as a model, gained significant strength in its range against the PKK that was encoded as communist and atheist. The organization not only targeted the PKK but also brought with it a functionalization of the organization as a paramilitary power group. Hizbullah, which engaged in combat with the Kurdish political movement as well as bloody revenge with its own factions, made a name for itself by murdering certain famous people such as feminist Islamist writer Konca Kuriş and the founder of the Zehra Foundation, İzzettin Yıldırım.

> Another militant Islamist group was İBDA-C (Great Eastern Islamic Raiders' Front) led by charismatic figure Salih Mirzabeyoğlu whose real name is Salih İzzet Erdiş and also referred as "Commandant." İBDA-C, which has operated since the middle of 1970s, has started to pursue a more aggressive and radical political strategy in 1990s. İBDA-C, which was claiming that conditions for an Islamic revolution in Turkey were ready, was an organization that called for armed struggle and adopted independent cell organization and guerilla war. (Özçetin, 2014: 336)

However, when its goals to "take the state over by force" and "Islamify the public by force" started to fade out in the '90s, the Islamist movement in Turkey started to spend more energy for its struggle on a legal plane. In other words, the Islamic opposition adopted "bypassing the state" (Davis and Robinson, 2012) as its main strategy after a short-term period of radical-constitutive violence strategy.

III. THE PARLIAMENT AND CIVIL SOCIETY

RISE AND TRANSFORMATION OF POLITICAL ISLAM IN THE PARLIAMENT

The '90s was definitely a period in which Islamists discovered the answer to what is political, organized the trajectory of their political strategies more successfully than before 1980 and understood the *benefits* of being active in the political field. An authentic idea of the pre-politics period embodied in the form of "establishing an Islamic state" (Aktay, 2005: 22) was abandoned after the period from 12 September also increased the visibility of political Islamism in the public sphere of Turkey. However, this visibility emerged in two axes: The first axis was the process conducted by the military regime for instrumentalizing the religion against the Kurdish movement in the East and the communism threat in the big cities, according to the traditional state pragmatism. The dominant complex, which parried the challenge from the left, started to pursue "glasnost" that was mostly based on controlling religious groups. Even the definition of Turkishness had unprecedented Islamic references in the 1982 Constitution. The second axis was that the state and military structured Kemalist restoration in accordance with loyalty to secularism (Çiğdem, 2005: 30). But this *dual strategy* adopted by the state to control the religion helped the Islamic opposition develop politically, which established the religion of Islam as the ideological background of its own project. Besides the popularity of political Islam in the Middle East, the fact that central parties in Turkey lost their credibility to a large extent and the ability of an Islamic organization to establish pragmatic alliances (the fact that it has had an ideological continuity through pro-Kurdish discourse and radical right in the Southeast) influenced this development (Bozarslan, 2004: 115).

The RP, which obtained the best achievement of political Islam so far by receiving more than 19% of the votes in local elections in 1994, receiving 24% of the votes and 158 seats in parliament in general elections in 1995, created an important breaking point in the political field by synthesising religious and secular rhetoric. The RP, which was approved by its grassroots due to its "fair order" project with a tendency to Islam and claimed to be an economic-political model different from capitalism and socialism, became open to interests of the capital through the quick rise of the Muslim bourgeoisie (Ayata, 1996: 51). The party therefore moved from a statist and protectionist position to a political strategy including an open market economy and integrating Turkey into the global economy (Şen,

1995). Despite all those politically flexible moves, the RP put the cat among the pigeons. In military documents, the concept of "separatist terrorism" was replaced by "reactionary threat." Even Erbakan was accused of sabotaging the national defence by secretly supporting the PKK. Then, as discussed previously, his party was closed and the main actors of political Islam were moved away from politics. The FP (Virtue Party) later represented political and ideological developments related to transformation in the social and cultural environments. However, the actors of political Islam after 28 February[148] started to use a new political language and strategy, and worked to strengthen their positions in the political field with a new context provided that they eased their criticism against the current order and intensified their relations with the capitalist class. After the 1997 crisis, the new generation of Islamists challenged the leadership of Erbakan. This revealed that ideological and class differences between Islamists were as keen as to be not limited within only a party alone. Thereby, "rebels [have] founded their own organization, [the] Justice and Development Party in 2001" (Tuğal, 2007: 108-109).

THE ILLUSION OF CIVIL SOCIETISM

In the 1980s, Turkey passed through a period at the center of mobilization in the form of the "rise of civil society" in which civilization or civil societism desired to cut itself loose from the state and its peremptoriness and the military's sovereignty. In the following years after the military coup, the notion of "civil society" materialized as *a new political actor* that organized itself in the form of reacting to, and making a stand against, the state and considered the legitimacy of the state apparatus arbitrary on the level of social actors and collectivities (Groc, 2009: 195). However, this multifaceted process did not go beyond the frame of "non-state organized field of rights and freedoms" in the sense of intellectual production, and the actors of civil society failed to attach civil initiatives onto the social struggle fields of the country. Therefore, the rhetoric of civil society did not implement meanings ascribed on itself into public processes due to the ongoing anti-democratic influence on social life by the statist mentality and institutional domination.

---

148   The 28 February military memorandum, which took place in the literature by the name of "postmodern military coup," reveals a period in which the military applied a discharge within the political field by preferring a secular life style and regime identity over political Islam's increasing identity policies. The civil wing was negated with adjectives such as "separatist" and "reactionary." The TSK attempted to look after its own interests by means of bypassing the regime's foundational ideology and obtained an opportunity to instrumentalize the notion of security.

If so, in the nature of the political field, what could be the primary reasons why civil society did not develop and evolve into a semi-ideology, "civil societism"? In our opinion, the first reason is that elites and intelligentsia, which hold the monopoly of Westernization and live in cities, utilize opening up to the West as a *class determinant* and use *symbolic violence* on rural people lacking material and symbolic resources. Through this situation that Tanıl Bora defines as "neoliberal chauvinism," the cultural and political conflict between two class positions gained the continuity and dynamics required for making a genuine civil society deactivated from the very beginning (Bora, 2003: 433-452; Bozarslan, 2004: 126-127). It is possible to consider as a second reason that the military transformed NGOs into *tools of a new political engineering* by settling in the center of politics again after its interventions on 28 February 1997. Many organizations were converted into representations of bureaucratic mentality within society via paramilitary "civil" society organizations attached to military-bureaucratic powers (Bozarslan, 2004: 127). Therefore, non-governmental organizations were conceived as *channels* replacing politics that caused NGOs to start acting *like a party* by applying macro-political goals. This type of civil-societism ultimately reproduces problems of substitutionism (Bora and Çağlar, 2007: 346).

As a result, the multifaceted traces of ANAP's policy in the economic-political field, the fact that Islamism became *a legitimate component* of the society, the rise of the white collar class, and the cultural production area building new connections through meta-markets by involving depolitized young generation have left their mark on the very first phase (1983-1991) of this stage of the political field. The second phase (post-1991) witnessed social and political appearances accompanying a constant crisis in the political field because coalition governments did not provide political stability, illegal activities of the state were revealed by an accident (Susurluk scandal), there were everlasting corruptions, social separation was maximized, the birth of "crime bosses" from old paramilitary actors became a new phenomenon, and the Kurdish problem was not solved, causing the country to enter a critical economic crisis in the early 2000s. In this regard, the AKP took the opportunity to establish a new hegemony in the severest economic crisis of the history of the Republic, in an atmosphere where the Kurdish problem deepened and in the course of processes in which the military worked to exert its authority again on the political field.

CONCLUSION

Would you be able to settle easily as such if I have not ensured continuity of the state through methods I know? If I did not save your beloved free market, if I did not prepare the ground with a sword blow for "capitalist arena" to be built, if I did not deactivate communists, your nightmares through methods you are judging now, if I did not open the main road by causing public opposition, labor unions, political parties, political associations, drawbacks against capitalism to collapse in a single day, if I did not make striking workers work next day, you could not even come this far... Every state is built through violence; it is protected through violence in case of emergency; if it were not for my client would you be able to protect it? Don't you resort to violence as well in states of emergency? Fine, Diyarbakır prison is my client's work but what about Roboski? (Gürbilek, 2015: 31)

We emphasized an essential truth in this brief study in which we examined the political history of late Ottoman Turkey through a certain motive (*political violence repertories*): There is a strong connection between multi-layered compulsory activities, which were the reflection of a departure process from the emperorship and struck almost all collectivities, and the *economy of violence* created by the integrist "national identity equation," which was established by the Republic. One end of this connection, which we believe has not been examined properly yet, comprises the state's traditional strategies (*reproduction of power*) in terms of building hegemonic capacity, and the other end is formed by various violence relations from the society to the state. Therefore, activities performed by Unionism, the real founder of the new nation state, and by the Kemalist governmentality, the follower of Unionism, which have constantly blown up the boundary between coercion and violence transformed violence practices in modern Turkey into a basic *political apparatus*. Therefore, we reiterate the argument constituting the raison d'être of our study: *Political violence is one of the major elements necessary to comprehend the history of Turkey.*

It is not possible to find any class layer, religious sect, secular political power, or members of a bureaucratic arena within Turkish political life that does not acknowledge the foundational dynamic of violence. With Kurdish revolts gradually increasing since the 1920s, the youth and labor movements in the '60s, the violence with a civil war atmosphere in the '70s and the PKK's uprising after the '80s illustrate that the state has been obliged to travel back and forth between monopolizating of legal coercion and applying illegal coercion since the day it was founded. Accordingly, all civilian political structurings that had teeth in the history of the country, since they were obliged to grow up in this economy of violence, established a certain political syntax that degrades what is political to *congregational causes*. These two processes feeding each other have transformed the state arena into a "fragmented tyranny," in the words of Charles Tilly, and have assimilated the political stage with a *scenery of violence*.[149] To conclude, in the equation of "state capacity versus democratization capacity" the odds are always stacked against democratization capacity.

On the other hand, political violence repertories surely do not become mobilized in layers of political arena only. A *lynching culture* growing in daily life by becoming concrete within the boundaries of society and a political culture suitable for paramilitary structuring have been highly effective on Turkey's history. The fact that the pro-resistance movement has been acknowledged as a norm, so to speak, in the last stage of the Ottoman Empire, the traumatic grudge transferred to Anatolia by an enormous migration wave created by the Balkan wars and, in relation, the participation of collective political actors in the Armenian genocide, the discharge of non-muslims through pogroms, the demonization of all ideological routes that took form against Kemalism and many other reasons have minutely constructed foundational mechanisms of communities in Turkey to resort to violence.

Herein, the paramilitarism peculiar to Turkey should also be considered as a separate analysis object. This is because political collectivities that have entered into a rapid organization process on military grounds and started to act as the state can only be revealed within the continuity of Ottoman/Turkish history. The fact that the state gave authority to outside actors (clan leaders, organizations like Special Organization, gangs within the state) to use force

---

149 While we write these lines (28 May 2015), a political party (HDP, Peoples' Democratic Party) working to get into parliament was exposed to physical assaults/pogroms 128 times in the last month, and a Kurdish movement wishing to legalize itself was not even tolerated.

SWORDS AND REMAINS

and therefore gave up its monopoly over coercion instruments has caused the paramilitary in Turkey to be constructed and then to gain autonomy. The fact that the mechanisms *normalizing* the violence (from the inequality of women and men to the existence of tribes, from forms of domestic violence to symbolic violence settings) has been established within the social life has constituted the essential basis for the Kemalist cosmology to be constructed over a Schmittin political apprehension.

Now, to get back to the question we asked in the introduction: *Is Turkey in a post-political violence period now?* We have seen that the late 1990s corresponded to a critical stage in this matter and the movements that produce systematic political violence have either been marginalized or transformed. Factions of the Turkish left that reproduce political violence have liquidated through military methods and have become marginalized. The marginalization has occurred as a result of the extension of legal access facilities to symbolic resources for socialist politics and the climate providing legitimacy to revolutionary violence being dissolved in the eyes of the left masses. In the Kurdish movement, this critical stage has materialized through the revision of goals on total war and independent Kurdistan, the *relative* decrease of pressure on Kurdish legal parties, and their entering into a negotiation period, even if it is fragile. With regards to the Islamist movement, the critical stage has appeared with political violence actors who stand up for the idea of Islamic revolution and are connected with the AKP network, directly or indirectly.[150]

In the first stages of the AKP government in which political violence instruments have been disabled or deactivated, mechanisms activating state coercion have been paused, even though they have not been discontinued entirely. Cases such as *Ergenekon*, which have been conducted through the rhetoric of settling accounts with perpetrators of the "dirty war" in the '90s and in general, with "the state within" (which by the way, 28 February was decisive for the AKP in this settling), have been welcomed with a certain political consensus as developments that will break the influence of the violence economy which has left its mark on the political arena. In this process, matching with economic welfare, the AKP has increased its vote rate up to 50%. However, because cases have been overextended and have become contextless by being transformed into a political leverage by opponents, the

---

150   For a study examining this transformation of radical Islamists through Gramsci's "passive revolution" concept, see Tugal, 2009.

AKP has tended to build a political hegemony based on the economic and political consensus. And this political hegemony was shaken by the Gezi Resistance while the AKP considered itself most powerful and believed that it was no longer in need of continuous production of consent wanted by that consensus.

The Gezi Resistance is surely a chain of events including many aspects and still waiting to be discussed on various levels. Regarding our subject, the importance of the Resistance is that it was shaped by a certain political and collective violence form, although its actors deny that consciously: "What made Taksim Square being occupied through barricades for thirteen days was the political violence presented in mass during the first stage of agency" (Çeğin and Özcan, 2014: 155). The direct factor for the reason why this collective political violence form was revealed was the unbalanced use of violence by police; the essential mechanisms of the coercion were at work from actions of the police to private law sanctions and to paramilitary practices fed by a lynching culture.

It does not seem possible that the collective violence form, which generated Gezi, would be directed into an illegal political form. On the contrary, the social energy released flowed into legal parties and increased turnout at elections. However, according to the political syntax that was created by the Turkish state's constitutive and then law-preserving violence, and has been constantly reproduced during educational stages of various organizations, *the reproduction of the traitor* still proceeds uninterrupted. Therefore, although the cyclical composition of its field varies, the Turkish state with implicit Schmittian political apprehension is based on a socio-political memory and organizational components that could adapt themselves, before you know it, to the concept of total civil war, giving the impression of an increase in democratization capacity. Under these circumstances, it is not possible to talk about a post-political violence period. And given its capacity to open enormous rooms to maneuver, the stance that the Kurdish movement will take in the near future is of vital importance to the violence economy in Turkey.

APPENDIX

Politics as War:
AKP, Kurdish Movement and
Re-Raising of Political Violence

A year and a half ago when we had completed this book you are holding at the moment, we could not have predicted that one of the central themes of our book, *state coercion*, would have transformed into "a suicide strategy which demolishes rationality" (Bozarslan, 2016: 74). However, social sciences do not operate on a logic of prophecy under any circumstances after all. Even though the aforementioned strategy has become evident since 2013, a *Führerprinzip case* wrecking Turkey's internal and external political logic started to permeate by year 2016 and it is an issue today, discussed by a good number of researchers. As for us, considering our study's problematics we will examine the forms that politics in Turkey has been taking on lately. In fact, what we will focus on is the militarization of Kurdish question, gradually intensifying coercive practices of the state and transformations occurred in the structure of Turkey's regime.

Military operations, started in Turkey's Kurdistan after the general election on June 7, 2015 when AKP's leadership in the Turkish parliament since 2002 was terminated and legal Kurdish politics led by HDP overcame the parliamentary threshold of 10%,[151] were mostly evaluated within the thematic frame of back to the 90's by the opponents. In our opinion, this is a deficient analysis. Despite its roughness, the state coercion in the 90's was not able to transform into a total destruction due to divisions and tensions in the field of the state (because numerous compartments from TSK to security forces were separated into certain factions). However, the state's coercion mobilized in the last year (as can be seen in the detailed reports below) has, beyond doubt, a more comprehensive character. Power configuration under the authority of Recep Tayyip Erdoğan contains a more compact potential

---

151 After the military coup on September 12, 1980, the new national election threshold in Turkey was introduced as %10 with the law, dated June 10, 1983, numbered as 2839. The main purpose here was to prevent the groups, seen as threats to the state, from pursuing legal politics.

of violence as compared to power structures of the 90's. As a matter of fact, it is possible to propose that this total destruction strategy directed towards Kurds has formed an idiosyncratic alliance, ranging from legal political parties except AKP to numerous political formations (from neo-Kemalists to Islamic sects, from old counter-guerilla teams to ordinary people). Yet interpreting this course only based on upheavals in the country's internal politics such as termination of the Negotiation process (which will be elaborated below) is misleading. Today, a construction program comes into question in terms of Kurdish movement. New balances emerged in the Middle East and Rojava Revolution, started with People's Protection Units' (YPG) seizure of Kobane (Ayn el-Arap) on July 19, 2012 and Afrin and Derik on the next day, triggered a more severe warfare than the 90s unquestionably. These developments representing a historical opportunity in terms of Kurdish movement led the Turkish state appeal to a strategy, which has goals beyond political aspects. In the light of these, first of all, we will examine AKP's power grabbing process, which begins in 2002 and gains strength gradually. Here, we will deal with the process of AKP's erection of hegemony, inner-state revenges and developments in the Kurdish question. But the chief objective of our analysis is to grasp how the Turkish state enabled the traditional state coercion after 2013 and what its dimensions are.

I. AKP'S ERECTION OF HEGEMONY

AKP came into power in the early 2000s by benefiting from the center-right block's disintegration and the political vacuum constituted as a result of highly dissociated ideological paths. It was argued by its ideologists that AKP appeared on the political stage as the representative of a "conservative democratic" identity; both it kept its distance from the radical Islamic movement, where it was born, and avoided performing traditional right-wing political reflexes. This new political party, backed by the liberals through its connections with the platforms such as EU, some leftist intellectuals, Fethullah Gülen Community representing cultural İslam in Turkey and a wide spectrum of the political right, got strength progressively even by making use of some conjunctural advantages.

The political elites developed a free market-centered, cultural consumerism-dominated "majoritarian governmental model" in the political level by activating a definite victimhood discourse (Balta, 2015). AKP's negotiable flexibility from the viewpoint of regional powers in addition to EU and USA played a significant role in its rise. Briefly stated, for establishing a new hegemony AKP took the opportunity of a political atmosphere where there was the gravest economic crisis of the republican history, the Kurdish question was quite intensified and the army was trying to re-exert its authority in the political field.

AKP dissolved the apolitical atmosphere of the 90s and assured that it would generate solutions for the problems, notably for income distribution, human rights, Kurdish question, EU and Cyprus issues, by positioning itself outside the mentality of "the state politics" and hence won the elections with outstanding success one after another. This situation increased public countenance for AKP and Tayyip Erdoğan (Çiğdem, 2009: 135). And in this direction, basically aspiring to "bring the country's politics into its principal axis", AKP conceived that it was critically necessary to provide a solid basis of legitimacy for maintaining the party's subsistence within the political field and opted for establishing conservatism discourse on these three lines: (1) emphasizing the local sensitivities, (2) a warm message given to the international public through a western ideological reference like conservatism, which does not have any legitimacy problem, and (3) the message of "we do not have any alliance with political İslam" targeting the Kemalist *doxa* (Yıldız, 2004: 55).

Engaging in a competition with its rivals in the political field through these three grounds of its conservative democrat discourse, AKP chose the way of passivizing the political Islam's demands by constructing the party's ideological and cultural elements within a right-wing conservative frame in accordance with the global capitalist[152] preferences.[153] It means that all the political Islamic formations, targeting the political supremacy after 1980, generated the consent of the groups, shaping the arguments opposing the system, by challenging the hegemonic logic of the political field in Turkey and achieved to aggregate conservative-poor segments of the society into the circle of neo-liberal paradigm. This "absorption" process, started by National Vision tradition, was ranged up by AKP and by virtue of this process together

---

152 According to the results of the research conducted by Korkut Boratav, Turkish economy under AKP's power has benefited from the international capital movements increasingly and still continues to gain favor of it. Between the years of 2004 and 2008 the total amount of foreign capital accumulated in Turkey increased to 131 million dollars. See Boratav, 2007.

153 For an important contribution from critical sociological perspective on this issue, leaving *mainstream* general political perspective aside, see Tuğal, 2009.

with its organizational insight, establishments and political language it uses, *İslamism* has not been seen as "massive central resistance" against capitalism any more.

In this line, Cihan Tuğal's ethnographical analysis, taking Gramscian relationship between "political society" and "civil society" into consideration, provides a partially explanatory framework. In this analysis, Tuğal formulates this new hegemonic establishment of AKP's power as "passive revolution of the capital."[154] As Tuğal's research based on Sultanbeyli-İstanbul suggests, this "absorption" process was configured within a mechanism operating in six levels (Tuğal, 2009: 236-250).

At the first level, which is related to political society, the issue was reduction of political Islam's intensity of radicalism in AKP's trajectory ("absorption of leadership"); this radicalism was mobilized on the layers ranging from micro-individual to macro-structural level. At the second level, functioning as "absorption of binary power", centralization of the power occurred by deactivating mainstream Islamic political culture. Third level was more influential than the first two: it was the transformation of mentality targeting the articulation of grassroots panislamist organization, initiated along with RP, with Turkish nationalism's *doxa* or, in Tuğal's words, "absorption of collective imagination." The mechanism operated at this third level also conforms to AKP's vision of European Union and "global competition."

AKP's strategies within civil society are in parallel with the mechanisms functioning in political society. At the first level, the concern is "absorption of everyday life", which appeared as isolation of conservative-religious *habitus* from "pure religiosity form" and its hybridization with capitalism's practices. The second level is materialized as *absorption of spaces* by means of Islamic aesthetical forms. And the third level is related to *economical absorption*; i.e. taming of religious poor's possible opposition. Through the agency of these mechanisms AKP made use of the potential of demobilizing the population. According to Tuğal, even if AKP did not islamize the regime by executing "passive revolution", it succeeded in islamizing public space though partially.

---

154 Italian thinker Antonio Gramsci's passive revolution [rivoluzione passiva] concept points briefly as the following: it is a process, during which any mass mobilization is passivized and then its demands are appropriated by the existing system; therefore mobilized establishments and classes are articulated with the dominant body. It also corresponds to an operation, under which dominant powers implement revolutions' discourse mechanisms and symbols as well as structural transformations in order to eliminate any possibility of revolution. And assuredly this implementation is realized providing that their revolutionary content is entirely cleared. For discussions related to this concept, see Morton, 2007; Showstack Sassoon, 2001.

It is no doubt, Tuğal's theses offer important insights about the connections between AKP and the capital.

However, we think that this analysis excludes some points, which we find important in terms of our own argumentation regarding the political field. For instance, Tuğal formulates AKP as a "break" with respect to relations between mainstream İslamic politics and the capital; yet it is required to ask this question here: Is this assumed *break* is the break of İslamic politics or a break constructed by *class formation* which began after 1950? We see the answer of this question as an ignored concern in the main itinerary of the work. On the other hand, another problem in Tuğal's work is that Islamic politics is approached as *a monolithic entity* while dealing with Islamic mobilization. Tuğal does not touch upon the secular state's strategy against İslam after 1980 sufficiently. Especially, this analysis cannot clarify exactly the content of this strategy oscillating between *repression* (controlling the charm of Islam in the eye of public) and *reconciliation* (instrumentalization of the religion in the political field if needed) and the way that this situation changes ideological structure and base of the Islamist movement. In fact, AKP referred to some strategies which would change the system, while being transformed by the system itself. Therefore, dynamics of this transformation in the field is not considered in this work relationally.

The Islamist movement having relatively theocratic dispositions had challenged nationalist *doxa* in the 90s. After the year 2000, AKP left its claims increasingly and exhibited a successful political performance with its promise of providing religious solidarity and freedom to both urban and rural poor. At this juncture, it is essential to emphasize these additional points: while AKP establishments achieved to hold representational monopoly of conservative sensitivities, they could legitimize "rights and freedom" discourse promised to its voters together with a nationalist mode of thinking. Furthermore, AKP pursued a tactic of stressing its conservative democratic identity which prevented itself from being targeted by the army. Thus, AKP put potential political opportunities on its own agenda by fabricating a pluralist political discourse in the process of hegemony-erection. In this way, it succeeded in melting conservatism, nationalism, liberalism and multiculturalism in the unique pot of existing political discourse.

After this period, in the first half of 2007 EU opposition in AKP started to rise. During this phase (2004-2007), in which a big stroke of tension and polarization was re-established, media columnists' stand-taking revolving around nationalist *doxa* solidified these polarization lines. In fact, the media threw each other's hat into the ring to produce political opinions for the sake of constituting Schmittian "friend-enemy dialectics". In the interim, a great deal of events happened targeting to destabilize the political field, ranging from the attack to the council of state (May 17, 2006) to the assassination of Armenian writer Hrant Dink (January 19, 2007), from information channels-led neo-nationalist mobilizations to Ergenekon arrestments,[155] which were unclear in every respect.

The alliance of CHP and MHP attempted to abolish the hegemony erected by AKP with a particular support of the urban elites and the rural nationalist population. Nevertheless, this counter-strategy, cultivated by nationalist media mobilization and Republic Protests [Cumhuriyet Mitingleri], would effect in quite opposite way in the elections that took place on July 22, 2007. The results of the general elections went down like a bomb among AKP-opponents since AKP qualified an incredible rise, CHP made no progress and MHP increased its voting rate.

Strengthening its hegemonic stance AKP pursued a politics welshing its promises, given before the elections, in the first period after 2007. A raft of issues started to become chronical problems in the political field: Oscillations between conservatism and democratism leaving suspense in the practical field, concrete failures in the steps taken in the Kurdish question, lack of veritable attempts related to constitutional amendment, retreats in European perspective and many others. These circumstances paved the way of AKP' failure in the elections on March, 2009 in comparison with the preceding ones, although AKP set out to construct a new historical block from 2007 onwards. Progressive weakening of AKP's voter potential in the elections of 2004, 2007 and 2009 demonstrated that AKP's way of making politics as building contact with Islamic communities by actively utilizing municipalities would be interrupted.

For some pundits, DTP (Democratic Society Party) would present an alternative perspective on the Kurdish question. As a matter of fact, DTP attained a significant success in the elections of 2009, especially under favor of AKP's reference to a statist discourse. However, DTP was closed down by the constitutional court on December 11, 2009, as an outcome

---

155 It is a case concerning "secret government set-up" in Turkey, which initiated on October, 2008, lasted 6 years and 2 months and abated on April 21, 2016 eventually.

of the state's reactions on the Kurdish question. CHP-MHP alliance could not exhibit a remarkable action since it was not able to be an alternative to AKP. Consequently, "period after 2000" –no matter which perspective is applied- was a course of time, during which the dynamics constituting the political field were premeditated through social tensions inherited by the period before 2000. Moreover, this phase went down in history also with AKP's shaping of its own political programs and discourses for establishing hegemony, continuance of Kurdish question as a bitter issue and evolution of Kurdish community into an alternative nationalism and, most essentially, with the fact that leitmotifs of nationalist *doxa* inscribed in the field appear gradually in a more disorganized fashion.

But what would be the fundamental reasons why this process of so-called liberalization was not so long-lasting and why this *u turn* towards an authoritarian political line was made? Some developments dissolved the coalition gathered around AKP gradually such as incremental initiation of conservatist interventions into highly secularized everyday life after 2000, international realm's and regional dynamics' acquisition of a conflicting character, and intention to overcome the effects of domestic economic crisis on the hegemony by taking measures of security state practices. A good number of former political alliances of AKP was dragged into new enemy positions, from Gülen Community establishments as one of the most significant agents of fragmental tyranny within the state to liberals providing full support to the party in terms of EU negotiations.

Middle East's restructuring process is decidedly one of the key cause behind this disorder. AKP undertook to be an active competitor in this restructuring process pursuant to its nostalgic "neo-Ottomanism" politics. In fact, as Evren Balta (2015) proposes, this was a manifestation of "Sunnite brotherhood project". The goal was fighting for being a founder of Sunnite stroke in Middle East, which would be divided into Sunnite and Shiite lines. It was also envisaged that the Kurdish question could be solved around this project. Kurds has been included in the circle of Turkish identity as being Muslim but excluded from the circle as being Kurdish since the foundation of the republic. In order to expand this circle on the basis of Sunnite brotherhood, AKP introduced the Negotiation process. Because this was considered as the only way to release the Kurds from PKK, which is a secular movement (Balta, 2015). However, the civil war erupted in Syria leading to decline of the entire project. Furthermore, since Kurds got strength and became an alternative to Salafi movement in Syria and by means of Kobane upheavals on October 6-7, 2014, Sunnite brotherhood project and Negotiation process were terminated. These developments also triggered an ever-growing civil war in Turkey.

II. CIVIL WAR PROSPECTS

According to Hamit Bozarslan (2015: 19), a chain of events "bewildered" people living in Turkey and fear was turned into a governmental technique. Among these events we can count: redefinition of Turkey's internal and external politics on the basis of religious sects between the years 2011 and 2015, Gezi Park protests, battle of Erdoğanism and Gülenism in the realm of the state, triumph of AKP in the elections on March 30, 2013 and on August 10, 2014, and election of Erdoğan for presidency as "One Man" who is juridically unamenable but embodies the power of execution in the last analysis. The internal target of this governmental technology was again Kurds. By the time HDP as the representative of the Kurdish movement got into the parliament by overcoming the parliamentary threshold of 10% for the first time and this led up the democratic politics, a civil war was again put into practice in Turkey's East.

The Turkish State has seen Kurdish question as a *security issue* since the beginning and tried to command the peace process with a security state attitude instead of addressing to the Kurdish movement. The sharpest example of this was security implementations followed by the armed conflict between Islamic groups and PKK in many Kurdish districts and cities on October 6-7, 2014. Internal Security Law, which got through and imposed despite strong social opposition after Kobane upheavals, became an indicator of Schmittian state of exception in the country.

No sooner did the peace process end than the places in Turkey's Kurdistan, especially the ones that PKK deploys, were bombed. In the locations where Kurds have organizational strength, arrestments increased rapidly. Political figures and elected parliamentarians were also arrested. In return, politicized lower class Kurdish youth declared autonomy and started seeking ways of building their own independent local structures (Küçük, 2015). Remilitarization of Kurdish question made PKK's redetermination of violence as politics unavoidable.

Subsequent to the elections held in June, AKP fell short of its expectations and Kurds made a historical accomplishment in Rojava region; both sides ignored the possibility of peace and behaved provocatively to settle accounts with each other on battlegrounds. In the wake of the suicide attack happened in Suruç,[156] HPG killed two special operation officers while sleeping[157] in reprisal for the attack on the grounds that they organized ISIS's border crossing. And hence, peace process, lasting inconsistently since 2012, came to the end literally.

After the collapse of the peace process, certain municipalities possessed by HDP/DBP declared autonomy one after another.[158] And against the judicial/military operations that the state initiated in these places and then generalized Kurdish armed forces (HPG-YPG-YDG/H-PKK) began to apply the methods specialized in Kobane defense in Kurdish cities located within the borders of Turkey.[159] Among these methods are tunneling,[160] entrenching, sabotage, sharpshooting, antihandling, hanging curtains between streets and so on. As can be predicted, Turkish state and its armed forces started to implement more rigid techniques, going beyond the counter-guerilla tactics used throughout the 90s (village evacuation, setting forests on fire, execution of villagers, armed combat with PKK guerillas on the mountains, etc.) in order to cope with PKK/HPG/YDG-H's new strategies. Turkish armed forces' implementations are based on, first of all, declaration of curfew in a certain region (district, quarter, etc.), then blockading of the region through gunfire and ultimately, entrance of special operation forces (PÖH-JÖH) into the region and start of infantry war by using more traditional methods. Introduction of warfare into metropolises and curfews became an integral part of the war concept of this new era. Sharpshooting, prohibition of health services in the blockaded districts and killing civilians in the basements during the curfew were applied as an absorbing and destructive military tactic and as state politics.

Now, we would like to approach this new conflicting atmosphere generated after the elections in June by considering Cizre, Silopi, Nusaybin, Sur, and Yüksekova; all these regions were identified with the new concept of violence applied by Turkish Armed Forces.

---

156 http://www.aljazeera.com.tr/haber/suructa-canli-bomba-saldirisi-31-olu
157 http://www.bbc.com/turkce/haberler/2015/07/150722_canli_turkiyede_bugun
158 http://www.milliyet.com.tr/dbp-den-gerilimi-tirmandiracak/siyaset/detay/2099960/default.htm
159 http://www.rethinkinstitute.org/wp-content/uploads/2016/02/hendek_son-5.pdf
160 http://www.hurriyet.com.tr/pkkli-teroristlerin-kazdigi-40-metrelik-tunel-ortaya-cikarildi-40041151

DIYARBAKIR-SUR: THE BLOCKADE

As we mentioned above, main feature of the war experienced in this new era depended on a strategy, defined by the autonomy declaration. Kurdish armed forces, whose actions were guerilla type hit-and-runs throughout the 90s, declared autonomy in certain regions, under favor of high spirit they obtained through achievements in Kobane and subsequent to the changed situation in Middle East for their benefit. Moreover, Kurdish armed forces started to implement a military strategy oriented to defense of certain lands. This went beyond the former strategy as armed hit-and-run actions which would prevent the state from commanding. At the heart of this strategy lain providing total emancipation of certain regions, so that the idea of autonomy as free lands would be materialized. The borders of these regions were determined by traps and trenches; behind them there were armed youth and more professionally-trained guerillas' barricades tried to defense streets, houses and even rooms.

Against this militaristic strategy as an attempt to materialize autonomy, the state committed violence in such a way that above all these regions were strictly enclosed and rendered without any outside connection except the state's sophisticated violence apparatuses. Thus, curfews were announced and the regions were isolated in order to correct through sophisticated violence.[161] Historical Sur district of Diyarbakır with its contiguous houses, narrow streets and high yard walls was the place where Turkish and Kurdish armed forces experimented their new war concepts upon each other in extreme levels. The curfew in Sur, announced by the state on December 11, 2015, lasted for more than four months and ended on March 13, 2016. [162]

During the operations, more than 70 Turkish Armed Forces members and more than 200 Kurdish armed forces members died/were killed.[163] Unfortunately, the civilians living in the region paid the actual penalty of the blockade and maybe the first time in the republican history a district connected to a city center was precluded totally.

CIZRE: THE DEEP FREEZER AND THE BASEMENTS

Another place where one of the harsh gunfights between Kurdish armed forces and Turkish law enforcement officers took place was Cizre. The whole array

---

161 http://sendika10.org/tag/sur-direnisi
162 http://www.sabah.com.tr/gundem/2016/03/17/diyarbakir-surda-sokaga-cikma-yasagi-kaldirildi
163 http://www.sozcu.com.tr/2016/gundem/pkk-operasyonlarinin-bilancosu-1131227/

of warfare tactics mentioned above was implemented by both sides and the most influential tactic of the Turkish forces which felt the state's coercion in people's bones was the blockade, applied through curfews.

Curfews transcended to be mere precautions. They became phenomena representing the state's violence in most explicit way and were embodied by means of certain impositions of the state:

(1)   13 years old girl, named Cemile Çağırga, who did not conform to the curfew sanction, was killed and then, again because of the curfew, she could not be buried. Her dead body had to be kept in the deep freezer in her family house for a few days. [164]

(2)   Still in Cizre, an ambulance on its way to a place where there was gunfight was commenced fire almost certainly by the law enforcement officers and one of the medical staff was shot in the head and killed.[165]

(3)   The major case materializing the state's violence was the experiences in two basements. The ambulances trying to reach some wounded citizens sheltered in the basements were commenced fire. Thus, the wounded people deprived of health services died. According to the claims of Şırnak Deputy Faysal Sarıyıldız and Diyarbakır Bar's members, the rest of people survived in those basements were killed by artillery shooting and chemical weapons.[166]

Consequently, during the operations lasted more than 70 days a hundred thousand people, which corresponds to almost whole population of the district, left the region; more than 20 law enforcement officers and hundreds of civilians and PKK members died. [167]

SILOPI: SNIPERS

In the frame of the new warfare concept, advanced by the state in Kurdish cities, the most effectively used agency was certainly the sharpshooting. This came to the fore mostly in Silopi, especially through allegations regarding existence

---

164   http://www.bbc.com/turkce/haberler/2015/09/150913_cizre_cemileninolumu_hatice_kamer
165   http://www.diyarbakirbarosu.org.tr/filemanager/cizre%20raporu.pdf
166   http://www.cumhuriyet.com.tr/haber/turkiye/477359/Cizre_de_bodrum_kati_ve_cevresine_operasyon__Onlarca_olu.html
167   http://www.sozcu.com.tr/2016/gundem/pkk-operasyonlarinin-bilancosu-1131227/

of possibly targeted civilians. In August of the year 2015, four civilians were killed within one day and local community found the sharpshooters of Turkish Armed Forces responsible for these killings.[168] But indeed, subsequent to the fact that 50 years old Taybet İnan was shot by the sharpshooters, the state's violence created through sharpshooting drew both national and international attention. By the time Taybet İnan returning home from visiting her neighbor was shot, one of her relatives, intended to go and take her, was also shot by a sharpshooter and killed; her husband was wounded. Due to the sharpshooting, it was impossible to take and save Taybet İnan who was lying suffering on the ground. She passed away agonizing the day after and her dead body was waited for a week to be buried on the street.[169]

Silopi was one of the regions where state forces started and finished operations at the earliest. According to the official sources, a security officer died and by the end of the 37th day, curfew ceased. Besides, tens of people from Kurdish armed forces and civilians died. It is estimated that approximately twenty thousand people migrated from the city.

NUSAYBIN-YÜKSEKOVA: FREE FIRE

Following the termination of peace process and the start of warfare, Kurdish armed forces implemented the method of tunneling, as stated before, which they never used previously since they learned it in Kobane. Quite particularly and effectively they applied it in order to develop logistical and militaristic tactics.

Nusaybin[170], located at Syrian border of Turkey, and Yüksekova[171], located at İranian border, are the districts where PKK dug tunnels frequently and used these tunnels as a replenishment technique and as a tactic. Since this tactic facilitates trapping and disappearance, Turkish state performed so much artillery shootings in these districts that it never did before to get through this tactical mastery of the tunneling with minimum casualty.

---

168 http://www.imctv.com.tr/silopide-keskin-nisanci-endisesi/
169 http://www.telgrafhane.org/silopide-katledilen-taybet-ananin-oglu-annemin-cenazesi-gunlerdir-sokakta/
170 http://www.mazlumder.org/tr/main/faaliyetler/basin-aciklamalari/1/mardin-ili-nusaybin-ilcesinde-meydana-gelen-h/12479
171 http://hakkari.mazlumder.org/tr/main/faaliyetler/basin-aciklamalari/1/mazlumder-hakkri-subesinin-yuksekova-ilcesind/10454

SILVAN-DARGEÇIT...

There were two other districts, Silvan and Dargeçit, where curfews took quite longer than expected, civilian deaths occurred, people could not meet their basic human needs like health services, electricity and water. As claimed by Amnesty Organization, in these districts like the others in warfare some basic human rights were violated through the state's violence. Thus, according to the reports provided by Amnesty Organization, the right of peaceful assembly was violated and civilians were exposed to disproportionate force; the right to move freely and the principle stating that the state is responsible for protecting right to live were both violated. In addition to these, incidents like chemical teargasses and over-pressurized water cannons, whose usages were banned according to the international agreements, became routinized as part of everyday life. [172]

III. TO BE CONTINUED

Turkey has been fighting with armed Kurdish movement since 1984 and this fight sometimes erupts and sometimes weakens. In the period between the years 2012 and 2015 peace was most likely to happen. Nevertheless, accomplishments of Kurds militarily in Syria and politically in Turkey on the one hand and AKP's loss of its stance because of ISIS in Syria and as a result of the elections in Turkey on the other hand, peace environment was abolished and a new wave of warfare emerged. During this war both sides inserted violent instruments and repertoires that they never used before. While Kurds dug trenches, trapped the barricades and tried to secure the regions where they declared autonomy with armed youth by introducing a new wave of violence; the state tried to maintain its hegemony and eliminate armed Kurdish movement by sharpshooting, artillery shooting, chemical weapon usage and curfews lasting for months. At this stage, PKK's both urban and rural guerilla activities are going on with a considerable strength. In fact, some elements of radical left in Turkey also gathered around PKK. However, as for a socio-scientific analysis of this new wave of violence is yet too early.

---

172 https://www.amnesty.org.tr/icerik/2/1777/uluslararasi-af-orgutu

REFERENCES

Ağaoğulları, Mehmet Ali (1987) "The Ultranationalist Right", *Turkey in Transition* (eds. Irvin C. Schick and E. Ahmet Tonak), Oxford: Oxford University Press, pp. 177-217.

Ahmad, Feroz (1977) *The Turkish Experiment in Democracy 1950-1975*, London: Hurst & Co.

Akça, İsmet (2006) *Militarism, Capitalism and the State: Putting the Military in its Place in Turkey*, Doctoral Dissertation, Department of Political Science and International Relations, İstanbul: Boğaziçi University.

Akçam, Taner (1992) *Türk Ulusal Kimliği ve Ermeni Sorunu*, İstanbul: İletişim.

Akçam, Taner (2003) "Türk Ulusal Kimliği Üzerine Bazı Tezler", *Modern Türkiye'de Siyasal Düşünceler vol. 4*, İstanbul: İletişim.

Akçam, Taner and Ümit Kurt (2012), *Kanunların Ruhu: Emval-i Metruke Kanunlarında Soykırımın İzini Sürmek*, İstanbul: İletişim.

Akçura, Belma (2006) *Derin Devlet Oldu Devlet*, İstanbul: Güncel.

Akdeniz, Eylem and Emrah Göker (2011) "The Historical 'Stickiness' of Nationalism Inside Turkey's Political Field", *Turkish Studies*, Vol. 12, No: 13, pp. 309-340.

Akkaya, Ahmet Hamdi (2013) "Kürt Hareketinin Örgütlenme Süreci Olarak 1970'ler", *Toplum ve Bilim*, No. 127, pp. 88-120.

Aktay, Yasin (2005) "Sunuş", *Modern Türkiye'de Siyasi Düşünce vol. 6: İslâmcılık* (ed. Yasin Aktay), İstanbul: İletişim, pp. 13-26.

Alış, Ahmet (2009) *The Process of the Politicization of the Kurdish Identity in Turkey: The Kurds and the Turkish Labor Party (1961-1971)*, Masters diss., Bogazici University, İstanbul, Turkey.

Alış, Ahmet (2012) "Kürt Etnobölgesel Hareketinin Doğuşu, Kitleselleşme Süreci ve Türkiye İşçi Partisi: 1959-1974", *Türkiye Siyasetinde Kürtler: Direniş, Hak Arayışı, Katılım* (ed. Büşra Ersanlı, Günay Göksu Özdoğan, Nesrin Uçarlar), İstanbul: İletişim, pp. 57-91.

Altınay, Ayşe Gül and Tanıl Bora (2009) "Ordu, Militarizm ve Milliyetçilik", *Modern Türkiye'de Siyasi Düşünce cilt 4: Milliyetçilik* (ed. Tanıl Bora), İstanbul: İletişim, pp. 140-154.

Ayata, Sencer (1996) "Patronage, Party and State: The Politicization of Islam in Turkey", *Middle East Journal*, No. 50, pp. 40-56.

Aydın, Suavi (2006) "Cumhuriyet'in İdeolojik Şekillenmesinde Antropolojinin Rolü: Irkçı Paradigmanın Yükselişi ve Düşüşü", *Modern Türkiye'de Siyasi Düşünce, vol. 2, Kemalizm*, İstanbul: İletişim, pp. 344-369.

Aydınoğlu, Ergun (2007) *Türkiye Solu (1960-1980)*, İstanbul: Versus.

Balta, Evren (2015) "Eşik", http://www.birikimdergisi.com/haftalik/7294/esik#.V3I07fmLTIV

Bargu, Banu (2014) *Starve and Immolate: The Politics of Human Weapons*, New York: Columbia University Press.

Barker, Colin (1991) "A Note on the Theory of Capitalist State", *The State Debate* (ed. S. Clarke), London: Houndmills, pp. 204-213.

Barkey, Henri and Graeme Fuller (1997) "Turkey's Kurdish Question: Critical Turning Points and Missed Opportunities", *Middle East Journal*, No. 51, pp. 59-79.

Batuman, Bülent (2013) "70'ler: Siyasetin Odağındaki Kent, Kentin Odağındaki Siyaset", *Toplum ve Bilim*, No. 127, pp. 68-87.

Belge, Murat (2007) "Türkiye'de Sosyalizm Tarihinin Ana Çizgileri", *Modern Türkiye'de Siyasi Düşünce vol. 8: Sol* (ed. Murat Gültekingil), İstanbul: İletişim, pp. 19-48.

Berkes, Niyazi (1974) "The Two Facets of the Kemalist Revolution", *Muslim World*, 64, pp. 292-306.

Berktay, Halil (2008) *Yaşadığımız Şu Korkunç Otuz Yıl*, İstanbul: Kitap.

Beşikçi, İsmail (1992) *Doğu Anadolu Mitingleri'nin Analizi (1967)*, Ankara: Yurt.

Bora, Tanıl (2003) "Nationalist Discourses in Turkey", *The South Atlantic Quarterly*, No. 102/2-3, pp. 433-451.

Bora, Tanıl and Kemal Can (2004a) *Devlet, Ocak, Dergâh: 12 Eylül'den 1990'lara Ülkücü Hareket*, İstanbul: İletişim (7th Edition).

Bora, Tanıl and Kemal Can (2004b) *Devlet ve Kuzgun: 1990'lardan 2000'lere MHP*, İstanbul: İletişim.

Bora, Tanıl and Selda Çağlar (2007) "Modernleşme ve Batılılaşmanın Bir Taşıyıcısı Olarak Sivil Toplum Kuruluşları", *Modern Türkiye'de Siyasi Düşünce vol. 3: Modernleşme ve Batıcılık* (ed. Uygur Kocabaşoğlu), İstanbul: İletişim, pp. 336-347.

Bora, Tanıl and Ümit Kıvanç (1996) "Yeni Atatürkçülük", *Cumhuriyet Dönemi Türkiye Ansiklopedisi, vol. 13*, İstanbul: İletişim, pp. 777-780.

Boratav, Korkut (1991) *Türkiye'de Sosyal Sınıflar ve Bölüşüm*, İstanbul: Gerçek.

Boratav, Korkut (2007) "Dünya Ekonomisinde Değişimler ve Türkiye'ye Yansımalar", *http://bagimsizsosyalbilimciler.org*

Bourdieu, Pierre (2012) *Sur l'État*, Paris: Seuil et Raisons d'agir Éditions.

Bozarslan, Hamit (1999) "Network-Building, Ethnicity and Violence in Turkey", *Abu Dhabi* (ECSSR, 1999).

Bozarslan, Hamit (2000a) "Ortadoğu ve Türkiye'de 'Milli Din' İslam ve İslamcılık", *Birikim*, No. 129, pp. 61-73.

Bozarslan, Hamit (2000b) " 'Why the Armed Struggle?' Understanding The Violence in Kurdistan of Turkey", *The Kurdish Conflict in Turkey: Obstacles and Chances for Peace and Democracy* (eds. Ferhad İbrahim and Gülistan Gürbey), New York: Saint Martin Press, pp. 17-30.

Bozarslan, Hamit (2004) *Türkiye'nin Modern Tarihi*, trans. Heval Bucak, İstanbul: Avesta.

Bozarslan, Hamit (2005a) "Bazı Karşılaştırma Unsurları: Ermenilerin ve Yahudilerin Yok Edilmesi", *Birikim* 193–194, pp. 59-77.

Bozarslan, Hamit (2005b) "Türkiye'de devlet, komitacılık ve çetecilik konusunda birkaç hipotez", http://www.ozguruniversite.org/index.php/guencel-yazlar/239-tuerki-yede-devlet-komitaclk-vecetecilik-konusunda-birkac-hipotez

Bozarslan, Hamit (2007a) "İbrahim Kaypakkaya", *Modern Türkiye'de Siyasi Düşünce vol. 8: Sol* (ed. Murat Gültekingil), İstanbul: İletişim, pp. 517-523.

Bozarslan, Hamit (2007b) "Türkiye'de Kürt Sol Hareketi", *Modern Türkiye'de Siyasi Düşünce vol. 8: Sol* (ed. Murat Gültekingil), İstanbul: İletişim, pp. 1169-1207.

Bozarslan, Hamit (2009a) "Kürd Milliyetçiliği ve Kürd Hareketi (1898-2000)", *Modern Türkiye'de Siyasi Düşünce vol. 4: Milliyetçilik* (ed. Tanıl Bora), İstanbul: İletişim, pp. 841-870.

Bozarslan, Hamit (2009b) "İktidar Yapıları, Zor ve Şiddet", *21. Yüzyıla Girerken Türkiye* (ed. Semih Vaner), İstanbul: Kitap, pp. 222-246.

Bozarslan, Hamit (2009c) "İfade Özgürlüğünün Berisinde ve Ötesinde", *Türkiye'de İfade Özgürlüğü* (eds. T. Koçak, T. Dogan, Z. Kutulada), İstanbul: BGST, pp. 274–281.

Bozarslan, Hamit (2009d) "Türkiye'de Siyasi Şiddetin Fikri Kaynakları", *Modern Türkiye'de Siyasi Düşünce, vol. 9, Cilt, Dönemler ve Zihniyetler*, İstanbul: İletişim, pp. 370–385.

Bozarslan, Hamit (2012) *Ortadoğunun Siyasal Sosyolojisi*, trans. Melike Işık Durmaz, İstanbul: İletişim.

Bozarslan, Hamit (2014) "Sunuş", *Türkiye'de Siyasal Şiddetin Boyutları* (eds. Güney Çeğin and İbrahim Şirin), İstanbul: İletişim, pp. 9-30.

Bozarslan, Hamit (2015) *Türkiye Tarihi*, trans. Işık Ergüden, İstanbul: İletişim.

Bozarslan, Hamit (2016) "Hamit Bozarslan'la Faşizm Üstüne", *1+1 Express*, No. 142, pp. 74-84.

Can, Kemal (2009) "Ülkücü Hareketin İdeolojisi", *Modern Türkiye'de Siyasi Düşünce cilt 4: Milliyetçilik* (ed. Tanıl Bora), İstanbul: İletişim, pp. 663-685.

Cangızbay, Kadir (2000) *Hiçkimsenin Cumhuriyeti*, Ankara: Ütopya Yayınevi.

Cangızbay, Kadir (2008–2009) " 'Bizim Cumhuriyet' ", *Doğu Batı*, no. 47, pp. 145-151.

Çayan, Mahir (2004) *Bütün Yazılar*, İstanbul: Boran.

Çeğin, Güney (2013) "Türdeşleştirme Projesinin Müphem Cüzü. Dersim, Devlet Raporları ve Kartografik Şiddet", *Bauman Sosyolojisi* (eds. Zülküf Kara), İstanbul: Ayrıntı, pp. 227-243.

Çeğin, Güney (2014) "Tek Parti Döneminde Rejimin Militarist Özerkliği", *Türkiye'de Siyasal Şiddetin Boyutları* (eds. Güney Çeğin and İbrahim Şirin), İstanbul: İletişim, pp. 31-55.

Çeğin, Güney and Ahmet Özcan (2014) "Politik Şiddetin Kavranışına Dair Bir Soruşturma: 'Gezi Olayları' Weber'in 'Devletin Meşru Şiddet Tekeli' Tezinin Tahrifatından Gayrı İncelenebilir mi?", *Gezi ve Sosyoloji: Nesneyle Yüzleşmek, Nesneyi Kurmak* (eds. Vefa Saygın Öğütle and Emrah Göker), İstanbul: Ayrıntı, pp. 149-157.

Çelik, Nur Betül (2006) "Kemalizm: Hegemonik Bir Söylem", *Modern Türkiye'de Siyasi Düşünce vol. 2: Kemalizm* (ed. Ahmet İnsel), İstanbul: İletişim, pp. 75-92.

Çiğdem, Ahmet (2005) "İslâmcılık ve Türkiye Üzerine Bazı Notlar", *Modern Türkiye'de Siyasi Düşünce vol. 6: İslâmcılık* (ed. Yasin Aktay), İstanbul: İletişim, pp. 26-34.

Çiğdem, Ahmet (2009) *D'nin Halleri: Din, Darbe, Demokrasi*, İstanbul: İletişim.

Cizre, Ümit (2005) *Muktedirlerin Siyaseti*, İstanbul: İletişim.

Çubukçu, Aydın (2007) "TDKP-'Halkın Kurtuluşu': Gerilladan Partiye", *Modern Türkiye'de Siyasi Düşünce vol. 8: Sol* (ed. Murat Gültekingil), İstanbul: İletişim, pp. 724-736.

Davis, Nancy J. and Robert V. Robinson (2012) *Claiming Society for God: Religious Movements and Social Welfare*, Indiana: Indiana University Press.

Demirel, Ahmet (2007) *Birinci Meclis'te Muhalefet: İkinci Grup*, İstanbul: İletişim (4th edition).

Deringil, Selim (1998) *The Well-Protected Domains: Ideology and the Legitimation of Power in the Ottoman Empire 1876–1909*, London: I. B. Tauris.

Deringil, Selim (2003) "They Live in a State of Nomadism and Savagery: The Late Ottoman Empire and the Post-Colonial Debate", *Comparative Studies in Society and History*, Vol. 45, No. 2, pp. 311-342.

Dilek, Oğuz (2014) "Türkiye Kapitalizminde Zorun Rolü: Rızasız Bir Toplum Sözleşmesi Olarak 12 Eylül Darbesi", *Türkiye'de Siyasal Şiddetin Boyutları* (eds. G. Çeğin and İ. Şirin), İstanbul: İletişim, pp. 347-369.

Dündar, Fuat (2008) *Modern Türkiye'nin Şifresi: İttihat ve Terakki'nin Etnisite Mühendisliği (1913-1918)*, İstanbul: İletişim.

Dündar, Fuat (2011) *İttihat ve Terakki'nin Müslümanları İskan Politikası (1913-1918)*, İstanbul: İletişim.

Düzel, Neşe (2008) "Zafer Toprak: 'Atatürk Fransa'nın 3. Cumhuriyeti'ni kurdu' ", *Taraf Gazetesi*, http://www.taraf.com.tr/nese-duzel/makale-zafer-toprak-atat-urk-fransanin-3-cumhuriyetini.htm

Eldem, Edhem (1999) "Istanbul: From Imperial to Peripheralized Capital", *The Ottoman City between East and West* (eds. Edhem Eldem, Daniel Goffman, and Bruce Masters), Cambridge, Cambridge University Press, pp. 135-207.

Eldem, Edhem (2007) "26 Ağustos 1986 'Banka Vakası' ve 1896 'Ermeni Olayları'", *Tarih ve Toplum Yeni Yaklaşımlar*, İstanbul: İletişim, pp. 113-146.

Elias, Norbert (1978) *What is Sociology?*, London: Hutchinson.

Epözdemir, Şakir (2005) *Türkiye Kürdistan Demokrat Partisi 1968/235 Antalya Davası Savunması*, İstanbul: Pêrî.

Ercan, Harun (2010) *Dynamics of Mobilization and Radicalization of the Kurdish Movement in the 1970s in Turkey*, Masters diss., Koc University, İstanbul, Turkey.

Erdoğan, Necmi (2006) "Neo-Kemalizm, Organik Bunalım ve Hegemonya", *Modern Türkiye'de Siyasi Düşünce vol. 2: Kemalizm* (ed. Ahmet İnsel), İstanbul: İletişim, pp. 584-601.

Ergil, Doğu (1980) *Türkiye'de Terör ve Şiddet: Yapısal ve Kültürel Kaynakları*, Ankara: Turhan.

Ergut, Ferdan (2014) "Devlet ve Politik Şiddet: Latin Amerika ve Türkiye'de Gerilla Hareketleri", *Türkiye'de Siyasal Şiddetin Boyutları* (eds. Güney Çeğin and İbrahim Şirin), İstanbul: İletişim, pp. 207-224.

Eroğul, Cem (1987) "The Establishment of Multiparty Rule: 1945-71", *Turkey in Transition* (eds. Irvin C. Schick and E. Ahmet Tonak), Oxford: Oxford University Press, pp. 101-143.

Fanon, Frantz (1963) *The Wretched of the Earth*, New York: Grove Press.

Fanon, Frantz (2008) *Black Skin, White Masks*, New York: Grove Press.

Fırat, Bahar Ş. (2014) "Türkiye'de 'Doksanlar': Devlet Şiddetinin Özgünlüğü ve Sürekliliği Üzerine Bir Deneme", *Türkiye'de Siyasal Şiddetin Boyutları* (eds. G. Çeğin and İ. Şirin), İstanbul: İletişim, pp. 369-403.

Findley, Carter V. (1980) *Bureaucratic Reform in the Ottoman Empire: The Sublime Porte, 1789–1922*, Princeton: Princeton University Press.

Giddens, Anthony (1985) *The Nation-State and Violence*, Berkeley: University of California Press.

Goloğlu, Mahmut (1972) *Devrimler ve Tepkileri (1924-1930)*, Ankara: Turhan Kitabevi.

Goodwin, Jeff (2005) "Revolutions and Revolutionary Movements", *The Handbook of Political Sociology* (eds. Thomas Janoski, Robert Alford, Alexander Hicks and Mildred A. Schwartz), Cambridge: Cambridge University Press, pp. 404-422.

Goodwin, Jeff (2006) "A Theory of Categorical Terorism", *Social Forces*, Vol. 84, No. 4, pp. 2027-2046.

Groc, Gerard (2009) "Demokrasi ve Sivil Toplum", *21. Yüzyıla Girerken Türkiye*, (ed. Semih Vaner), İstanbul: Kitap, pp. 193-222.

Gündoğan, Cemil (2005) *The Kurdish Political Mobilization in the 1960s: The Case of the 'Eastern Meetings'*, Masters diss., Middle East Technical University, Ankara, Turkey.

Gündoğan, Cemil (2007) *Kawa Davası Savunması ve Kürtlerde Siyasi Savunma Geleneği*, İstanbul: Vate.

Gündoğan, Cemil (2012) "Geleneğin Değersizleşmesi: Kürt Hareketinin 1970'lerde Gelenekselle İlişkisi Üzerine", *Türkiye Siyasetinde Kürtler: Direniş, Hak Arayışı, Katılım* (eds. Büşra Ersanlı, Günay Göksu Özdoğan and Nesrin Uçarlar), İstanbul: İletişim, pp. 93-150.

Gunes, Cengiz (2012) *The Kurdish National Movement in Turkey: From Protest to Resistance*, London and New York: Routledge.

Gürbilek, Nurdan (2015) *Sessizin Payı*, İstanbul: Metis.

Hakan, Sinan (2013) *Türkiye Kurulurken Kürtler (1916–1920)*, İstanbul: İletişim.

Hanioğlu, Şükrü (1986) *Osmanlı İttihad ve Terakki Cemiyeti ve Jön Türklük*, İstanbul: İletişim.

Harris, George S. (1965) "The Role of the Military in Turkish Politics, Part I", *Middle East Journal*, No. 19, pp. 54–66.

Hirsch, Joachim (2005) *Materialistische Staatstheorie: Transformationsprozesse des kapitalistischen Staatensystems*, Vsa Verlag.

Hobsbawm, Eric (2000) *Bandits*, New York: The New York Press (4th edition).

Işıklı, Alpaslan (1987) "Wage Labor and Unionization", *Turkey in Transition* (eds. Irvin C. Schick and E. Ahmet Tonak), Oxford: Oxford University Press, pp. 309-332.

Jacoby, Tim (2005a) *Social Power and the Turkish State*, London: Routledge.

Jacoby, Tim (2005b) "Semi-Authoritarian Incorporation and Autocratic Militarism", *Development and Change*, 36/4, pp. 641-665.

Jacoby, Tim (2011) "Fascism, Civility and the Crisis of the Turkish State", *Third World Quarterly*, Vol. 32, No. 5, pp. 905-924.

Jessop, Bob (2008) *State Power: A Strategic-Relational Approach*, Cambridge: Polity.

Jongerden, Joost and Ahmet Hamdi Akkaya (2010) "Born from the Left: The Making of the PKK", *Nationalisms and Politics in Turkey: Political Islam, Kemalism and the Kurdish Issue* (eds. Marlies Casier and Joost Jongerden), New York: Routledge, pp. 123-142.

K. Eriksen *et.al.*(1991) "Governments and the Education of Non-Dominant Ethnic Groups in Comparative Perspective", *Schooling, Education Policy and Ethnic Identity* (ed. J. Tomiak), New York: New York University Press, pp. 389-417.

Kadıoğlu, Ayşe (1996) "The Paradox of Turkish Nationalism and the Construction of Official Identity", *Turkey: Identity, Democracy and Politics* (ed. S. Kedourie), London: Frank Cass., pp. 177-193.

Kadıoğlu, Ayşe (1999) *Cumhuriyet İradesi Demokrasi Muhakemesi*, İstanbul: Metis.

Karpat, Kemal (1985) *Ottoman Population 1830–1914*, Madison, WI: University of Wisconsin Press.

Kaygusuz, Özlem (2016) "Bir Siyasal İdare Tekniği Olarak Güvenlik ve AKP Döneminde Ulusal Güvenlik Devleti", *Praksis*, No. 40, pp. 85-121.

Kazancıgil, Ali (2009) "Devlet: Türk Modernliğin Merkezi Aktörü", *21. Yüzyıla Girerken Türkiye* (ed. Semih Vaner), İstanbul: Kitap, pp. 119-153.

Kazgan, Gülten (1995) *Yeni Ekonomik Düzende Türkiye'nin Yeri*, İstanbul: Altın.

Keleş, Ruşen and Artun Ünsal (1982) *Kent ve Siyasal Şiddet*, Ankara: SBF.

Keyder, Çağlar (1987) "The Political Economy of Turkish Democracy", *Turkey in Transition* (eds. Irvin C. Schick and E. Ahmet Tonak), Oxford: Oxford University Press, pp. 27-65.

Keyder, Çağlar (2004) *Türkiye'de Devlet ve Sınıflar*, İstanbul: İletişim.

Kısacık, Raşit (2010) *Kawa: Kürt Sorunu ve Etnik Örgütlenmeler 1*, İstanbul: Ozan.

Klein, Janet (2011) *The Margins of Empire: Kurdish Militias in the Ottoman Tribal Zone*, Stanford: Stanford University Press.

Koçak, Cemil (1997) "Siyasi Tarih (1923–1950)", *Türkiye Tarihi: Çağdaş Türkiye 1908–1980, vol. 4* (ed. Sina Aksin), İstanbul: Cem, pp. 83–173.

Korsch, Karl (1974) "The Crisis of Marxism", *New German Critique*, No. 3, pp. 7-11.

Köse, Ali Osman (2014) *Sol'un Tarihinde Kara Bir Leke: Sol İçi Şiddet*, İstanbul: Boran.

Küçük, Bülent (2015) "Kürt Siyasetinin Dönüşümü ve Yapısal Paradokslar", http://t24.com.tr/yazarlar/bulent-kucuk/kurt-siyasetinin-donusumu-ve-yapisal-paradokslar,13178

Küçük, Murat (2007) "Türkiye'de Sol Düşünce ve Aleviler", *Modern Türkiye'de Siyasi Düşünce vol. 8: Sol* (ed. Murat Gültekingil), İstanbul: İletişim, pp. 896-934.

Küçük, Murat (2013) "Sol ve Aleviler: Yeryüzünü Kızıl Taçlar Bürüye", *Sol ve İlahiyat: Dini Soldan Okumak* (eds. Kazım Özdoğan and Derviş Aydın Akkoç), İstanbul: İletişim, pp. 269-282.

Kühn, Thomas (2007) "Shaping and Reshaping Colonial Ottomanism: Contesting Boundaries of Difference and Integration in Ottoman Yemen, 1872-1919," *Comparative Studies of South Asia, Africa and the Middle East*, Vol. 27, No. 2, pp. 315-331.

Kürkçü, Ertuğrul (2007) "Sosyalist Harekete Silâhlı Mücadelenin Girişi", *Modern Türkiye'de Siyasî Düşünce 8. Cilt: Sol* (ed. Murat Gültegingil), İstanbul: İletişim, pp. 494-509.

Kushner, David (1977) *The Rise of Turkish Nationalism, 1876–1908*, Londra: Frank Cass.

Laçiner, Ömer, (1976) "1971 Öncesi Dönem ve THKP-C Hareketinin Eleştirel Analizi 1", *Birikim*, Vol. 4, No. 22, pp. 7-28.

Landau, J. M. (1974) *Radical Politics in Modern Turkey*, Leiden: E.J. Brill.

Landau, J. M. (1981) *Pan Turkism in Turkey: A Study in Irredentism*, London: C. Hurst.

Lewis, Bernard (1993) *Modern Türkiye'nin Doğuşu*, Ankara: TTK.

Mann, Michael (1992) "The Autonomous Power of the State: its Origins, Mechanisms and Results", *States, War and Capitalism Studies in Political Sociology*, Cambridge MA, Oxford UK: Blackwell.

Mann, Michael (1993) *The Sources of Social Power, vol. 2*, Cambridge: Cambridge University Press.

Mann, Michael (2002) *Explaining Murderous Ethnic Cleansing: Eight Theses*, Paper prepared for the International Sociological Association Conference, Brisbane, Australia.

Mann, Michael (2005) *The Dark Side of Democracy: Explaining Ethnic Cleansing,* Cambridge: Cambridge University Press.

Marcus, Aliza (2007) *Blood and Belief: The PKK and the Kurdish Fight for Independence*, New York: New York University Press.

Mardin, Şerif (1991) *Türkiye'de Din ve Siyaset*, İstanbul: İletişim.

McAdam, Doug (1986) "Recruitment to High Risk Activism: The Case of Freedom Summer", *American Journal of Sociology*, Vol. 92 No. 1, pp. 64-90.

McDowall, David (1992) *A Modern History of the Kurds,* London, I. B. Tauris.

Minassian, G. F. and A. Avagyan (2013) *Ermeniler ve İttihat ve Terakki İşbirliğinden Çatışmaya*, trans. Mutlucan Şahan, İstanbul: Aras.

Morton, A.D. (2007) *Unravelling Gramsci: Hegemony and Passive Revolution in the Global Political Economy*, London: Pluto Press.

Öğütle, Vefa Saygın and Hüseyin Etil (2014) "1970-73 Türkiye'sindeki Devrimci Şiddet Momentinin Politik ve Sosyalbilimsel Bir Analizi", *Türkiye'de Siyasal Şiddetin Boyutları* (eds. Güney Çeğin and İbrahim Şirin), İstanbul: İletişim, pp. 249-316.

Ongun, Selin (2015) "DHKP-C'nin Karar Mercii Yurtdışında", an Interview with Hanefi Avcı, *Cumhuriyet*, May 28, 2015.

Özbudun, Ergun (2011) *Otoriter Rejimler, Seçimsel Demokrasiler ve Türkiye,* İstanbul: Bilgi Üniversitesi Press.

Özcan, Ahmet (2014) "Son Kürt Eşkıyaları: Kürt Meselesinde 'Adi' Şiddetin Olağanüstülüğü, Siyasallığı ve Yasa Yapıcı Mirası", *Türkiye'de Siyasal Şiddetin Boyutları* (eds. Güney Çeğin and İbrahim Şirin), İstanbul: İletişim Yayınları, pp. 165-206.

Özçetin, Burak (2014) "İslamcılıktan Yeni-İslamcılığa: İslam, Şiddet ve Devrim", *Türkiye'de Siyasal Şiddetin Boyutları* (eds. G. Çeğin and İ. Şirin), İstanbul: İletişim, pp. 317-347.

Özdemir, Şennur (2006) *Müsiad: Anadolu Sermayesinin Dönüşümü ve Türk Modernleşmesinin Derinleşmesi*, Ankara: Vadi.

Öznur, Hakkı (2004) *Derin Sol: Çatışmalar, Cinayetler, İnfazlar*, Ankara: Alternatif.

Özoğul, Hakan (2011) *Cumhuriyetin Kuruluşunda İktidar Kavgası*, trans. Zuhal Bilgin, İstanbul: Kitap.

Öztürk, Sırrı (2001) *İşçi Sınıfı, Sendikalar ve 15-16 Haziran*, İstanbul: Sorun.

Paker, E. Balta (2010) "Dış Tehditten İç Tehdide: Türkiye'de Doksanlı Yıllarda Ulusal Güvenliğin Yeniden İnşası", *Türkiye'de Devlet, Ordu ve Güvenlik Siyaseti* (eds. Evren Balta Paker and İsmet Akça), İstanbul: Bilgi Üniversitesi Press, pp. 407-431.

Parla, Taha (2001) "Kemalizm Türk Aydınlanması mı ?" *Modern Türkiye'de Siyasi Düşünce vol. 2: Kemalizm* (ed. Ahmet İnsel), İstanbul: İletişim, pp. 313-317.

Parla, Taha (2007). *Türkiye'de Anayasalar*, İletişim.

Pekdemir, Melih (2007) "Devrimci Yol", *Modern Türkiye'de Siyasi Düşünce vol. 8: Sol* (ed. Murat Gültekingil), İstanbul: İletişim, pp. 743-778.

Samim, Ahmet (1987) "The Left", *Turkey in Transition* (eds. Irvin C. Schick and E. Ahmet Tonak), Oxford: Oxford University Press, pp. 147-176.

Sapolya, E.B. (1974) *Ziya Gökalp: İttihat ve Terakki ve Meşrutiyet Tarihi*, İstanbul: İnkilap and Aka.

Sarıoğlu, Sezai (2007) "12 Eylül Sonrası Devrimci Sosyalist Hareket Üzerine", *Modern Türkiye'de Siyasi Düşünce vol. 8: Sol* (ed. Murat Gültekingil), İstanbul: İletişim, pp. 1004-1030.

Sarısözen, Veysi (1988) "Çevrek Yüzyıl Önce Kurduğumuz Örgüt: FKF", *Sosyalizm ve Toplumsal Mücadeleler Ansiklopedisi*, İstanbul: İletişim.

Sartre, Jean-Paul (1963) "Preface", Frantz Fanon, *The Wretched of the Earth*, New York: Grove Press.

Schick, Irvin C. and E. Ahmet Tonak (1987) "Conclusion", *Turkey in Transition* (eds. Irvin C. Schick and E. Ahmet Tonak), Oxford: Oxford University Press, pp. 365-378.

Sezgin, Ümit (1987) *Aydınlatılmamış Cinayetler*, İstanbul: İletişim.

Showstack Sassoon, A. (2001) "Globalisation, Hegemony and Passive Revolution", *New Political Economy*, 6, 1, pp. 5-17.

Skocpol, Theda (1979) *States and Social Revolutions: A Comparative Analysis of France, Russia and China*, Cambridge: Cambridge University Press.

Sommier, Isabelle (2008) *La Violence Révolutionnaire*, Paris: Presses de la Fondation Nationale des Sciences Politiques.

Sommier, Isabelle (2012) *Devrimci Şiddet*, Türkçeye çeviren Işık Ergüden, İstanbul: İletişim.

Stoddard, P. H. (1963) *The Ottoman government and the Arabs, 1911 to 1918: a preliminary study of the Teşkilât-ı Mahsusa*, unpublished dissertation, Princeton University.

Suny, R. G. (1993) *Looking Toward Ararat: Armenia in Modern History*, Bloomington: Indiana University Press.

Şen, Serdar (1995) *Refah Partisinin Teori ve Pratiği*, İstanbul: Sarmal.

Taşkın, Yüksel (2009) "Anti-Komünizm ve Türk Milliyetçiliği: Endişe ve Pragmatizm", *Modern Türkiye'de Siyasi Düşünce cilt 4: Milliyetçilik* (ed. Tanıl Bora), İstanbul: İletişim, pp. 618-634.

Tekeli, Şirin (2009) "Kadınlar: Cumhuriyetin Sevilmeyen Cinsi", *21. Yüzyıla Girerken Türkiye* (ed. Semih Vaner), İstanbul: Kitap, pp. 246-278.

Tilly, Charles (1985) "War Making and State Making as Organized Crime", *Bringing the State Back In* (eds. P. Evans, D. Rueschemeyer, T. Skocpol), Cambridge: Cambridge University Press, pp. 169-187.

Tilly, Charles (1990) *Coercion, Capital and European States AD 990-1990*, Cambridge MA, Oxford UK: Blackwell.

Tilly, Charles (1998) "Social Movements and (All Sorts of) Other Interactions – Local, National and International – Including Identities", *Theory and Society Special Issue on Interpreting Change at the End of the Twentieth Century*, 27(4), pp. 453-480.

Tilly, Charles (2003) *The Politics of Collective Violence*, Cambridge: Cambridge University Press.

Toksöz, Meltem (2007) "Adana Ermenileri ve 1909 'İğtişâşı'", *Tarih ve Toplum Yeni Yaklaşımlar*, İstanbul: İletişim, pp. 147-157.

Toprak, Binnaz (1987) "The Religious Right", *Turkey in Transition* (eds. Irvin C. Schick and E. Ahmet Tonak), Oxford: Oxford University Press, pp. 218-235.

Tuğal, Cihan (2007) "Nato'nun İslâmcıları", *NLR* (II) 44, pp. 5-34.

Tugal, Cihan (2009) *Passive Revolution: Absorbing the Islamic Challange to Capitalism*, Stanford: Stanford University Press.

Tunçay, Mete (1989) "Tanzimat Fermanı", *Tarih ve Toplum*, No. 71, pp. 266-267.

Tunçay, Mete (2005) *Türkiye Cumhuriyeti'nde Tek Parti Yönetimi'nin Kurulması*, İstanbul: Tarih Vakfı Yurt (4th edition).

Tunçay, Mete (2006) "İkna (İnandırma) Yerine Tecebbür (Zorlama)", *Modern Türkiye'de Siyasi Düşünce, vol. 2, Kemalizm*, İstanbul: İletişim, pp. 92-96.

Tunçay, Mete (2007) *Cihat ve Tehcir*, İstanbul: Salyangoz.

Üngör, Uğur Ü. (2005) "'A Reign Of Terror' Cup Rule In Diyarbekir Province, 1913-1923, unpublished dissertation, University Of Amsterdam, Department Of History.

Ünlü, Barış (2011) "Frantz Fanon: Ezilenlerin ve Mülksüzlerin Düşünürü", *Ankara Üniversitesi Afrika Çalışmaları Dergisi*, Vol. 1, No. 1, pp. 9-41.

Ünlü, Barış (2014) "Kürdistan/Türkiye ve Cezayir/Fransa: Sömürge Yöntemleri, Şiddet ve Entelektüeller", *Türkiye'de Siyasal Şiddetin Boyutları* (eds. Güney Çeğin and İbrahim Şirin), İstanbul: İletişim, pp. 403-434.

Ünüvar, Kerem (2013) "'70'ler: '80'lerin Öncesi '60'ların Sonrası", *Toplum ve Bilim*, sayı 127, pp. 30-47.

van Bruinessen, Martin (2013) *Ağa, Şeyh ve Devlet*, trans. Banu Yalkut, İstanbul: İletişim.

Vaner, Semih (1987) "The Army", *Turkey in Transition* (eds. Irvin C. Schick and E. Ahmet Tonak), Oxford: Oxford University Press, pp. 236-265.

Vaner, Semih (2009) "Demokrasiyle Otoritarizmin Birlikteliği", *21. Yüzyıla Girerken Türkiye* (ed. S. Vaner), İstanbul: Kitap, pp. 153-193.

Weber, Max (2004) *Economy and Society*, Stanford: Stanford University Press.

White, Paul J. (2000) *Primitive Rebels or Revolutionary Modernizers?: The Kurdish Nationalist Movement in Turkey*, London: Zed Books.

Yasamee, F. A. K. (1993) "Abdulhamid II and the Ottoman Defence Problem", *Diplomacy and Statecraft*, no. 4, pp. 22-23.

Yeğen, Mesut (2004) "Türk Milliyetçiliği ve Kürt Sorunu", *Modern Türkiye'de Siyasi Düşünce, vol. 4, Cilt, Milliyetçilik*, İstanbul: İletişim, pp. 880–892.

Yeğen, Mesut (2007) "Türkiye Solu ve Kürt Sorunu", *Modern Türkiye'de Siyasi Düşünce vol. 8: Sol* (ed. Murat Gültekingil), İstanbul: İletişim, pp. 1208-1236.

Yerasimos, Stefanos (2009) "Toprak Saplantısı ya da Hayalet Uzuvların Acısı", *21. Yüzyıla Girerken Türkiye* (ed. Semih Vaner), İstanbul: Kitap.

Yerasimos, Stéphane (1978) "The Monoparty Period", *Turkey in Transition: New Perspectives* (eds. İrvin Cemil Schick ve Ertuğrul Ahmet Tonak), New York: Oxford University Press.

Yıldırım, Ali (2008) *FKF Dev-Genç Tarihi*, Ankara: Doruk.

Yıldız, Ahmet (2004) *"Ne Mutlu Türküm Diyebilene" Türk Ulusal Kimliğinin Etno-Seküler Sınırları (1919-1938)*, İstanbul: İletişim.

Yıldız, Ahmet (2006) "Kemalist Milliyetçilik", *Modern Türkiye'de Siyasi Düşünce, vol. 2, Kemalizm*, İstanbul: İletişim, pp. 210-234.

Yılmaz, Murat (2009) "Dündar Taşer", *Modern Türkiye'de Siyasi Düşünce cilt 4: Milliyetçilik* (ed. Tanıl Bora), İstanbul: İletişim, pp. 668-677.

Zürcher, Eric-Jan (1984) *The Unionist Factor: The Role of the Committee of Union and Progress in the Turkish National Movement 1905–1926*, Leiden: E. J. Brill.

Zürcher, Eric-Jan (1998) *Turkey: A Modern History*, London & New York: I.B. Tauris.

Zürcher, Erik-Jan (2007) *Cumhuriyetin İlk Yıllarında Siyasal Muhalefet: Terakkiperver Cumhuriyet Fırkası*, trans. Gül Çağalı Güven, İstanbul: İletişim.